BEYOND MARX AND MACH

SOVIETICA

PUBLICATIONS AND MONOGRAPHS

OF THE INSTITUTE OF EAST-EUROPEAN STUDIES AT THE

UNIVERSITY OF FRIBOURG/SWITZERLAND AND

THE CENTER FOR EAST EUROPE, RUSSIA AND ASIA

AT BOSTON COLLEGE AND THE SEMINAR

FOR POLITICAL THEORY AND PHILOSOPHY

AT THE UNIVERSITY OF MUNICH

Founded by J. M. BOCHEŃSKI (Fribourg)

Edited by T. J. BLAKELEY (Boston), GUIDO KÜNG (Fribourg), *and*
NIKOLAUS LOBKOWICZ (Munich)

VOLUME 41

K. M. JENSEN

University of Colorado

BEYOND MARX AND MACH

ALEKSANDR BOGDANOV'S

Philosophy of Living Experience

D. REIDEL PUBLISHING COMPANY

DORDRECHT : HOLLAND / BOSTON : U.S.A.

LONDON : ENGLAND

Library of Congress Cataloging in Publication Data

Jensen, Kenneth Martin, 1944–
    Beyond Marx and Mach.

    (Sovietica ; v. 41)
    Bibliography: p.
    Includes index.
    1.   Malinovskiĭ, Aleksandr Aleksandrovich, 1873–1928.
Filosofiia zhivogo opyta. 2. Philosophy. 3. Dialectical
materialism. 4. Experience. I. Title. II. Series.
B4249.M33F5434   197′.2   78–12916
ISBN 90–277–0928–9

Published by D. Reidel Publishing Company,
P.O. Box 17, Dordrecht, Holland

Sold and distributed in the U.S.A., Canada, and Mexico
by D. Reidel Publishing Company, Inc.
Lincoln Building, 160 Old Derby Street, Hingham,
Mass. 02043, U.S.A.

This book is dedicated to L. Boyd and
Dorothy V. Jensen and to the memory of
Lora H. Joseph

TABLE OF CONTENTS

ACKNOWLEDGEMENTS

I wish to express my appreciation to the following:
Professor Thomas Blakeley, for encouraging me to submit this manuscript to *Sovietica* and for his handling of it thereafter; Professor Karl Ballestrem, for reading an earlier version of it and for providing criticisms; Professor Marc Raeff, for counseling me on the topic and approaches to it; Professor Floyd Ratliff, for materials sent me on Ernst Mach and Bogdanov and for his moral support; and Professor Stephen Fischer-Galati, for taking up the burden of this work's supervision in its dissertation form. Although these individuals vouchsafed me considerable aid and good counsel, I am most deeply indebted to Pamela K. Jensen for support that was as much professional as it was wifely. Needless to say, none of the above share any responsibility for the contents of this work.

K.M.J.

INTRODUCTION

A. ALEKSANDR BOGDANOV

On April 7, 1928 the career of one of the most extraordinary figures of Russian and early Soviet intellectual life came to an abrupt and premature end. In the process of an experiment on blood transfusion, Aleksandr Aleksandrovich Malinovsky, better known as Bogdanov, had exchanged his blood with that of a critically ill malaria victim in hopes of saving both the patient and his blood. The outcome of this may be guessed: both doctor and patient died forthwith.[1] Although an extraordinary venture on Bogdanov's part, for it was part of a search for the means to immortality,[2] the transfusion experiment was only one of a host of startling things he had done in his thirty years in Russian politics and public life. In actuality, the activities and achievement of his two years as director of the Soviet Union's first institute for the study of blood transfusion seem virtually insignificant beside the events of earlier years.[3] It would be fair to say that Aleksandr Bogdanov stood in a singularly prominent position in the political and intellectual life of Russia from the turn of the century to 1930. Politically, he had been Lenin's only serious rival for leadership among the Bolsheviks before 1917. In the early years of the Soviet regime, Bogdanov stood head and shoulders above any other public figure operating outside the ranks of the Party. Only a handful of men, i.e., Plekhanov, Bukharin, Berdiaev and Solov'ev, can be compared to Bogdanov in the extent of their intellectual influence in those years. In no case was the intellectual career of any of these men so varied and so continually notable as that of Bogdanov. As we shall see in the biographical sketch which follows, the first three decades of the twentieth century found Bogdanov in positions of political, cultural, and intellectual leadership at every turn.

Bogdanov, like Lenin the son of an educator, was born on August 10, 1873 in Tula. His gymnasium studies highly successful, he entered the natural science faculty of Moscow University around 1892 and pursued studies there and in Kharkov, where he received his degree in 1899 as a physician specializing in psychology.[4] Bogdanov tells us in his autobiography that his

1

contempt for authority in educational institutions led him into radical politics in 1894.[5] As was usually the case with student radicals, he began his career as a populist but was soon converted to Marxism (1896). Between 1894 and 1904, Bogdanov agitated and wrote propaganda in association with various worker, student and social-democratic groups in Moscow, Kharkov, Tula and Vologda. During this time, he developed numerous contacts and strong ties among the Russian working class in the social-democratic party and literary circles.[6] Arrested numerous times between 1899 and 1901, he was finally sent into three-years' exile in Vologda. In those years (1901–1904), Bogdanov came into contact with many of the leading lights of Russian social-democracy through association with fellow-exiles in that city. In Vologda, he had the company of Berdiaev, then the leading figure among the Legal Marxists, V. Rudnev (pseudonym Bazarov), the co-translator of Marx's *Kapital,* I. I. Skvortsov-Stepanov, the other translator, A. V. Lunacharsky, the future Commisar of Education and others.[7] In this context, Bogdanov the propagandist, organizer and theoretician rose to the ranks of the well known in Russian radicalism. In those years, he took the pseudonym Bogdanov most often, although he was known to use Maksimov, Rakhmetov, Reinert, Riadovoi and Verner as well.[8] While Maksimov stuck with him for a time, he became universally known as Bogdanov and retained the usage to the end of his life.[9]

The term of his exile expired, Bogdanov, who had been attracted to the Bolsheviks during the debates of 1903–1904, joined Lenin in Switzerland in the Summer of 1904. Almost immediately, he rose to the position of second-in-command and became the faction's principal leader in Russia. Both Georges Haupt and Karl Ballestrem suggest that Bogdanov brought Lenin out of political isolation at a time when he was set off from the rest of the social-democratic movement by bringing him the contacts and talent to issue a Bolshevik paper.[10] The contacts were apparently Bogdanov's very numerous political and intellectual associates in Russia. The talent was provided by Bogdanov himself and the three important figures he had brought into Bolshevism in 1904, Bazarov, Lunacharsky and Skvortsov-Stepanov.[11] From 1904 to 1908, Lenin and Bogdanov formed a firm bloc, with the latter acting as the former's man in Russia. Although occasionally at odds over the running of the Bolshevik committee in St. Petersburg and Bogdanov's experimentation in philosophy,[12] the two scrupulously avoided open disputes.

Although their partnership was continually reaffirmed, Bogdanov came to be regarded by many Bolsheviks, and certainly by Lenin himself, as a rival for leadership of the faction. Beginning in 1905, Bogdanov's activities in Russia greatly enhanced his importance. During the revolution of that year, he had been the chief Bolshevik in the St. Petersburg Soviet, where by all accounts he played an important role.[13] In addition, he was twice elected to the Central Committee of the Russian Social-Democratic Party and, as the only Bolshevik on the Committee, was the most visible member of the faction in Russia.[14] During the period of the first two Dumas, Bogdanov functioned as the engineer of Bolshevik involvement and held control of all local Bolshevik committees in Russia by way of his editorship of their journal, *Vpered.*[15]

In some ways, Bogdanov's rivalry with Lenin was merely circumstantial: Bogdanov was quite simply better known and better situated in the revolutionary movement. Gradually, however, this rivalry took on a more active character. After the closing of the second Duma, Bogdanov broke with Lenin over the issue of tactics regarding the third. He assumed active leadership of that large faction of Bolsheviks who favored insurrection over continued legal participation in politics. Lenin, of course, prevailed in the matter and dissuaded the Bolshevik Central Committee from Bogdanov's "Otzovist" course.[16] Although Bogdanov eventually went along with Lenin,[17] the die was cast for further difficulties between them. Bogdanov became in time the leader of those "left" Bolsheviks who continually pressed for revolution between 1907 and 1911. The strength of the left Bolsheviks is attested to by the fact that the group was eventually expelled (1909) in the first and most significant of Bolshevik splits. In this same period (1905–1909), Bogdanov asserted himself against Lenin in another way. He, along with Leonid Krasin, managed virtually complete control of Bolshevik finances. The two, who formed a triumvirate with Lenin after 1905, were extraordinarily adept at raising funds both legally and extralegally.[18] Bogdanov has been credited with being the chief architect of the infamous "expropriations" which gained the faction hundreds of thousands of rubles and something of a bad reputation.[19] The role of Bogdanov and Krasin as fund-raisers developed into their role as financial controllers. From 1907 on, Lenin found it increasingly necessary to circumvent the two in order to fund his projects. They apparently had other ideas as to where Bolshevik monies should go.[20] Interestingly, when Bogdanov and Krasin were expelled from the Bolshevik Central Committee in 1909, the former took the better part of the faction's funds with him. The monies found their way into the coffers of the *Vperedist* faction of left Bolsheviks and were used to fund the *Vperedist*-run Capri and Bologna Party Schools.[21] If the control of funds can be positively associated with power in a revolutionary movement, Bogdanov's role in Bolshevik finances attests to the extent of his rivalry with Lenin in those years.

As indicated, Bogdanov's partnership with Lenin did not break down until 1908–1909, when the two came into open conflict on theoretical issues. The polemic between Lenin and Bogdanov at that time comprises one of the most important chapters in both the career of Bolshevism and the development of Lenin as a theoretician. Between 1902 and 1908, Bogdanov had written and published several works of philosophy. Although Lenin regarded these positivist-inspired and, for that, at odds with the spirit and letter of Marxism, he opted to keep philosophical disputes out of party literature in order to maintain the unity of what was then a fragile organization. He took the position that ideological diversity was permissible as long as it was not politically and organizationally disruptive. The story of the ideological split with Bogdanov is too long and involved to present here,[22] but suffice it to say that the split with the left Bolsheviks over the matter of Duma involvement eventually brought an end to the ideological truce. In 1908–1909, Lenin demanded political, organizational and philosophical unity among the Bolsheviks and brought his discontent with Bogdanov and the rest to the radical public in the pages of *Proletarii*, the faction's principal organ at the time.[23] Subsequent to the polemics which ensued, Lenin engineered the expulsion of Bogdanov and Krasin from the Bolshevik Central Committee. The eventual outcome was the departure of Bogdanov and virtually all of the left Bolsheviks from the faction itself. In a sense, what Lenin had gained in 1904 he lost in 1909.[24]

The group led by Bogdanov and including Lunacharsky, Bazarov and others remained politically active, calling themselves the *Vperedist* group after the name of the journal they collaborated on between 1909 and 1911.[25] The *Vperedists*, although soon to dissolve, did in fact make a bid to wean the Bolshevik rank and file away from Lenin. Continuing to use the journal as a rallying point, the group moved on in 1910–1911 to establish the first social-democratic party schools. Held on Capri and in Bologna in succeeding years under Bogdanov's directorship, the schools taught everything from philosophy and history to organizational tactics.[26] Both attracted many of the more important Russian Marxist intellectuals as lecturers. The list includes not only the gifted likes of Bogdanov, Lunacharsky and Pokrovsky, but also Trotsky, Maxim Gor'ky and V. Menzhinsky.[27] In 1909–1911, it must have seemed to many social-democrats that the intellectual leadership of their movement had taken on a new and more virile form among the *Vperedists*.

More important than the loss of Bogdanov and the rest to Bolshevism and the opposition of *Vpered* was the fact that the ideological dispute caused Lenin to take several positions which would determine the character of Soviet politics and ideology. In chasing out the left dissidents, Lenin formulated the doctrine of *partijnost'* or the "partyness of philosophy."[28] This phrase, which makes firm the elemental connection between philosophy and politics, expressed the Leninist contention that all ideological divergence from the party line led inevitably to dangerous political and organizational dissidence. The result of the dispute with Bogdanov and the rest, then, was the tight intellectual discipline so characteristic of the Communist Party and the Soviet regime. While the Bolsheviks admitted and retained men of divergent views before 1909, thereafter they rejected and expelled them.

As important as the doctrine of *partijnost'* was to Lenin and Bolshevism in the ensuing years, it was but one of the doctrines and positions growing out of the split with Bogdanov. The conflict between the two led to the writing (1906–1907) of Lenin's only published work on philosophy, *Materialism and Empirio-Criticism* (1909).[29] While scarcely noticed at the time, the work would become part of the scripture of Marxism-Leninism. From it, Soviet ideologues took Lenin's statements on various matters regarding epistemology, philosophy of science, dialectics, etc., and built them into the foundation of official Soviet philosophy. In a sense, then, Bogdanov's effect on Lenin and Soviet ideology was greater than any other thinker save Engels and Hegel. As some scholars have suggested, Soviet dialectical materialism might well have taken on a substantially different character had it not been for the challenge of Bogdanov.[30]

In 1911, Bogdanov left *Vpered* and the Social-Democratic Party altogether. He tells us in his autobiography that he became tired of the squabbles of émigré intellectual life and wished to return to Russia.[31] One cannot help but suspect, however, that he passed through a period of intellectual crisis in 1910–1911. As we shall see, Bogdanov's work took a new turn in those years, and it was apparent that he now considered himself needed more as a theoretician than as a political leader.[32] The *Vperedists* dispersed quickly after his departure. While the circumstances of the group's dissolution are not known, it may well have been due to the lack of the sort of leadership necessary in so intellectually powerful a group. Many of the *Vperedists* remained politically active. Most of these returned to Lenin in time, although they remained to a large extent intellectually loyal to Bogdanov. The early years of the new regime found many *Vperedists* in positions of intellectual leadership. Lunacharsky and Pokrovsky headed the Commisariat of

Education and Gor'ky of course, became the very "conscience" of the revolution.[33]

Between 1911 and 1917, Bogdanov withdrew almost entirely from public life. Nevertheless, he continued to write propaganda pieces for *Pravda* and other workers' papers.[34] These years saw the beginning of several new projects, and, in essence, Bogdanov spent them in preparation for the considerable role he would play in 1917 and the early years of the new regime.

The February revolution found Bogdanov in Moscow. He had returned to Russia in 1914 and spent the war years as a doctor at the front.[35] Between the revolutions, Bogdanov founded the Proletarian Culture Movement *(Proletkul't)*, an organization the significance of which can hardly be overestimated. The matter of proletarian art, literature, education, philosophy and science had absorbed much of his energy between 1911 and 1917.[36] Thus, when the opportunity seemed best for the institutionalization of his ideas, Bogdanov was ready not only with doctrines but organizational plans as well. The movement grew rapidly and came to be the only mass organization besides the Party to flourish in those years. *Proletkul't* claimed upwards of 400,000 members organized into art, literature and crafts workshops. As an organization, it aspired to dictate in cultural matters as the Party did in political affairs.[37] While not opposed to the regime, *Proletkul't* agitated for a complete break with the "bourgeois" past which ran counter to the more moderate Party line. Because of its rabid "leftism" and the challenge it issued to the Party in its attempt to reign in cultural affairs, Lenin was forced to take positions on culture with which he otherwise might not have bothered. The challenge of *Proletkul't* pushed Lenin to assert the Party's rule in cultural matters as well as in philosophy. In 1921, *Proletkul't* was forced to abandon its independent status and to attach itself to the Commisariat of Education.[38] The old attack on Bogdanov began again with the republication of *Materialism and Empirio-Criticism* in that same year, and *Proletkul't* faded quietly away.[39]

Curiously, Lenin's opposition to *Proletkul't* and the renewed attack on Bogdanov's philosophical position did not drive him out of public life. In 1918, he had become the first director of the Socialist Academy for Social Science (after 1924 the Communist Academy) and continued in that position until 1923.[40] It is apparent that the Academy was important to Lenin and the Party, since it was proposed as a "proletarian" antidote to the bourgeois-controlled Academy of Sciences, Russia's greatest scholarly institution. In spite of the opposition to Bogdanov, who would have nothing to do with the

Party, he was given considerable range in the running of the Academy. There is, in fact, some evidence to suggest that the institution's program between 1918 and 1923 was "Bogdanovist" in significant part.[41]

Bogdanov remained a member of the Academy until his death. After 1918 he held forth as a professor at Moscow University and played an important role in *Sovnarkhoz*, the government's principal economic council.[42] So great was his stature in those years that at the time of Lenin's death he was asked to rejoin the Party by the triumvirs Zinoviev, Kamenev and Bukharin, who hoped to bring him into collaboration against Stalin.[43] This is all the more significant, since his thought had been indicted in 1923 as the inspiration of the Workers' Truth group which practiced illegal agitation against the regime.[44] Perhaps unfortunately, Bogdanov refused to join either the cause of the triumvirs or the Party. Whether or not he subsequently sought the protection of Stalin, as one commentator suggests,[45] it was clear that by that time his interests were very far removed from politics. In his autobiography, Bogdanov tells us that he devoted himself to purely scientific work after 1923.[46] While this was a broad category in his mind, since it included work in economic and social planning, it was certainly the case that he drifted steadily toward private research during the last five years of his life. The year 1926 might be taken to mark his ultimate move away from public life. In that year he founded the transfusion institute and worked quietly and productively there until his death.[47]

Bogdanov was widely eulogized for his numerous contributions to the revolution and Soviet regime. The lead in this came from the most imposing intellectual in the Party, Nikolai Bukharin, who wrote Bogdanov's obituary for *Pravda*.[48] This was most fitting, for Bogdanov's influence on Bukharin had been enormous, perhaps greater than it had been on any other individual with whom Bogdanov had come in contact.[49]

If the impact of Bogdanov's career as politician and public figure was great, the impact of his thought was even greater. The variety of his contributions to Bolshevism, Soviet planning and science is matched, if not over-matched, by the variety of his intellectual contributions. Bogdanov himself divided his intellectual career into work in five different areas, i.e., political economy, historical materialism, philosophy, proletarian culture and "organizational science".[50] In every area in which Bogdanov worked, he made extensive and highly original contributions. Most often, he was on the scene first and with the most to offer. As he was intellectually ambitious, so was he successful in producing widely influential works. His intellectual career and its influence may be briefly depicted as follows.

Between 1896 and 1899 Bogdanov was principally involved in the study of economics. Beginning in those years, he produced a series of Marxist texts which were revised and re-released numerous times.[51] His works on "political economy" became in time standard social-democratic reading and were officially adopted by the Soviets. It has been claimed that Bogdanov, more than any other writer, gave the generation of the revolution its education in Marxist economics.[52] I. I. Skvortsov-Stepanov was perhaps the only figure who had so much influence in this area, and even he functioned most often as Bogdanov's co-author.[53] Although his work in economics had the greatest effect on, if you will, the "introductory level", Bogdanov's impact was felt in the highest circles of Soviet economic planning, i.e., in *Sovnarkhoz*, the Socialist Academy, etc. In addition, it should be noted that Bogdanov's influence was very strong on the economic thought of Bukharin and his followers in the 'twenties.[54]

Between 1899 and 1910, Bogdanov produced a series of popular works intended to provide the working class with an historical-materialist worldview. While mostly Marxist economics and social theory, these works also brought the latest results of scientific research into historical-materialist perspective. As Karl Ballestrem suggests, Bogdanov's major works in this area, *Basic Elements of an Historical View of the World* (1899) and *Knowledge from the Historical Point-of-View* (1901),[55] sought to bring "scientific socialism" and natural science together in a broad perspective.[56] It is difficult to assess the extent of Bogdanov's influence as an historical materialist. If Bukharin's *Historical Materialism*, which is replete with "Bogdanovist" points-of-view is any indication, his effect in this area may well have been as great as his impact as a political economist.[57]

As a Russian Marxist theoretician, Bogdanov led the polemic against the Legal Marxists, attacking the likes of Berdiaev, Bulgakov and Struve for their neo-Kantian leanings.[58] As the leader of the struggle against "idealism" in Russian Marxism between 1902 and 1905, Bogdanov became the central figure of the "opposite", i.e., positivist, trend. Although he did not claim this position for himself and eschewed the label of "positivist", his influence on the career of positivism in Russian Marxism was considerable. The trend was strong until 1930, when the Party succeeded in proscribing it.[59] Some have suggested that had Bogdanov and others with positivist leanings not been the political opponents of Lenin, Soviet though might well have taken on the same empiricist and pragmatist coloring as Western European and American philosophy in the 'twenties and 'thirties.[60] As it was, the "mechanist" trend with which Bogdanov and the positivists were associated by its opponents nearly became the official line in the 'twenties.[61]

First in the context of, and later apart from the neo-Kantian polemic, Bogdanov produced numerous tracts of and about philosophy. Beginning from the study of epistemology under natural-scientific and critical-positivist influences (circa 1903), Bogdanov eventually broadened his philosophical position into a complete and many-faceted worldview, which he considered wholly new and different from those of the past.[62] This work greatly enhanced Bogdanov's impact in other areas of endeavor: in a sense it made him one of the strongest theoreticians among social-democratic leaders. Among those who were sympathetic to his worldview were such important Russian and Soviet intellectuals as Lunacharsky, Pokrovsky, Gor'ky and Bukharin. It might be said, in fact, that most of the intellectually serious social-democrats before 1917 held Bogdanov as philosopher in high regard. If Valentinov is correct, Bogdanov's treatises outsold all others at that time.[63] Given the continued popularity of his thought and that of his sympathizers, who held so many of the important positions in the early Soviet cultural establishment, it might be said as well that the "Bogdanovist" worldview remained the subject of serious consideration into the 'twenties.

As we noted above, from 1911 to 1917 Bogdanov devoted himself to constructing a theory and program of proletarian culture.[64] In a sense, the Capri and Bologna Party Schools were his first experiment in directing proletarians toward the creation of their own culture. Between 1917 and 1921, his work in this area intensified with the flourishing of *Proletkul't*. Bogdanov must be considered a principal architect of the vision of the new art, literature, music, etc., as it appeared in Russia after 1917.[65] As in the case of his economic and historical-materialist work, he had created in *"proletkul'tism"* an idea which stood alone in breadth and depth at that time. *"Proletkul'tism"* endured through the 'twenties, and from time to time Bogdanovist cultural ideas were manifest among those who opposed the Soviet regime's compromises with bourgeois technical and intellectual elements.[66] In addition, Bogdanov's notions spread as far West as England, where a clearly Bogdanovist proletarian culture movement developed in the 'twenties.[67]

While philosophy had been Bogdanov's largest intellectual interest before 1910, his concern shifted thereafter to science; the last 18 years of his career in print were devoted primarily to the study of the "science" of organization. It was in this area that Bogdanov was at his most ambitious and original. The years 1913–1922 saw the appearance of three volumes attempting to create a "universal science of organization" which Bogdanov saw as the science of sciences demanded by the development of automated production and the rise of the proletariat.[68] While the "universal organizational science" was not

widely acclaimed in itself, Bogdanov's notions on organization found their
way into Soviet economic planning via the Socialist Academy and the thought
of Bukharin.[69] From 1922 to his death, work after work on organizational
science appeared. As late as 1926, Bogdanov showed an optimism for the project which could only have come from some significant support among Soviet
intellectuals.[70] Later his work on "organization" would be praised as an
important beginning to Russian research in cybernetics.

B. TOWARD A NEW APPROACH TO BOGDANOV AND
THE RUSSIAN MACHISTS

The sketch of Bogdanov's career and thought above is meant to introduce the
subject of our study and to provide evidence of the breadth and diversity of
his intellectual concerns. We wish to propose the need to restudy Bogdanov
under an approach which takes him in and for himself, that is, according to
his broadest intentions and outside of and beyond the context in which past
scholars have placed him. Most commonly, students of Bogdanov have turned
away from the considerable undertaking of his thought in and for itself after
a partial sketch in favor of assessing the effect of his political and philosophical struggle with Lenin on the development of the Party and Soviet
ideology.[71] While his impact in this regard is indeed that fact about
Bogdanov's career and thought which is of the most enduring importance, its
employment as a focus at the expense of others has led to the obscuring of
the complete phenomenon of Bogdanov. In all of the major studies, he is ever
Lenin's rival, either in the actual sense or in the sense that he is deemed the
exponent of the sorts of politics and thought with which Lenin and Leninists
had no truck. When his thought is allowed to speak for itself, it is generally
only so much as is necessary to show the points of conflict with Lenin. Even
his biographer, while claiming to view Bogdanov as a singularly original
thinker, structures his assessment of Bogdanov's thought according to Lenin's
reaction to it. For Dietrich Grille, "Bogdanovism" is a set of doctrines
determined more by Lenin's opposition than by anything else.[72] Taking the
struggle with Lenin as a focus as they do, the major studies fade rapidly when
it comes to the discussion of aspects of Bogdanov's thought which cannot
be tied in directly with the struggle. It is assumed by some commentators that
Bogdanov's thought had a certain unity and that his half-dozen or so
intellectual concerns were part of a single greater one.[73] Curiously, no one
has attempted to back these assumptions with a study of the actual facts.

Usually, his thought is reduced down to the epistemological point of view with which Lenin took issue in *Materialism and Empirio-Criticism*.[74]

The need to study Bogdanov under the broader approach of his thought in and for itself is suggested, most obviously, by the extent to which he functioned and theorized outside the context of the dispute with Lenin and the fact that no one has allowed his works to speak wholly for themselves. There is, however, another circumstance which makes his restudy seem all the more necessary and worthwhile. Scholarly concern with Bogdanov vis-à-vis Lenin and Soviet ideology has obscured more than the career and thought of one man. It has, in fact, obscured an extraordinarily interesting trend in the intellectual life of early twentieth-century Russia.

Part of the reason for the intensity of Lenin's opposition to Bogdanov's philosophical position was due to the fact that he did not stand alone in it. From the time of the polemic with the neo-Kantians until 1908–1909, Bogdanov stood at the center of a group commonly referred to as the Russian Machists. These thinkers, all Marxists united by their opposition to the neo-Kantianism of Berdiaev and company, shared (at least for a time) an affinity for empiriocriticism, the critical-positivist doctrine of Ernst Mach and Richard Avenarius which had been popular among European Marxists in general after 1880.[75] Although, as we shall argue more extensively below, the Russian Machists became over time highly independent thinkers, both Russian and Western scholars have come to consider the activities and thought of the group adjunct to the political and intellectual career of Bogdanov. Accordingly, Bogdanov has been taken to speak for the whole, and no attempt has been made to study the others in and for themselves. Furthermore, the distinction between Bogdanov's thought, which, as we shall see in this study, was only Machian in part and at a particular time, and that of the group has become so blurred that almost anyone who shared positions and points of view with Bogdanov has been taken to be part of the Machist trend.[76]

The term "Machist" came into use around 1905 when Lenin and Plekhanov recognized that Bogdanov and the others who polemicized against the neo-Kantians had been considerably under the influence of Machist criticial positivism. Finding themselves as much opposed to positivist Marxism as they were to the neo-Kantian variety, the two came to divide all opposition to "orthodoxy" between the "idealists" and the "Machists".[77] Subsequent to the philosophical conflict with Bogdanov, Lenin continually insisted on applying the term to those who were in league or sympathy with his opponent as well as to any Marxist at all who leaned in the direction of positivism, whether of the Machist variety or otherwise. This ideologically expedient name-calling continued in practice as long as Bogdanov's ideas and positivism presented a threat to the Party line in philosophy.[78]

Those thinkers labeled Machists in this fashion fall into three groups: 1) those who actually participated in the polemic against the neo-Kantians and espoused empiriocritical points of view in so doing, 2) those who shared one or another position with Bogdanov in intellectual matters at whatever time, and 3) those who were associated with Bogdanov either at the time of his political leadership or during the years of *Proletkul't*. If we consider who falls under the Machist designation, we discover immediately the total unreasonability of its use. Such singular thinkers as Lunacharsky, Pokrovsky, Gor'ky, Aleksandra Kollontai and Bukharin fall into the second group above and the third includes the likes of Trotsky and the wholly aphilosophical Krasin![79] Only the members of the first group may reasonably be considered Machists. They are Bogdanov, N. N. Vol'sky (pseudonym Valentinov), Ja. A. Ber'man, P. S. Jushkevich, Bazarov, P. Gel'fond and S. Suvorov, all of whom collaborated in the chief anti-neo-Kantian tract, *Essays of a Realistic World-View* (1904).[80]

Past scholarship, concentrating on Bogdanov, has had little to say about the rest. We know the most about Valentinov, since he came West after the revolution and produced several interesting memoirs.[81] These, however, tell us next to nothing about his thought and there are no studies regarding it. Jushkevich's thought has been discussed briefly by Gustav Wetter in conjunction with his study of Bogdanov in *Dialectical Materialism*.[82] The others remain totally unknown and uninvestigated. In dealing with the group as a whole, the tendency has been to emphasize Bogdanov's central place, and with that, to consider Russian Machism, like Bogdanov, for its negative contribution to Marxism-Leninism. In only one instance has the group's affinity for Machist critical positivism been studied further than Lenin's reaction to Bogdanov's thought makes necessary.[83] Even in that instance, the study is almost wholly conjectural since it is made without a general survey of Machist literature on the basis of what its author has learned about Bogdanov alone. In no instance has the Machist reaction to "Leninism" and other prevailing trends in Russian Marxist thought been investigated. That such a study and investigation are crucial to understanding the Machists goes without saying.

The most unfortunate deficiency of past scholarship is clearly its failure to consider the Machists in accord with their broadest and most basic purposes. That such an attempt is necessary is suggested by several facts about their career beyond the years of the neo-Kantian polemic. Although none of them gained the notoriety of Bogdanov before the revolution, they did a considerable amount of writing in those years. After the neo-Kantian polemic, Bogdanov and the rest went their separate ways intellectually. All came in time to renounce much of their earlier enthusiasm for empirio-criticism, and many shook off a good deal of their Marxism in the bargain. Each sooner or later came to assert the newness and originality of his thought. In 1908–1909 the "real" Machists, joined by others more appropriately called "Bogdanovists," produced two collective works, *Essays in the Philosophy of Marxism* and *Essays in the Philosophy of Collectivism*, which dealt with a host of social, political, economic, cultural and philo-sophical issues not associated with positivism or Marxist doctrines per se.[84] Lenin, however, chose to regard these collections as part of the Bogdanov-led "Machist" menace growing in Russia since 1902 and held forth against their authors on this ground in *Materialism and Empirio-Criticism*.[85] What in fact brought these men together in 1908–1909 was a common distrust of all orthodoxies, whether Marxist, positivist or otherwise, and a common concern that contemporary reality should be brought under a radically new sort of critique which such orthodoxies would not allow. Consequently, the collections show their authors to be very far from unanimity in philosophical points of view. Lenin was correct in considering Bogdanov and the rest a "revisionist" threat to orthodox Marxism, but the extent of their revisionism went well beyond whatever affinity for Machist critical positivism they still possessed in those years.

In proposing to deal with Bogdanov's thought in and for itself, we also suggest the way in which the Russian Machists need to be approached. If there is more to Bogdanov's thought than an epistemological position of which Lenin did not approve, there is similarly more to the thought of the Machists than their affinity for empiriocriticism suggests. Because of their indepen-dence and the diversity of their thought, one ought to take them, first separately and then as a group, according to their basic self-conceptions and broadest intentions. Their relations with the neo-Kantians, Lenin and even Bogdanov must be treated as secondary. The employment of such an approach would most certainly yield interesting results. For one thing, the reasons for the appeal of Machist critical positivism and other species of "scientist" thought among Russian intellectuals also favorably disposed toward Marxism would obviously be given a more substantial character. For another, we would be afforded a more complete understanding of a major dissident faction of Russian Marxists, the influence of which was considerable on numerous important figures of the revolutionary and early Soviet periods.

What might be the most interesting result of such an approach, however, lies in a broader context than the history of Russian Marxism. Since each of the Machists came to regard himself as an original thinker with universal concerns, a study of the group in and for itself might reveal its members as wide-ranging and serious commentators on the character of life and thought in the early twentieth century. One might find that Bogdanov and the rest comprise a group of thinkers more broadly and, perhaps, more intimately in touch with reality in that promising and disturbing time than most of their better-known and politically more successful contemporaries in the Russian radical intelligentsia. While this conjecture is largely inspired by the study of Bogdanov which follows, even a superficial perusal of the major Machist writings suggests that the concerns and intents of these men were exceptionally broad and ambitious and that their thought was conceived as a radically new response to the conditions of contemporary life and thought. Accordingly, any thorough-going study of one or another of the Machists ought to take the breadth of approach that the phrase "the thinker in and for himself" implies and be prepared to draw broad conclusions.

C.   STUDYING BOGDANOV

It is the intention of this study to make a beginning at the study of Bogdanov's thought under the approach discussed above. The particular way in which we have chosen to take Bogdanov in and for himself needs some explanation, since what we attempt here falls considerably short of a complete study.

Clearly, the proper way in which to approach any thinker is by way of a thorough-going consideration of the entire corpus of his writings with the intention of establishing his basic self-conception and fundamental intents. While such a consideration is possible in dealing with most of the Machians in a monograph-length work, in the case of Bogdanov it is not: the number of his works is simply too great for a relatively short study.[86] While all of the Machians were prolific writers, no one matched Bogdanov in the sheer volume of pages written. A survey of Machist literature reveals, in fact, that he was responsible for nearly half of it. Alongside the enormity of the task of taking the whole of Bogdanov's writings into consideration at once, there is the added difficulty of their diversity. Upon reviewing the corpus of his works, one is tempted to take Bogdanov's autobiographical statement at face value. There, he portrayed himself variously as political economist, historical materialist, philosopher, theoretician of proletarian culture and philosopher of science, as if these·were entirely separate vocations thrust upon him by the demands of his career in science, politics and public life.[87] Indeed, it is difficult to glimpse a basic self-conception and fundamental purposes in such diverse works as *A Short Course in Economic Science, Basic Elements of an Historical View of Nature, Empiriomonism,* 'What is Proletarian Poetry?' and *Tektologiia: The Universial Science of Organization.* It is perhaps for this reason that past scholars have avoided seeking out the pattern and meaning of the whole of his thought in favor of showing his career in print as a series of turnings from one concern to another prompted by changes in his life and the effects of new influences.[88]

For a time, it appeared to this writer that the only way to take Bogdanov seriously in and for himself was to attempt a work-by-work, influence-by-influence study in the hope that an overall picture would eventually emerge. It was decided to begin with a look at Bogdanov the "philosopher", the epistemologist under the influence of Mach, following the suggestion of other of his students that Bogdanov's thought was first and foremost part of the critical-positivist trend in the late nineteenth and early twentieth centuries.[89] The study of *Empiriomonism,*[90] Bogdanov's principal work on philosophy, however, presented a difficulty which forestalled the study. From reading the three volumes of the work, it was apparent that Bogdanov's arguments on philosophy were made in conjunction with, and dependent upon, a host of social, economic, historical and scientific arguments which were obscure on account of their transfer without adequate explanation from Bogdanov's earlier works. It was clear that Bogdanov the philosopher could not be considered apart from Bogdanov the economist, sociologist, historical materialist and philosopher of science. It seemed that nothing short of a complete study of Bogdanov's works would facilitate understanding him in and for himself.

Fortunately, unwillingness to abandon the topic eventuated in the realization that there was a way in which Bogdanov's basic self-conception and general purposes could be studied short of the complete investigation of his work. In looking through some of Bogdanov's minor works on philosophy, which this writer had acquired on microfilm title by title, he came upon a lecture entitled 'From Religious to Scientific Monism'. In delivering this, perhaps to his colleagues in the Socialist Academy at the time of his departure from the directorship, Bogdanov canvassed his entire career in print, citing his conclusions on various matters (indeed, a universe of them) as evidence in making an argument for the end of philosophy and the sort of knowledge which would supersede it as that most necessary for the advance of mankind in both labor practice and thought. In brief, the lecture formed a rather complete statement of worldview, self-conception, general and enduring purposes, and was an assessment of a life's work in the bargain. It appeared, then, that this lecture was an important key to understanding Bogdanov in and for himself. It seemed that from so broadly conceived a work coming roughly in the wake of Bogdanov's ultimate intellectual achievement, the universal science of organization, one might turn to survey the corpus of his writings with an idea of the basic things for which to look.

As it turned out, however, 'From Religious to Scientific Monism' led not to an intellectual biography but to another sort of study felicitously more within the scope of a monograph-length work. It was discovered that the lecture had been appended to the 1923 edition of *The Philiosophy of Living Experience,*[91] a work written in 1910 and first published in 1913, which had previously appeared to this writer, who had not been led to believe otherwise by past scholars, to be a popular restatement of Bogdanov's position in philosophy created for the benefit of his partisans and potential supporters at the time of *Vpered.* In considering the reason for the reissue of both the work and lecture under the same cover, it was discovered that the latter was nothing more than a restatement of the former in abbreviated form. Apparently, Bogdanov had appended the lecture to show that the 1910 work fully expressed the positions he held in 1923. Indeed, comparison of the later edition of *The Philosophy of Living Experience* to that of 1913 revealed that no revision whatever had occurred. Here, then, was a much more substantial key to Bogdanov's thought and a highly unusual one, considering that although written in mid-career its arguments and positions endured without change from the time of *Vpered* into the last five years of his life. What was perhaps even more unusual about *The Philosophy of Living Experience* was that it assessed accurately and in advance the character of Bogdanov's work after 1910 by setting the "universal science of organization" as the task ahead of him. Thus, it appeared that the work as a personal statement was not only one of self-assessment but one of self-direction as well.

As a consequence of these discoveries, it was decided to focus the study of Bogdanov's thought in and for itself on *The Philosophy of Living Experience.* Upon consideration of the scope and intentions of the works, any thought of going beyond its explication and analysis seemed too ambitious. It became apparent that the work was nearly as broad and diverse in its concerns as the whole of Bogdanov's thought itself. Within its pages, one finds a study of the conditions of life and thought in the early twentieth century, the exposition of a philosophical worldview issued in response to those conditions, an assessment of the career of philosophy, an historical-materialist study of the career of labor practice and knowledge, and a projection of the future of mankind. Although the discussion of all this seemed quite enough for one study, another feature of the work suggested the reasonability of studying it alone. In contrast to 'From Religious to Scientific Monism', *The Philosophy of Living Experience* contained several long chapters assessing and criticizing empiriocriticism and Marxist materialism.[92] This aspect of the work suggested that its study would not only provide a general portrait of Bogdanov's thought but also a substantial insight into how he regarded intellectual competitors of far greater stature than Lenin. In short, *The Philosophy of Living Experience* promised a great deal toward the understanding of what Bogdanov conceived himself and his thought to be.

D. *THE PHILOSOPHY OF LIVING EXPERIENCE*

In introducing the study of *The Philosophy of Living Experience*, we should note straightway that the treatment of this single work is in no way intended to replace the complete study of Bogdanov's thought which ought to be done. This work begins the study of Bogdanov in and for himself by taking what must be considered his broadest and most diverse work it and for itself. Hopefully, our treatment of *The Philosophy of Living Experience* will be more substantial a beginning than another sort of partial study.

We propose to explicate and analyze the work in accord with its particular intentions and effects. It is our intention to take the arguments of *The Philosophy of Living Experience* as seriously as Bogdanov did himself and to regard the work as it was hoped to be received. We will refrain, therefore, from passing judgment on the quality of its arguments or the accuracy of its assessments. Further, we will avoid searching for and identifying the sources of Bogdanov's ideas beyond that which the work itself gives us. It is clear that *The Philosophy of Living Experience,* like *Empiriomonism,* has its immediate sources in the works which preceded it. Without a complete study of Bogdanov's earlier works and their sources, most conclusions we might reach regarding the sources of his thought in *The Philosophy of Living Experience* would very likely be unreliable. We do not deny that a proper study of Bogdanov's thought must involve the investigation of the career of various influences in his writings. Inasmuch as our study deals with a single work derivative of others, it seems more appropriate to give indications of sources and influences without concluding broadly on what they indicate about the whole of Bogdanov's thought.

Since the matter of his relationship to Marx and Mach is of particular interest to one wishing to understand Bogdanov's self-conception, and since the two are discussed more directly and extensively in *The Philosophy of Living Experience* than in other of his works, it is tempting to take the chapters devoted to them as ultimate statements regarding their influence on Bogdanov. While that they may be, we have no way of knowing from the work under consideration what the influence of Marx and Mach amounted to prior to 1910. Again, we will elaborate the way in which the influence of Marx and Mach appears in the work and will leave the matter of their total influence open.

In this study, we will proceed largely without the aid of past scholarship on Bogdanov's thought. The principal reason for this is to allow *The Philosophy of Living Experience* to speak for itself. There are, of course, numerous treatments of Bogdanov's thought which describe and analyze positions transferred over into the work from earlier writings.[93] While these treatments are not inaccurate, they tend to present the tenets of Bogdanov's thought as evidence to support arguments that he was an empiricist of this sort, a Marxist of that — or a Machian critical positivist but for something or other, etc. While this is often illuminating, it ignores the fact that Bogdanov conceived of himself as a thinker independent of all trends in past thought. To say that this or that position is a materialist, empiricist or Marxist one, relates it more to the corpus of materialism, empiricism or Marxism than it does to the corpus of Bogdanov's thought itself. We submit that since Bogdanov considered his worldview unique, the only way to appreciate fully the meaning of his positions is to take them as unique tenets in systematic relation with other unique tenets. Thereby, we may discover the unity and basic intentions of his thought.

Another reason why we will proceed without the aid of others is for the simple reason that next to nothing is forthcoming with regard to *The Philosophy of Living Experience*. The work is cited quite often in explications of Bogdanov's epistemological point of view, since it is restated there in concise form.[94] In no instance, however, has a commentator attempted either to depict the context into which the statement of epistemological position is put in *The Philosophy of Living Experience* or to investigate the work in and for itself. The most extensive mention of the work comes in Grille's biography, where it is briefly considered as the first announcement of Bogdanov's intention to create a "universal science of organization".[95] It is difficult to understand why the work has been ignored, if only because it contains criticism of Marx. We expect that the oversight has again been due to the concentration on Bogdanov's struggle with Lenin. *The Philosophy of Living Experience* was written, after all, not only after *Materialism and Empirio-Criticism* but also after Bogdanov's reply to Lenin in *Belief and Science* (1910).[96] Since it came after the polemic had subsided and was not in itself polemical, scholars may quite simply have been inclined to write it off as a popular restatement of positions already well known and lacking in substance compared to the works in which those positions originally appeared.

We have already noted the ambitious character and great diversity of the work. While it would be inappropriate to offer a disquisition on the scope, effect and general intentions of the work here, the reader must be given some introduction to its construction, language and style. As we proceed, it will become apparent that the work is more than anything else a collection of independent essays. This is not to say that it lacks coherence, for each essay has a purpose and effect contributory to the whole. It is to say, rather, that the numerous and diverse concerns of *The Philosophy of Living Experience* are dealt with in segregation from one another in order to facilitate their complete development. Thus, we have an opening essay discussing the contemporary problem of philosophy and the need for its solution followed very tardily, in the next-to-the-last chapter of the work, by the exposition of Bogdanov's worldview as that solution. In between, we find two essays on the origins and development of religious and secular thought, a chapter on the basic character and methods of materialism and idealism, two chapters on the history of philosophy concentrating on the materialist line, and then two chapters assessing the meaning and significance of empiriocriticism and Marxist materialism. In the work's final chapter and conclusion, we find an essay on the end of philosophy and the future of knowledge beyond it.

How these various parts fit together and what they were meant to achieve both in themselves and as a whole will be revealed as we proceed. We mention the work's contents and construction here to warn the reader to expect a many-sided work showing something less than a high degree of system and continuity. In accord with the segregation of its concerns, we have chosen to deal with each part of the work separately and in turn, that is, to take each essay and chapter in and for itself and to conclude upon it in limited fashion before attempting to describe its place in the whole. While we might have divided our study into as many chapters as the work has separate parts, we have chosen to divide it roughly in half, taking the three essays and three chapters which comprise the first half of the work together into one chapter under the title 'The Contemporary Problem of Philosophy and Philosophy's

Career', and the succeeding chapters one by one in chapters of the same title, i.e., 'Empiriocriticism', 'Dialectical Materialism', 'Empiriomonism' and 'The Science of the Future'. For the sake of analyzing the whole, we have deemed the first half of the work introductory to the second, for in it numerous positions are taken from which not only the exposition of Bogdanov's solution to the problem of philosophy proceeds but also the assessment and critique of Marx and Mach. In a sense, all but the final chapters of the work are introductory and more will be said of that when we reach the chapters dealing with the second half of the work.[97]

The language of *The Philosophy of Living Experience* is straightforward and clear for being, as we shall see, highly personalized. We will use Bogdanov's own language with a minimum of augmentation. For one thing, it would be difficult to compare his terminology with any other. For another, using Bogdanov's own language will serve to convey the tone of the work and better facilitate taking its content in and for itself. Bogdanov's style, although not consistently so, is more literary than it is philosophical or scientific. *The Philosophy of Living Experience* must have been a pleasant change from the usual diet of theoretical tracts for the work's natural audience, the Russian proletariat and revolutionary intelligentsia. We say this not simply because of its language and style, but because the work deals with important questions of the time largely outside the usual theoretical contexts of Marxism, populism, etc. In it, Bogdanov is concerned with charting new directions for life and thought which other theoreticians did not describe. Furthermore, he presents a series of interesting and often ingenious explanations and schemes which must have caught and held his readers.

The arguments of *The Philosophy of Living Experience* are rather loose but lack little for that. As the work's style is literary, so is its argumentation. Because Bogdanov provided extensive point-by-point summaries for most of the essays and chapters, there is little difficulty in coming to an essential understanding of what he argues in a given case. These summaries, however, present certain problems for one who wishes to condense the material of an entire chapter or essay. As often as not, Bogdanov leaves important arguments out of his summaries. In some instances, the summary seems more like a second essay on the same topic, because its content and argumentation are significantly different from the body of the essay or chapter. For the sake of clarity and concision, therefore, we will impose our own structure on the essays and chapters in an attempt to bring their bodies and summary statements into conjunction. In addition, we will reorganize, abbreviate and supplement when necessary in order to bring out and link together Bogdanov's principal arguments. In some instances our structure will closely parallel Bogdanov's own. In others, the two will diverge to a certain extent. Hopefully, this will give our explication and analysis coherence without misrepresenting the work.

Because our intention is to explicate and analyze *The Philosophy of Living Experience* in and for itself, we will not proceed under the direction of a thesis more specific than that the work may be concluded upon as the presentation of a worldview set in several frames or contexts which ought to be considered to a certain extent part of that presentation. These frames or contexts may be designated as follows: the conditions of life and thought as Bogdanov saw them in his time, the career of religious and secular thought, the career of labor practice and knowledge, and the meaning and significance of the thought of Marx and Mach. Because Bogdanov spent nearly as much time and effort in constructing these as he did in presenting his worldview and did so in essays and chapters segregated from one another, they ought to be accorded some status apart from their role as frames and concluded upon as well.

If our study of *The Philosophy of Living Experience* under the approach discussed succeeds, we may achieve a number of useful and interesting things beyond revealing the significance Bogdanov accorded his own thought. First, and most obviously, we will certainly acquire a new "criticial line" on Bogdanov which, although it is Bogdanov's own, might serve as a tool of analysis for future studies and form a perspective against which an objective view can be measured. Secondly, our study may afford an expanded perspective on Bogdanov, inasmuch as it proposes to regard him, as *The Philosophy of Living Experience* suggests, in general aspect, that is, as "thinker" or "philosopher" rather than as the representative of one or another narrower sort of intellectual undertaking. With this, we may discover something with regard to the manner in which Bogdanov responded to the realities of his own time, if not modern reality per se. Given who Bogdanov was and the period in which his thought was conceived, these are things we would be compelled to look for even if *The Philosophy of Living Experience* did not give so open an accounting. Finally, we may be able to secure for Bogdanov a more fully defined place from the *fin de siècle* onward. Although this would be tentative inasmuch as it rests on conclusions from the study of a single work, we ought to be able, at least, to place Bogdanov with regard to whatever trends of thought *The Philosophy of Living Experience* suggests.

CHAPTER I

THE CONTEMPORARY PROBLEM OF PHILOSOPHY
AND PHILOSOPHY'S CAREER

As we have noted above, the first half of *The Philosophy of Living Experience* forms a lengthy and complex introduction to the remainder of the work. Our purpose in this chapter is to sketch out and explicate that introductory material so as to show how it guides the reader toward, and prepares him to accept, the critiques of Marx and Mach and the exposition of "the philosophy of living experience" which follows. The title of our chapter reflects its simple thesis. We submit that, in his brief initial essays and in the three chapters which follow them, Bogdanov established the criteria according to which "the philosophy of living experience" would be formulated. Inasmuch as the first half of the work is introductory to the chapters on Marx and Mach as well, we submit that these criteria were also intended to form the basis for Bogdanov's criticism.

The first half of *The Philosophy of Living Experience* is by and large a discussion of the meaning and career of philosophy. That discussion has two aspects. The first of these, which is found in the first of the three introductory essays, is a treatment of the "problem of philosophy" for contemporary man. There, Bogdanov dealt with the relationship between philosophy and life as it was in his own time. The intent of this essay was to establish the general sense and purpose of philosophy for contemporary man and, by extension, for the man of the future. Inasmuch as Bogdanov considered the sense and purpose of philosophy to have been always the same, the essay also serves to establish his basic perspective on its significance in the past. The second aspect of the larger discussion, which is pursued in the remainder of the first half of the work, is an analysis of the character of past thought from the earliest worldviews to nineteenth-century materialism. In this, Bogdanov attempted to show what philosophy had been and, by arguing its socially and historically determined and, therefore, limited character, what contemporary philosophy and the philosophy of the future should *not* be.

Although Bogdanov's essays and chapters may be divided into the two parts mentioned above, we have chosen to divide them into four. Part of the reason for this is that by so doing the text is more easily organized in exposition. Our first part or section, entitled "Philosophy and Life", deals

22

with the first essay which has as its subject the problem of philosophy. Our second section, entitled "The Rise and Development of Worldviews", explicates the second and third of the initial essays. We have done this, since the second and third together form a sort of bridge between the first and the three chapters on the career of philosophy which follow. In these essays, Bogdanov sought both to establish the social and historical bases for his initial arguments, and to set down the social and historical analysis he would apply to the history of thought. In our third section, "What is Materialism?" we deal with Bogdanov's chapter on the basic methods and procedures of past thought. In this chapter, he applied his social and historical point of view in an attempt to establish the basic features of the several "lines" of philosophy's development. In the last section, "Ancient and Modern Materialism", we consider at once the last two chapters of the first half of the work, since these chapters form a continuous narrative on the character of philosophy (or at least of its most important manifestations) from the pre-Socratics to the era of Marx and Mach. In this narrative, we see Bogdanov attempt to justify his earlier conclusions on the methods and procedures of thought.

If the reader considers the length of this chapter, he may be moved to ask why, when the material covered is largely introductory and, therefore, of secondary importance in *The Philosophy of Living Experience,* does it deal with that material in such detail? There are several important reasons for this. First, we wish to be faithful to the character of the work, to its general scope, purposes and development. If Bogdanov had not thought it vital to deal at length with the meaning and role of philosophy and the character of past thought, he would not have done so. We submit that his reasons for this went well beyond the one which suggests itself immediately, i.e., that his audience, the Russian proletariat and revolutionary intelligentsia, needed ample preparation to accept any argument whatever regarding philosophy. Bogdanov must have felt that his perspectives on the meaning of philosophy and its career demanded lengthy explanation to establish their validity. In addition, because his purpose was to offer a genuinely new worldview and one which comprehended the enormous contents of human experience, Bogdanov must have deemed it necessary to show the extent and depth of his dealings with the diverse aspects of that experience. In line with his intention to set forth a new philosophy, Bogdanov must also have felt it necessary to justify its succession. In effect, the lengthy discussions of the first half of the work serve to put all philosophical perspectives prior to those of Marx and Mach behind Bogdanov. If he were going to relegate the bulk of philosophical tradition to obsolescence, he must have felt the need to provide an extensive and many-sided analysis to justify it. Bogdanov's own world-view would take philosophy beyond Marx and Mach in his estimation: in the first half of the work, he established that he would not return to previous thought in so doing.

The second of our reasons for going into the first half of *The Philosophy of Living Experience* in such detail is that the independent character of its parts requires it. Without detail and added explanation in most cases, the separate essays and chapters would make little sense. Thirdly, it should be noted that the first half of the work is, after all, a summation of Bogdanov's conclusions from more than a decade of study and writing on everything from economics and history to philosophy and science. Considering that summation in detail gives us a substantial appreciation of the breadth and character of Bogdanov's concerns, at least during the first half of his career. Obviously, "the philosophy of living experience" set forth in the second half of the work arose on the basis of his many-faceted research. This suggests the best reason of all for detailing the first half. One can look upon the pro-positions and perspectives set down there as the productions of a thinker proceeding from the point of view of the "philosophy of living experience". We submit that the order of the work could easily have been reversed in the writing. Bogdanov might have stated the problem of philosophy, shown his response to it, and then gone on to deal with past thought, Marx, Mach, etc., from the perspective of his own worldview. This is not to say that the work should read back-to-front. Doing so would undoubtedly make its explication doubly difficult, and of course, the true progress of the work would be obscured.

With these purposes, theses and justifications of approach behind us, we proceed to the matter at hand.

A. PHILOSOPHY AND LIFE

Bogdanov presented the problem of philosophy for contemporary man in the form of an essay on the relationship between philosophy and life. In this essay, however, he clearly intended to do much more than state the problem. First, Bogdanov set out to establish what philosophy is and why man needs it to live. Secondly, he gave an analysis of its relationship to "human experience" with an eye toward establishing what was "scientific" and, therefore, the most complete and useful sort of philosophy, and what was not. Thirdly, he proposed to evaluate what philosophy had become over time and to suggest the rudiments of a solution to the problem of its inappropriateness to contemporary life. This essay, "What is Philosophy? To Whom and For What is it Necessary?", [PLE, pp. 3–19] * is for that a microcosm of the work it introduces, or, what might be better said, an essay of the same scope and intents. As we shall see, however, *The Philosophy of Living Experience* is by no means simply an expansion of this essay. In fact, one must labor to correlate the arguments of the whole work with those of its introduction. We submit, therefore, that this essay should be taken as Bogdanov's statement of the problem of philosophy and as an indication of the scope and general intentions of the larger work. The reader is urged to fasten onto the general principles reiterated by Bogdanov in the essay's summary (and repeated at the end of this section) and not to be unduly concerned with carrying the other arguments of the essay forward as he reads on.

In the beginning, Bogdanov sought to gain the attention and confidence of his immediate audience, the Russian proletariat and revolutionary intelligentsia, by treating the relationship of philosophy and life as an elementary matter. He made it out to be something every reasonable man, every class-conscious proletarian, either understood already or could readily understand. To do this, he called upon two "proletarian philosophers" to bear him out. Referring to and commenting upon the unpublished writings of Fedor Kalinin and Nikifor Vilonov, he proposed to discuss philosophy's true relationship to "human labor, struggle and thought".[1] He proceeded toward this via a critique of what philosophy had become, inspired principally by the writings of Kalinin on the subject.

Bogdanov argued that the prevalent doubt as to the importance and utility of philosophy was due to the way in which it was and had been practiced in the present and immediate past. The philosopher, he said, had become over time a man wholly detached from life, a professional specialist studying thought in and for itself. The questions with which he dealt were narrow and, as such, had at best only an indirect bearing on the human condition. Therefore, he said, philosophy had become obscurantism and the province of the few. As obscurantism, it was rightly eschewed, especially by proletarians. [PLE, p. 4] Bodganov, of course, was not prepared to leave philosophy in the hands of contemporary specialists. Such philosophy was simply improper, outmoded and, therefore, "false". [PLE, p. 4] He would show that there

* Hereafter, references to the text of *The Philosophy of Living Experience* (1923 edition), will be made in this manner.

were analyzable social and historical reasons why this was the case, but for the moment he concerned himself with showing the correct relationship of philosophy and life, with defining, if you will, "true philosophy".

True philosophy, he said, could not be associated with the study of thought in and for itself, since its object was the entirety of human experience. Furthermore, Bogdanov asserted, as the content and meaning of human experience was a universal concern, so philosophy has its original and ultimate practitioner in every man. [PLE, p. 4] Taking his lead from Kalinin in this, Bogdanov argued that philosophy had its beginnings on the personal level. Where Kalinin had noted that every aspect of a man's life "passes through the prism of his own philosophy", [PLE, p. 4] Bogdanov asserted that "each man has his philosophy, whether he wants it or not". [PLE, p. 19] The true relationship between philosophy and life was, therefore, elementary; every conscious, living being practiced philosophy in one way or another. Bogdanov implied that man's concern with the content and meaning of his experience was grounded in the struggle for existence. Each man had his philosophy because he needed it to live. As Bogdanov stated on the essay's summation, philosophy was the necessary "tool of guidance" (*orudie rukovodstva*) for human thought and practice. [PLE, p. 19] [2]

Bogdanov built steadily upon these notions of every man as philosopher and philosophy as a "tool of guidance". He based his explanation of the relationship between the philosopher and his "tool" on a social and historical view of human experience. This view is particularly important for understanding Bogdanov's analysis. He defined individual philosophy and the philosophies of collections of individuals, from small groups to social classes, in terms of the portion of the whole of human experience on which they were based. Furthermore, he defined philosophy and science in similar terms. Bogdanov made the quantity of experience the crucial element in judging the validity and utility of all thought, from individual worldviews to the highest levels of philosophy and science. The term "experience" itself is not defined in any substantial way here. What Bogdanov regarded "experience" to be is not so important in this argument as who possesses how much of it. Therefore, we may take the word in its most ordinary sense for the time being. Later, we will see the full extent of its meaning for Bogdanov. [3]

Not at all curiously, Kalinin held many of the same views of the relationship of individual and collective philosophies, and Bogdanov quoted him at length, commenting on and expanding his ideas. Kalinin referred to individual thought as "private philosophy" (*domašnaja filosofija*), that is, an implement produced by individual needs on the basis of individual experience, verified and shaped by individual practice. [PLE, p. 4] When individuals gathered in the distant past, he said, their private philosophies were united to form folk wisdom or everyday philosophy, a limited form of systematized thought based on collective experience. [PLE, p. 4] In the proverbs of folk wisdom Kalinin saw generalizations which served as "tools of guidance" for the collective. "In unity there is strength", he noted, was a generalization of man's relationship to man which in turn implied the relationship of collective man to the struggle for existence. [PLE, p. 5] Bogdanov picked up the matter at that point using the example of Marx's "scientific-philosophical formula, ... the basic idea of the proletarian social-historical worldview: 'social consciousness is determined by social being.'" [PLE, p. 6] While it is a scientific-philosophical formula, he stated, it is like the proverb a creation of collective experience. However, unlike the proverb, it is based on a much greater part, approaching the whole, of collective experience. That, according to Bogdanov, was the reason for calling it "scientific". [PLE, pp. 6–7] Proverbs, philosophical generalizations and scientific laws all arise from collective experience and collective need and are verified and shaped by collective practice. Those determined by the greatest experience and need and verified and shaped in the broadest use, he said, have the greatest scientific content. Furthermore, as human experience grows, generalizations based on human experience become more meaningful, more useful and therefore more scientific. [PLE, pp. 7–8]

In this manner, Bogdanov argued that philosophy must be related to its experiential base in order to be judged and evaluated. His use of the term "scientific philosophy" demands additional comment here. For Bogdanov, worldviews based on the whole of human experience at any given time may be every bit as scientific as any of the natural sciences. As we shall see below, that which makes areas of study sciences is that they comprehend the whole of human experience in those areas. If you will, Bogdanov held that at any given time philosophy in its highest and most complete form was scientific.

Leaving his scheme of the relationship between the various sorts of philosophy and "human experience", Bogdanov went on to detail the character of the scientific point of view. He asserted that

the scientific point of view is that which corresponds to the highest level of its time, [that] which takes into account all of the accumulated experience in a given sphere of knowledge. [PLE, p. 9]

It was easily discernible, he said, why Marx's *Capital* was taken by many as a model of scientific study. According to Bogdanov, Marx used an enormous amount of material gathered from "both study and practice", applied to it the most contemporary methods, which were themselves created and prepared by the collective efforts of many researchers, and "united and bound those ideas which expressed all tendencies of development in contemporary society". [PLE, p. 9] For Bogdanov *Capital* was, therefore, the product of collective experience evaluated by collectively formulated methods. "And so", he concluded,

here is what "scientificalness" amounts to: applying in mental work all the socially gathered plentitude of knowledge and skill. The same thing applies, obviously, to scientific philosophy. [PLE, p. 9]

In Bogdanov's opinion, it was not at all difficult to discover who possessed "all the accumulated experience", the scientific point of view, in any given case:

It is possessed not by this or that separate individual, but by the whole of society, or, if society is not unified and [is] broken into classes, then [the possessor] is the most progressive class in this realm of class collectives. [PLE, p. 9]

How, then, would Bogdanov view Marx's *Capital,* the product of an individual, as a model of the scientific point of view? His argument as to why certain individuals appear to be ahead of their time, why they appear to be alone in possession of the scientific point of view, makes this question easy enough to answer.

Bogdanov might have used Marx as an example but chose, instead, Copernicus. Clearly, Bogdanov noted, the heliocentric notion which Copernicus espoused did not correspond to the common experience of the time. It did, however, correspond to all of the accumulated experience in the area of astronomy. [PLE, p. 10] He argued here that men like Copernicus had simply gained access to the "accumulated experience" of mankind and had given it some particular shape while others had not. And so the relationship of the individual to the accumulated experience of mankind was clear for Bogdanov: an individual might be the "codifier" or "agent", but the possessor of the scientific point of view was ultimately the progressive class.

Bogdanov asserted that the scientific point of view, while appearing in the past and present to be the province of the few, actually corresponded to the "highest level of cultural development" at any given time. [PLE, pp. 10–11] That, he said, was what "the accumulated experience of mankind" implied. Our thinker noted that the progressive classes of the past had never been anything but a small part of the whole of mankind. He saw no reason, therefore, why the scientific point of view should have been anything but the province of the few. The rest of society was not progressive and common everyday thought naturally lagged behind its scientific counterpart. [PLE, p. 11]

At this point, it might seem that Bogdanov was attempting to justify the lag, to portray the detachment of scientific thought from the other aspects of life as an inevitability. Such was not the case. Bogdanov felt that the appearance of the proletariat as the progressive class guaranteed an end to the detachment and the disappearance of the lag. His argument proceeded in roughly the following manner. As the progressive class would come to correspond in numbers to the whole of mankind, so would the whole of mankind become the possessor of the scientific point of view. "Scientific philosophy" would become more and more directly related to the experience, the lives of all men. [PLE, p. 11] Clearly, Bogdanov's mass man of the future would be anything but common. As we shall see better later in this work, Bogdanov's proletarian, because of his role in advancing production, would need science and "scientific philosophy" in order to cope with everyday life.[4] Thus, for Bogdanov, science, scientific and common philosophy converge as the proletariat grows. It was clear that he saw in Marx's work evidence of the beginning of that convergence. [PLE, p. 11]

Having defined philosophy vis-à-vis human experience and having suggested its integral relationship to life, Bogdanov went on to speak about the practice of philosophy in his own time. While he saw the convergence of science, scientific and common, everyday philosophy as an inevitability, Bogdanov demanded that the philosopher work actively toward that end. One gets the impression here that he was as concerned with converting the "bourgeois specialist" to his point of view as he was with encouraging proletarians to pursue "scientific philosophy" on the basis of their progressive class experience.

Bogdanov again admonished his readers that the experience of the progressive class, the proletariat, demanded that philosophy be taken into "systematic union" with every aspect of human life.

If one takes from scientific philosophy only bits and pieces and masters them, not taking them in systematic union with other parts of socially accumulated experience, then bad, unreliable "private philosophy" is the result. [PLE, p. 11]

To apply Marx's being-consciousness formula without his theory of social classes, he said, amounted to "private philosophizing". [PLE, p. 11] The unity of philosophy and life had to be uppermost in the scientific philos-

opher's mind. Furthermore, Bogdanov asserted, the developmental character
of the relationship of philosophy and life in the proletarian era had to be
considered. If, for instance, Marx's formula of being-consciousness were
taken as an absolute, rigid law rather than as a tendency of development
based on the experience of a developing class, then all proletarians would
have to be socialists by definition. Of course, Bogdanov asserted, this was not
the case because class-consciousness was developmental and began on the
"private" level. With more class experience, more proletarians become
socialists. [PLE, p. 12] According to Bogdanov, therefore, Marx's concept of
being-consciousness, as an integral part of socialism, expressed a tendency of
development; it gained more scientific depth and character as the proletariat
developed. [PLE, p. 12] It was apparent, of course, that Bogdanov considered
the generalizations of scientific philosophy in his own era to be developmental
and therefore subject to revision over time.

Continuing his argument for change in the practice of philosophy,
Bogdanov asserted that philosophical specialization of the bourgeois sort had
to be overcome. True, he said, specialization was an historically necessary
phenomenon. The growth of specialization in production and thought had
been a progressive feature in the bourgeois era. [PLE, p. 12] Equally necessary in light of proletarian class experience, said Bogdanov, was the integration of all aspects of human experience into a unified system. The scientific
philosopher, he said, could begin to meet both needs by simply conceiving
and communicating his thought in readily understandable language. [PLE,
p. 12] Obviously, Bogdanov believed a unified system of thought based on
the whole of human experience should be universally understandable.

Our thinker used the professional reception of Mach and Avenarius to
illustrate how unfortunate the use of specialized terminologies could be. We
will repeat this illustration in full, since it is the first indication in *The
Philosophy of Living Experience* of Bogdanov's opinion of Mach. One might
argue on the basis of this that he regarded Mach's approach to philosophy
something of a model for contemporary thought.

One prominent natural scientist and philosopher, Ernst Mach, a thinker very independent and deep, attempted to set forth his views in comparatively popular, generally
understandable language. And what happened? Philosophers simply did not understand
him and regarded him with the greatest scorn. But, soon after, another philosopher,
Richard Avenarius, appeared. He not only used special "philosophical" language but, not
satisfied with it, worked out a new terminology exclusively his own which surpassed [the
terminologies] of his predecessors and contemporaries in difficulty of comprehension. In
essence, he professed views very close to the ideas of Mach. An honest man, he
repeatedly referred to him [Mach] in his work. The specialists recognized Avenarius as a

prominent philosopher, [and] thanks to him, it was deemed necessary to have another look at Mach. These same views, which they did not want to know in their popular formulation, appeared serious and valuable when translated into the miserable [*užasnyj*] language of Avenarius. [PLE, pp. 12–13]

In addition to making this suit for clear communication of the results of science, Bogdanov also asserted that the sciences demanded methodological unification in the proletarian era. Quoting and commenting on the notions of Vilonov in this regard, he now suggested that the task of philosophy was to unify human experience into a "strict, structured system of universal understanding". [PLE, p. 15] What "strict" and "structured" meant here is especially important. He agreed with Vilonov that the material for this system had to be taken from "all the sciences and all branches of labor". [PLE, p. 15] Here, Bogdanov indicated that part of the process would involve collecting the results of the specialized sciences into a unified whole. This gave Bogdanov's concept of the true philosopher's role a more concrete character. Furthermore, he implied that in the proletarian era all other aspects of life would come more and more under scientific scrutiny. Marx, after all, had shown that technology, economics and the relations of production were subject to scientific investigation. [PLE, p. 15] For Bogdanov, the task of the true philosopher, then, was to integrate the results of the traditional special sciences and the new social sciences into a system of scientific laws which express the relationships of the whole. [PLE, p. 15]

Bogdanov concluded his essay with a note on the relationship of philosophy and the class struggle. Philosophy in its highest or "scientific" form was not empty and detached from life, he said:

[I]t is the daughter of labor and struggle, it grows with them and with them it changes. When a mighty class enters the arena of history, a class to which history entrusts a new [and] grandiose task, a new philosophy must also arise. [PLE, pp. 15–16]

This statement is the first of a whole series of statements which made up Bogdanov's argument regarding the social and historical character and conditionality of all philosophy, past, present and future. Although he had a great deal to propose in this regard, our thinker limited his comments to the ability of the bourgeoisie and proletariat to understand the historical role of philosophy. According to Bogdanov, the role of philosophy in the class struggle was something the bourgeoisie did not and, indeed, could not understand. Because of this, bourgeois philosophy made pretenses to being absolute and eternal. [PLE, p. 16] As a tool of classes which rise and fall, said Bogdanov, philosophy necessarily could not produce absolute and eternal truths but only relative and temporary ones. He asserted that proletarians were aware of this fact as well as of the role of philosophy as a "tool of guidance" in the class struggle.

[Since they] are accustomed to using material tools in labor and realize that they make them by their own hands, it is easier for the proletarians to grasp the essence of those mental tools which they themselves produce. [PLE, p. 16]

To confirm this fact, he said, one need only look at what the few proletarian philosophers have written with regard to the matter of truth. There followed in the text a long quote from Vilonov on the matter which indicated that he at least rejected the possibility of absolute truth and error. [PLE, pp. 16–17]

Bogdanov concluded the initial essay of *The Philosophy of Living Experience* with a six-point summary. We repeat it here to make his position on the problem of philosophy and the relationship of philosophy and life readily accessible for future reference.

1. Every man, whether he wants it or not, has his philosophy. It is a necessary tool of guidance in practice and thought.
2. Common everyday philosophy is based on parts of collective experience. It is controlled by the narrow individual experience of each personality. Scientific philosophy is based on the fullness of collective experience and is controlled by collectively produced methods. The first is incomparably less successful than the second and leads to many unfortunate mistakes.
3. Scientific philosophy need not necessarily be ponderous, cloudy and obscure in exposition. These are only the characteristics of the sectarian philosophies of contemporary specialists. Such specialization contradicts the task and sense of scientific philosophy.
4. Like all products and tools of human activity, philosophy changes and is up-dated. Therefore, the philosophical truth of one time is necessarily different from the philosophical truth of another. There may be no absolute and eternal philosophical truths.
5. Just as the basic vital tasks of different classes are different, and since each tool should correspond to its task, so the philosophy of one class will not serve another. In its strivings each class must work out its own philosophy — otherwise, its struggle will proceed without organized guidance.
6. Class philosophy is the highest form of its collective consciousness. [PLE, p. 19]

What can be said in conclusion about the problem of philosophy as it is set forth in Bogdanov's discussion of philosophy and life? Clearly, the problem is that philosophy has ceased to be a tool of guidance for practice and thought, for life, in the present. The solution is reflected in the statement of the problem: present-day thinkers must reconstruct philosophy as such a tool by re-encompassing and re-evaluating human experience in all of its contemporary aspects. Inasmuch as the whole of human experience has become or is becoming the exclusive possession of the proletariat, the philosopher must follow the lead of Marx and grasp the realities of proletarian life. In doing so, he must integrate the practical experience of the proletariat together with the experience generated by the sciences. The realities of life, of "production", in the present demand this. At the same time, philosophers must not be blind to the role of philosophy in the class struggle and construct thought in accord with the new demands and historical task of the class which leads the progressive development of mankind.

B.   THE RISE AND DEVELOPMENT OF WORLDVIEWS

With these statements on the meaning and role of philosophy behind him, Bogdanov commenced a long, two-part discussion on the rise and development of religious and secular worldviews. We will combine the material of the second and third introductory essays in our explication of this discussion without mentioning where one ends and the next begins.[5] There is no need to do so, since the one flows directly out of the other. We have suggested above that these essays form a bridge between the discussion of philosophy and life and the chapters on the history of thought. As a bridge, they do several things in connecting the two parts of the first half of the work. First, they serve to legitimize Bogdanov's argument that philosophy is a "tool of guidance" serving humanity in the struggle with nature by showing that philosophy and the species of systematized thought preceding it have ever been such tools. This suggests that a study of past thought might prove useful in the search for a solution to the problem of philosophy in the present. Secondly, these essays purport to uncover the origins and determiners of worldviews and the formal causal principles associated with them. This suggests the fundamental way in which past thought should be approached to yield information germane to the appropriate character of philosophy as a tool in the present. Finally, the discussion of the rise and development of worldviews provides an overview of the history of society and thought from earliest times to the present. Bogdanov's perceptions on the history of philosophy find their place within the more general scope of this overview.

Bogdanov's discussion of worldviews had four principal parts or aspects which we will treat in turn. In the first of these, he sought to establish the origins of thought and how it came to be systematized into worldviews. With this, he again suggested thought's fundamental purposes and how and why it was related to the real world. In the second, Bogdanov set forth the essential features of the earliest, i.e., religious, worldviews and the origins of causal notions. Thirdly, our thinker described the decline of religious worldviews and the succession of secular thought with its substantially different character and causal notion. Finally, he dealt briefly with the relationship of religious and secular thought, describing the problems created by the religious legacy in a secular world.

Bogdanov began his essay with an elliptical remark to the effect that if man in the epoch of civilizations has his worldviews, it must not always have been so. He pointed out that before philosophy came religion and that, before religion, there existed no systematic knowledge whatsoever. [PLE, p. 20] Bogdanov's periodization of the history of thought comprised three principal phases: the primitive or pre-religious phase, the religious phase and the secular. Not at all curiously, this corresponded to and depended upon his major stages in the history of society: the primitive, the authoritarian and exchange stages. [PLE, p. 20] This scheme was clearly quasi-Marxist, since it purported to reflect the general progress of production.[6] As in any such scheme, the relationship of men in each of Bogdanov's stages was determined by their roles in production. Correspondingly, language and thought, the religious and secular worldviews, arose as superstructure resting on the relations of production and were accordingly determined by them. [PLE, p. 20]

Bogdanov did not feel that inarticulate, primitive man could be said to have had a worldview, a "proper system of knowledge". [PLE, pp. 20–1] He did not argue that inarticulate man lacked a form of knowledge but only that it was in no way systematic. Systematic knowledge implied that the products of individual minds had been brought together and ordered. According to Bogdanov, this could not have occurred before the existence of language and the social relations on which language is based. [PLE, p. 21] The primitive stage of society, he asserted, was marked by the gathering of men into groups to advance the struggle with nature. Correspondingly, he saw the primitive phase of the history of thought marked by the appearance of that one tool which facilitated collective action, language. The elements of language, which Bogdanov took to be the same things as the elements of thought, arose from the involuntary sounds which accompanied work. These elements, which he called "word-ideas" (slova-ponjatija), came to serve as designations for the acts of labor. [PLE, p. 22] Once they had arisen, he asserted, word-ideas began a life of their own as they were related in regular ways to form language. However, he saw their meanings and relationships to one another tied directly to the practical demands of the collective struggle against nature.

[PLE, p. 38] As it was necessary to designate the acts of the struggle by word-ideas, Bogdanov said, so was it necessary to designate the things which struggling man encountered. Things, he claimed, are fundamentally the "stable points of the application of activity, human or natural". [PLE, p. 38] According to Bogdanov, word-ideas born in and associated with human labor were, therefore, carried over to nature to name things. After Max Mueller, Bogdanov called this "the basic metaphor", and he stressed the notion that language fundamentally expressed human actions and the objects to which those actions were applied. [PLE, pp. 23—4]

The sum of word-ideas did not automatically comprise a worldview in Bogdanov's opinion; they were only "the simplest expressions of technical rules (*pravila*) and representations of the facts of experience". [PLE, p. 38] Primitive word-ideas thus comprised the elements of knowledge, but they were not immediately subject to systematization. Bogdanov maintained this because he believed primitive man lacked a structured work relationship on which to base a model of causality. For him, causality was the basic law or structuring device of a worldview and the reflection of basic forms of labor organization. [PLE, pp. 24—5]

Bogdanov's primitive man worked in leaderless collectives. Labor was accomplished on the basis of a mutual aid for the satisfaction of immediate individual needs. [PLE, p. 25] As society progressed, he asserted, the struggle with nature became more complex and sophisticated. It was discovered that collective labor, organized for the good of the whole rather than for separate individuals, made the struggle easier and more fruitful. The role of organizing labor in this way naturally fell on the individual who possessed the most expertise. Initially, this "organizer" was only differentiated from the rest by his knowledge of the work process; he was at the same time an "implementor". [PLE, pp. 25—26] Gradually, Bogdanov claimed, various other roles in the collective accrued to him. First, because he was the organizer of production, he became the distributor of its fruits. Then, as labor and production became more complex, he had to give up his role as implementor to concentrate his energies on organization. [PLE, p. 28] The relationship of organizers and implementors, as portrayed here, consituted Bogdanov's concept of "authoritarian cooperation". [PLE, p. 29] This form of collective cooperation was the fact which distinguished the authoritarian period in human society. As we shall see, that period for Bogdanov lasted until the appearance of exchange economy and the rise of the bourgeois class.

In this phase, said Bogdanov, authoritarian cooperation gave man his first definite model for a notion of causality, i.e., a way in which to ascertain the "permanent bonds of phenomena".

Following the process of labor, in which the organizer's [act] necessarily draws after it the act of the implementor, men presented every stable sequence of facts in nature and among themselves according to this same scheme; this is the authoritarian form of causality. [PLE, p. 30]

Bogdanov identified authoritarian causality, then, with the notion that all which occurs in the world of men and nature is caused by active human or like-human agents acting upon passive objects.

For Bogdanov, the authoritarian form of causality permitted the elements of knowledge to be ordered and the relations of phenomena to be established for the practical benefit of man. Implicit in his view was the notion that authoritarian causality, as the basis for the explanation of all phenomena, served to reinforce authoritarian cooperation in production. Authority and obedience were seen as the order to the world. [PLE, p. 31–2]

In this earliest form of causal explanation, Bogdanov purported to have discovered the origin of the spirit-matter duality which had plagued human thought ever since. In order for authoritarian causality to operate successfully, he said, no act could be seen as uncaused. When the observed actions of men and things had no apparent cause, Bogdanov asserted, man in the authoritarian period assumed the causes were there anyway. [PLE, p. 39; also p. 33] By this he meant that an active agent was taken as the cause of an event even when none was perceived. Such agents were simply considered to be invisible, to be "spirits". [PLE, p. 38] Similarly, he continued, when no action was apparent, "things" were assumed to be not acted upon and, therefore, to be the antithesis of spirit, inert matter. [PLE, p. 38; also p. 33] According to the authoritarian worldview, said our thinker, matter was subordinated to active spirit just as the passive implementor was subordinated to the active organizer in authoritarian labor cooperation. [PLE, p. 38; also p. 34]

Bogdanov saw all of the relationships of authoritarian society bound up with conservative tendencies; all of life was regulated by tradition. This tradition, like the authoritarian notion of causality, had its origins in the organizer-implementor relationship. [PLE, p. 39] According to Bogdanov's scheme of social development, the organizer of production could not rely for long on expertise as justification of his authority. As production advanced and society became more diverse, others could make claim to expertise. The organizer, then, had to resort to the tradition of past organizers to justify his position. [PLE, p. 39] Bogdanov found the origins of religion in the building of this tradition.

The authority of distant ancestors grew with each generation and proceeded to the level of deification. Deified ancestors were looked upon as organizers of all human practice, as the source of all knowledge. [PLE, p. 39]

Once the "legacy of ancestor-organizers" took form, said Bogdanov, the authoritarian system of knowledge became a total worldview. It should properly be called the religious worldview since the source of all truth, knowledge and causation was assigned to deity. [PLE, p. 39]

According to Bogdanov, the authoritarian-religious system of knowledge was a complete monistic worldview, because it "seized all the experience of men" at a time when the authoritarian relationship in production "seized all of their social-labor life". [PLE, p. 40] It is apparent here that Bogdanov applied to the religious worldview the same criteria which he had applied to philosophy in the previous essay. The religious worldview, he said, based on "all the experience of men", represented the scientific point of view in its time. [PLE, p. 40] He obviously found the religious worldview temporarily valid since it functioned as a "tool of guidance" unifying knowledge and assuring the success of the collective struggle with nature by supporting the authoritarian form of cooperation.

Again in a manner similar to his portrayal of the fall of contemporary philosophy away from the scientific point of view, Bogdanov depicted the decline of the religious worldview in terms of changes in social relations. For him, the religious worldview was valid as long as all human experience lay within the limits of authoritarian tradition. However, he said, there came a time when all of the aspects of human life did not conform to the authoritarian order of things. The "accelerated development of technique" and the rise of exchange economy led to greater social differentiation and changes in the organizer-implementor relationship. [PLE, p. 41; also p. 54] While he detailed a number of changes in this context, it is fair to say that Bogdanov viewed the detachment of the organizer-authority figure from direct participation in production as the crucial feature in the decline of authoritarian social relations and the religious worldview based upon them. Once the organization of production fell into the hands of the exchange, i.e., commercial, classes which had accompanied advancing production and the increase in social intercourse, the authority of the older type of organizer came to rest solely on tradition. Similarly, he asserted, the religious world-view became the worldview of the authoritarian organizer alone. [PLE, pp. 42–3] A new worldview, that of the new organizing class, grew up along-side the religious system of knowledge. This new worldview was "extra-religious" and, therefore, secular. In its furthest development, said Bogdanov, the extra-religious worldview took the form of philosophy and the various sciences. [PLE, p. 43]

Our thinker would shortly explain the necessity of a new sort of world-view for exchange society, but before this he made an interesting comment on one of the consequences of the rise of the new worldview alongside the old.

Little-by-little secular thought gained ascendancy in the practical everyday life of men and began to be considered the realm of "knowledge" in general. Religious thought was disengaged from the system of labor, assumed an "unearthly" character, and made up the special realm of "truth". [PLE, p. 54]

The implication here was apparently that in the time of uniform social organization and a single worldview based on that form of organization, truth and knowledge amounted to the same thing. With the rise of a new form of social organization alongside the old, each became a separate realm, at least in common experience. For Bogdanov, this separation was apparently his-torically necessary but something to be done away with in the present and future. Truth and knowledge were the possessions of the progressive classes. Religious thought as the realm of truth was as doomed as religious thought as a proper "tool of guidance".

Why, in Bogdanov's view, did the secular worldview come to prevail in practical, everyday life? It would be enough to say that Bogdanov saw it serving the new organizer-implementor relationship. The new organizer in society was not an individual descended from a line of "ancestor-organizers"; the new organizer was an entire class of men which had not previously existed. [PLE, p. 44] Bogdanov argued that it would be difficult for such a class to seek support for authority in the tradition of individual organizers and in a religious tradition which tended towards monotheism. [PLE, p. 45] Instead of relying solely on this reasoning, however, Bogdanov went on to assert that a new form of causality was worked out which structured the secular worldview in conformity with exchange relations and which took authority out of the hands of individual organizers, both human and divine, and placed it in the hands of an abstract force. [PLE. p. 46]

Economic necessity rules men in exchange relations – it defines their activities and the results of these activities. Men began to understand the bonds of all phenomena according to this form: they began to understand that an effect was not simply "subordinated" to its cause, but that both were subordinated to one another and were bound together out of necessity. This necessity in and for itself has no concrete contents

– it is only necessity. Such is the abstract form of the causal bond peculiar to exchange society. [PLE, pp. 54–5]

Bogdanov stressed that the abstract form of causality which accompanied the rise of the socially progressive class was itself "cognitively progressive". [PLE, pp. 46–7; also p. 55] Where the authoritarian form looked for the free will of an organizer, human or divine, in every cause-effect sequence, the new form set no such limits to the steps of cause and effect. According to Bogdanov, it viewed each cause-effect sequence as part of an infinite series of such sequences, a series governed by natural or logical necessity. [PLE, p. 48] Thus, abstract necessity as an explanation of the relationships of phenomena, he argued, was clearly superior to some anthropomorphized agent who intervened at every point. Bogdanov asserted that the new form of causality could explain away the chaotic relations of exchange society by replacing a more easily understood human or like-human agent with the less understandable "force". [PLE, p. 48] Clearly, he felt that authoritarian causality could not be successfully adapted to explain away the chaos; the ancestors and gods of the authoritarian worldview had a tradition of predictable human or like-human behavior to live up to.

The fact that Bogdanov saw the secular and religious worldviews in an unresolved struggle was a significant aspect of his perspective on the history of thought. Because the secular worldview was based on an "abstract and contentless" causal principle almost as "unearthly" as the authoritarian, he said, religion, which purported to have special knowledge of the abstract, the "unearthly", could not be disposed of so easily. [PLE, p. 50] Bogdanov saw in the history of systematized knowledge to his own time the struggle between the authoritarian and abstract notions of causality. In that struggle, he said, "knowledge passed through a whole series of transitional and mixed forms which have not vanished even now." [PLE, p. 55] In the history of philosophy, with its materialist, idealist, empiriocritical and dialectical-materialist moments, Bogdanov saw the lingering influence of the authoritarian legacy preventing the dominance of the abstract causal notion.[7] In reality, the monistic authoritarian-religious worldview had not yet given way to a similarly monistic but secular successor. [PLE, p. 48]

As we shall see, these notions formed part of a rather complex perspective on the career of causal notions and the bodies of thought based on them. It will become clear that Bogdanov considered abstract causality to be inappropriate for a secular monism, and he judged secular worldviews to his time incapable of being complete. He would claim to have discovered the appropriate causal notion, "labor causality", himself.[8] Although he would not permit abstract causality to be as conducive to the construction of a monistic system of knowledge as its authoritarian predecessor, he certainly judged it to be superior and progressive in its time. He considered worldviews based on it, that is, philosophies and sciences, to aspire to be, and to be in fact, steps toward a new monism.[9] None of them could be granted complete success, but some were clearly better than others as we shall see.

In conclusion, we might summarize the effects of the discussion above as follows. First, we see that for Bogdanov worldviews, whether religious or secular, are defined by, reflect and reinforce systems of production. Each successive worldview has its roots in human "practice" and "practice" is its principal determiner. The legacy of past thought is but a minor influence; that legacy, however, may be troublesome. Secondly, Bogdanov tells us that causal notions are basic to the creation of worldviews, since they make it possible to relate all of the diverse elements of thought to one another. Understanding causal notions permits us to see the basic connection between thought and the system of production it reflects and serves. Causal notions, like the elements of thought themselves, find their models in practice. The way in which a given worldview depicts causality is a reflection of the basic fact of labor organization at any given time. Thirdly, because worldviews and causal notions depend on the system of production, they change as it changes. New causal notions, new worldviews, arise to organize thought about changed reality. Finally, Bogdanov tells us that the history of society must be divided into three major parts: the primitive, authoritarian and exchange stages. The history of thought, inasmuch as it corresponds to and depends upon the character of society, must be seen in three stages: the primitive or unsystematic, the authoritarian-religious and the abstract-philosophical. The development of causality, similarly, must be seen as moving from a time when no causal notion existed, to the stage of authoritarian causality and on to the stage of abstract causal necessity. We should note here that, for Bogdanov, the history of causal notions, thought and society was not yet complete. All were about to or had already entered a new stage. We find here the beginnings of an argument regarding the impossibility of a secular monism arising in exchange society and bourgeois thought. The rest of that argument and an indication of how a secular monism might be gained would not be long in coming in *The Philosophy of Living Experience*. Clearly, Bogdanov intended to show his readers, the successors of exchange society, "traditional" philosophy and causal necessity as well as the long-awaited successor to the authoritarian-religious worldview as a monistic system of knowledge.

C. "WHAT IS MATERIALISM?"

As we have suggested, the foregoing statements on the social and historical character of worldviews are the embarkation point for Bogdanov's discussion of the history of philosophy. The three chapters devoted to this discussion make up a full third of *The Philosophy of Living Experience*. [PLE, pp. 56–173] Because of their length and scope, one is tempted to consider them a self-contained essay, a work within the work which is slightly off the point. Indeed, reading them does detract one a bit from the contemporary problem of philosophy which is the focus of the whole. If, however, the reader remembers that these chapters are, after all, part of a long introduction and considers that a critique is implied in them, the focus of the greater whole is not lost at all.

That Bogdanov wished to criticize past thought as inappropriate to present realities is made apparent in the first of the three chapters, "What is Materialism?" [PLE, pp. 56–85] There, Bogdanov makes it clear that a true appreciation of the basic types of philosophy and their methods is to be gained from a social-historical critique of the basic premise of materialism, i.e., the notion of matter as primary being. Such a critique would show that premise to be false from the contemporary perspective. In addition, that critique would give rise to a similar criticism of the basic premise of idealism. In effect, the chapter gives us Bogdanov's basic views on the character and methodology of all past philosophies which, as we shall see later, are deemed either materialist or idealist to the exclusion of a third alternative. We are taken beyond his arguments on secular worldviews to Bogdanov's specific positions on philosophers from the pre-Socratics to the nineteenth-century materialists. The two chapters which follow form a long narrative illustrating, in the assessment of specific philosophies ancient and modern, the reasonability of positions set forth in "What is Materialism?"

In this chapter, one begins to see Bogdanov the "philosopher of living experience" at work. His analysis is as much theoretical as it is social and historical. Perhaps more than any other part of *The Philosophy of Living Experience* this chapter typifies Bogdanov's attempt to bring philosophic invention and social-historical analysis together. In so doing, our thinker makes clear his perspectives on basic issues such as the nature of being, the proper character of philosophic methods, etc. In taking a stand on the relative value of materialism and idealism to the progress of thought toward a complete secular monism, he begins to show the reader something of the basic orientation the "philosopher of living experience" must have.

The chapter presents a half-dozen or so arguments. We shall deal with each in turn and hope that the general thrust of the essay will become apparent as we go along. Bogdanov begins the essay with a discussion of labor and its objects which generates a definition of "matter". The notion of matter as primary being is measured against this definition and materialism as a philosophy is characterized. From this, our thinker proceeds to analyze the relationship between labor and ideas which permits him to depict the "real" character of idealism. In its next arguments, the essay deals at length with the method by which both materialism and idealism explain the world. Here we are purportedly shown *the* method of all philosophy. Then, in a partial return to his discussions of "matter" and "idea" as primary being, Bogdanov attempts to explain why "matter" and "idea" are taken to be things-in-themselves by philosophers and offers, in effect, a critique of absolute being. Finally, he gives us the assessment of the relative value of materialism and idealism alluded to above.

"What is Materialism?" began with a series of arguments on the relation of human experience, nature and labor. Bogdanov developed his position slowly, building upon and reworking common, everyday conceptions. Following that process would take many pages, diverting our attention from the more important aspects of the chapter. Accordingly, we will attempt to summarize his conclusions. They should be readily understandable, since they correspond in content and terminology to the arguments of his introductory essays.

Bogdanov's position on experience, nature and labor is laid out in the following formulae taken from the essay's first paragraph and its final remarks:

Man calls nature the endlessly unfolding field of his labor, of his experience. [PLE, p. 56]

The system of experience is the system of labor, all of its contents lie within the limits of the collective practice of mankind. The sense of this practice is to organize nature in the human interest; such is the direction of social activity taken as a whole. [PLE, p. 83]

These formulae imply that 1) "nature" is the arena of "labor", 2) that neither concept can be conceived of without the other, 3) that the "field of labor" is the same thing as the field of human experience, 4) that the concepts "experience" and "labor" are integral, and 5) that the "collective practice of mankind" is directed toward the organization of nature, the "field of experience", for man's benefit. As we shall see, these formulae lie at the base of Bogdanov's own philosophy which he considered to be "the labor worldview".[10]

On the basis of these notions, Bogdanov pursued his definition of the concept "matter" and the argument that "matter" had a correlative relationship with labor. "Labor", he said, "is effort, [and] effort supposes resistance." [PLE, p. 83] Nature, being the object of all human effort, he continued, is therefore the realm of resistance. That realm might be called the "kingdom of matter" as long as one keeps the idea of resistance in mind. [PLE, p. 83] Matter for Bogdanov, then, was merely an abstraction, a metaphor designating that which resists human effort. Logically, that which resisted effort could be quite "immaterial" from Bogdanov's perspective. Indeed, such was the case. As he put it:

In the clash of two activities, each appears as matter to the other. So, in the battle of two armies, each views the other exclusively as a material obstacle which must be surmounted. [PLE, p. 83]

He criticized bourgeois philosophers for not seeing the "basic, elementary fact" that there may be no activity without resistance, and that matter, the resisting entity, cannot be conceived of without reference to the action directed towards it. [PLE, p. 57] He cautioned his readers to take "labor" and "matter" in the most general way: "labor" meant the collective practice of mankind, "matter" the sum total of resistance to that activity. [PLE, p. 58]

Interestingly, Bogdanov did not find his concept of matter to be significantly different from that of the modern physicist. For the latter, he said, matter is characterized by its inertia, that is, by its resistance to effort. [PLE, p. 58] Bogdanov saw the law of inertia as a metaphor which carried over to nature the forms of human effort and resistance. "Consequently", he said, "the scientific concept of matter ... corresponds fully to that general philosophical concept which we have set forth." [PLE, p. 58]

It was clear that Bogdanov felt this definition of matter was merely a restatement of something which had been universally recognized, or at least suspected. He credited Marx, along with the modern physicist, with having understood the metaphorical meaning of matter. Marx clearly saw that "matter is the object of production, wherein its essence is also to be found". [PLE, pp. 58–9] Therefore, Bogdanov said, Marx rightly called his philosophy "materialism", since it related social development to man's efforts to surmount resisting matter. [PLE, p. 59] For Bogdanov the appearance of materialist philosophies in general signaled recognition of the metaphorical meaning of matter. It was only to be expected that man should attach great importance to the "physical" objects which most directly resisted his efforts. [PLE, p. 59] Obviously, Bogdanov considered this a one-sided view; but as we shall see, it was a step in the right direction.

Leaving his discussion of matter for the moment, Bogdanov directed his attention to the other side of the relationship, to labor. He posited two levels of "social-labor activity": the technical (read: "elemental", "direct") level and the organizational level. [PLE, p. 83] This distinction served an important purpose for Bogdanov. As labor on the technical level became more complex, he asserted, man came to need organizational forms. These forms were the "concepts, thought, norms, all of those things which are called ideas in the broadest sense of the word". [PLE, p. 83] This, said Bogdanov, is the realm of "spirit", the realm of ideology. [PLE, p. 83] Direct labor had to do with "physical" nature, while the ideological process had its business with "organization", that is, with the organization of labor itself. [PLE, p. 59] For Bogdanov the technical was in no way subordinate to the ideological: they were correlates, the second meeting demands that arose in the first. More than that, Bogdanov saw no difference between technical and ideological labor. The ideologist exerted effort against resistance as well, he said; only that which resisted his efforts was the "labor nature of men" rather than physical objects. [PLE, p. 83] For Bogdanov, the "labor nature of man" constituted "matter" in the sense that "one action is considered matter in relation to another acting against it". [PLE, p. 83]

Bogdanov also considered his view of ideological labor to be universally recognized. Idealistic philosophy as well as religion, arising in the period when organization and authority were closely bound together, recognized the importance of ideological labor and organizational forms. Hence, the world of ideas was viewed as primary reality by many. Again, Bogdanov found this view one-sided; it detached organizational forms from the technical process of labor and, with that, from their true relationship with "matter". [PLE, p. 60]

For Bogdanov, materialism and idealism constituted the two principal "lines" of the history of thought from the pre-Socratics to Marx. [PLE, pp. 61–2] He implied that this was wholly understandable given the fragmented nature of exchange society and the prevalent notion of abstract causality. Paying obeisance to contentless necessity, he said, secular philosophies failed to recognize the correspondence between "spirit", "matter" and human action. [PLE, p. 63; also p. 85] Where abstract causal necessity ruled, human action was subordinated to it and was denied its proper relation to "spirit" and "matter". Any attempt, then, to come to grips with the relation of man to nature or man to man had to come down on one side of the dichotomy or the other. As long as society was fundamentally split into classes of "organizers" and "implementors", as long as "spirit" and "matter" were considered to be independent of one another, one was compelled to concentrate either on the object of human practice or on its organizational forms. [PLE, p. 63; also, p. 85]

How did materialism and idealism proceed in their explanation of experience according to Bogdanov? The answer to this is both interesting and crucial for an understanding of how Bogdanov himself proposed to proceed as the "philosopher of living experience". Materialism and idealism, he said, did not base their procedures on the simple reduction of experience to either matter or ideas. They did not attempt to show that all experience was material or ideal as such, nor did either philosophy attempt to remove one or the other side of experience from the field of thought. Rather, he asserted, "they relied on the fundamental method of supplementing experience, on *substitution*". [PLE, p. 64; also p. 85] "Fundamental" here meant "basic and eternal". While he would criticize the materialists and idealists for their form of substitution, he did not attempt to discredit substitution as a philosophical procedure per se. Indeed, he considered it proper and even vital to all philosophy. Basically, Bogdanov's concept of materialist and idealist substitution meant that all non-material or non-spiritual experience was taken to be an attribute of either matter or spirit. While it may seem at first glance that his concepts of "reductionism" and substitution amount to the same thing, such was hardly the case.

The origins of substitution, said Bogdanov, lay in the "symbolic [nature] of human intercourse". [PLE, p. 84; also pp. 65]

Man substitutes words, . . . the symbols of art, writing, etc, . . . for various forms of consciousness, feeling, striving and thought. The former are in no way similar to the latter but [they] are bound together in a most vital manner. [PLE, p. 84; also pp. 65–6]

While he gave no examples of this elemental form of substitution, what Bogdanov meant is clear enough. To illustrate his point, we might fabricate an example of our own. The word or concept "anger" would be for Bogdanov a "substitution" for certain human gestures and expressions. Obviously, all "angry" gestures taken together would be in no real way similar to "anger". Gestures are physical movements, "anger" is a word, a concept, an abstraction, a "substitution" for something else. The purpose of this elemental form of substitution, said Bogdanov, is to provide a means by which men can understand one another, by which men can explain "the sense and correspondence of their actions". [PLE, p. 84; also p. 67] He claimed that from the elemental level, the act of substitution was eventually carried over to all the other levels of experience and to nature "with an aim to accomplish their explanation, to give understanding and prediction" and, Bogdanov added, to aid the struggle against nature. [PLE, p. 84; also p. 67]

Materialists and idealists, while greatly complicating and expanding the practice of substituting, did nothing different from their most primitive predecessors in Bogdanov's view. Their procedures amounted to "taking an object and effectively changing it into something else, while at the same time admitting the essential difference". [PLE, p. 68] The materialist, for instance, says that that which is not matter is but a manifestation, property or attribute of it. Thought, he argues, is a manifestation of nerve processes in the brain, or, more usually, thought *is* nerve processes. The materialist here substitutes nerve processes for thought with which they have nothing real in common. Hence, thought is changed by the materialist into something else. Once this is accomplished, that which is not "material" per se may be integrated into the materialist worldview without discomfort. [PLE, pp. 69–71] Similarly, the idealist says that all that is substantial, sensual, is a manifestation of thought and the substantial may then find a place in his worldview. [PLE, pp. 71–2] Bogdanov disapproved of continuing this "strange" practice, but only in its materialist and idealist forms. Materialist-idealist substitution was deemed "strange" here because "matter" or "idea" as things-in-themselves were the substitutes. [PLE, p. 72] As we shall see, substitution had an integral place in Bogdanov's thought. He called his form of it "universal substitution," which implied that it did not employ any sort of thing-in-itself as a substitute, and sought to establish it as the successor to the materialist-idealist form.[11]

For the moment, we need to say a few more words about Bogdanov's view of materialist-idealist substitution. As has been suggested, he saw this form of substitution to be progressive in its time. Reductionism, he said, simply made no sense; neither "idea" nor "matter" could be banished from the field of thought. [PLE, p. 72] To illustrate this point, Bogdanov brought up Democritus. He agreed that this pre-Socratic felt acutely the bind of materialist reductionism and was one of the first to find the logical way out of it. Democritus, he said, knew that reductionism could not explain "spirit". He found that one might do so by saying that "spirit" was not matter per se, but a manifestation, an attribute, of it. [PLE, p. 72] For Bogdanov, Democritus' use of this sort of substitution was clearly an early sign of progress in the construction of worldviews. The sense of Bogdanov's position was that man would be in a sorry state had thinkers foundered on the rocks of reductionism. In his opinion, that one must substitute to communicate and understand was a fundamental fact. Materialists and idealists had done the right thing, but it would be wrong to assume that their particular form of substitution was either universally or eternally valid. [PLE, p. 72]

From his discussion of substitution, Bogdanov moved on to deal with "abstract fetishism", the force which encouraged materialist-idealist substitution. [PLE, p. 73] This term meant, simply, the positing of absolute concepts, like "matter" or "idea" which had essences outside human experience or which were defined apart from the relationship of human action and its objects. For the "fetishist", said Bogdanov, "matter" and "idea" were conceived as things-in-themselves. [PLE, p. 73] The character of this fetishism was clear, he said. "An idea which is objectively the result of past social activity and which is the tool of the latter, is presented as something independent, cut off from it [i.e., social activity]...." [PLE, p. 82] As we have seen, Bogdanov felt that materialist-idealist substitution would be impossible were the relationship of the concepts "idea" and "matter" to human activity recognized. The true relationship slipped from man's grasp, he said, with the rise of "abstract fetishism". "Abstract fetishism" itself arose from the organization of exchange society. [PLE, p. 74]

In exchange society, Bogdanov asserted, the individual loses consciousness of his membership in the collective. This was due to social fragmentation, to the formal independence of the various aspects of production, to market competition and the economic struggle in general. "Social activity as [society's] aim ceases to exist for the individual and is shattered into atoms of individual activity." [PLE, p. 85] In Bogdanov's view, thought in exchange society was necessarily individual thought. Individual thought could not help but see "idea" and "matter" as unrelated and absolute. The only action the individual knows is individual action. [PLE, p. 74; also p. 85] In truth, human activity in its collective form creates and defines "idea" and "matter". The individual, who does not know of collective activity, cannot conceive of this and is willing to accord "idea" and "matter" a superior sort of existence apart from any human action. [PLE, p. 74; also p. 85] Putting this in other words for Bogdanov, if one fails to understand human activity as social activity, then one has nothing to which the concepts of "idea" and "matter" can be related.

For Bogdanov, the development of the notion of thing-in-itself was a stumbling block in the way of a complete monistic philosophy. However, he saw the notion of "matter" as thing-in-itself to be, in an important sense, progressive. In spite of its shortcomings, said Bogdanov, philosophical materialism stood a step closer to a secular monism than did idealism. For that reason, its historical forms should be considered more progressive than idealism at any given time. [PLE, p. 75] Further, Bogdanov implied that as materialism was more progressive than idealism, so would "the philosophy of living experience" be more progressive than materialism for the same reasons. The reasoning behind these assertions is given in the following manner. The world of resistance or "kingdom of matter", said Bogdanov, is that toward which all collective activity is directed. For the materialist, the world of resistance is the realm of physical nature. For the idealist, on the other hand, that which resists is only the labor nature of men, a much smaller realm. The world of organizational forms, of "ideas", is created by a much smaller part of human activity working on a smaller segment of the world of resistance. Materialism is closer to a monistic system since it deals with a greater portion of the world of resistance. [PLE, p. 75] In addition, Bogdanov argued, idealism's products are abstract and contentless when taken by themselves apart from their relationship to direct labor and physical nature. The products of materialism, in contrast, always bear the mark of the direct labor process. [PLE, p. 76] Bogdanov's philosophy, as "the labor worldview", would apparently succeed all forms of materialism in grasping an even greater portion of the world of resistance. In taking thorough account of all of labor and all of its objects, "the labor worldview" would set the ideological or organizational activity of men in its proper place as the servant of direct labor. Ideological and direct labor would be bound together as the inseparable aspects of collective activity, and "matter" and "idea" would come together in the realm of resistance as aspects of the world of resistance. [PLE, p. 76]

Bogdanov credited both Marx and Mach with contributing to the critique of "fetishistic" materialism in a manner similar to his own. He attempted to show that his perspective was borne out in Marx's theses on Feuerbach. In the first, eighth, ninth and tenth theses, he said, Marx argued that a worldview which separated matter from human activity could only be contemplative, that is, without an active character. For Marx, Bogdanov said, passive philosophy was not a proper system of knowledge at all. Implicit in Marx's argument was the call to make materialism "active", that is, to bring the concept "matter" back into relation with human action. [PLE, p. 76–7]

Ernst Mach attacked the "fetishism" of matter from a different perspective than Marx, Bogdanov said, but the criticism was similar. Mach argued that the ordinary concept of matter was insupportable, because it had been cut off from action. [PLE, p. 77] Bogdanov repeated part of Mach's famous discussion on the Newtonian concept of mass to show that Mach understood masses, quantities of matter, to be defined in terms of force. He noted that Mach argued that force was defined in relation to mass.

[PLE, p. 78] Bogdanov did not go into Mach's attempt to get outside this circular process, but simply pointed out that for Mach matter had no meaning when divorced from action. [PLE, pp. 78–9] Mach's analysis of ordinary matter did not go far enough in Bogdanov's opinion. It is true, he said, that Mach understood that the concept of mechanical force had its basis in human effort, that mechanical force was a metaphorical concept. However, he did not see human effort in terms of collective labor or social activity. According to Bogdanov, Mach remained within the limits of individualistic thought. [PLE, p. 79] We shall pick up this criticism of Mach and the other Empirio-critics in the next chapter.

In concluding, Bogdanov returned to his argument that researching the real relationship of "idea", "matter", and human action was impossible in exchange society. This time he emphasized that which was possible, that is, substitution to explain the world as the sum of things-in-themselves and their attributes. [PLE, pp. 80–1] Of the two forms of substitution, the materialist was clearly the more progressive. He implied that from its stance one might see the true nature of idealism, of ideology, of organizational forms, and thereby begin to properly relate human action on its various levels to its objects. He concluded that materialism ". . . is nearer to a labor worldview, to a philosophy of living experience". [PLE, p. 85]

In summing up the material of this chapter, we might do well to divide that summary between Bogdanov's philosophical statements and his scheme for the history of philosophy. As regards the first, we may make the following points.

1. The concepts "labor" and "matter", "effort" and "resistance", "social or collective activity" and "nature" comprise Bogdanov's notion of what the world is. That which is, is either action or resistance. Because one cannot be conceived of without the other, the world may not be broken into separate or exclusive aspects. For this reason, "matter" and "idea" as things which resist can have no existence apart from human action. They cannot be things-in-themselves. Furthermore, they cannot be conceived as totally isolated realms of "being".

2. Materialism and idealism reflect partisanship for one or the other types of human labor activity, the direct or the ideological, as well as partisanship for one or the other part of the world of resistance, "physical" nature or man's "labor nature". Materialism and idealism both take a mistaken view of the world as the sum of "things-in-themselves" along with the manifestations or attributes of those things. In actuality, both types of human labor activity are the same and so are

their objects. There is no primary form of labor nor primary being.
3. Materialists and idealists explain the world by substituting matter for
   idea or idea for matter. In this way, the bind of assigning primacy to
   matter or idea is escaped.
4. Such substitution is a fundamental fact about the way man thinks, the
   way all philosophy has proceeded and must proceed in the future. Men
   substitute to understand one another and to relate the innumerable
   elements of the world. In its simplest form substitution amounts to
   using words and concepts to designate things. In its most complex
   form, it amounts to changing things and concepts into other things and
   concepts. The materialist does this when he says that thought is a
   manifestation of nerve processes. The idealist does this when he says
   that things are specific manifestations of general ideas. For Bogdanov,
   materialist-idealist substitution is inappropriate to contemporary
   philosophy, since it employs as substitutes "matter" and "idea" as
   things-in-themselves. The contemporary philosopher must substitute,
   but he must not view any given substitute as primary reality.

As far as the history of philosophy is concerned, Bogdanov tells us that
materialism and idealism are its two major lines and that each employs the
same method, i.e., substitution, in explaining the world. Both are flawed,
"fetishistic", and incapable of seeing the true relationship of "matter",
"idea", and human action. This is due to the fact that both reflect the
fragmented, individualistic character of human action in exchange society.
Without a proper view of action and the world which resists it, no monistic
worldview is possible. Materialism and idealism may aspire toward that goal
but cannot reach it. Philosophy, however, does show certain progressive signs.
Its use of a more complex sort of substitution is progressive. In addition,
materialism, by dint of its concern with a larger portion of the realm of
resistance, takes philosophy a step closer to a worldview which comprehends
the whole of that realm. Bogdanov tells us, in effect, that philosophy is
moving toward a grasp of that whole as well as a grasp of the whole of human
activity. When this is accomplished, a secular monism will have been created.
Materialism will have been succeeded as the progressive worldview and the
study of ideas put in its proper place.

D.   ANCIENT AND MODERN MATERIALISMS

We have said that the last two chapters of the first half of *The Philosophy of
Living Experience* discuss the history of philosophy from the pre-Socratics to

the nineteenth century. In light of the fact that they are entitled "The Materialism of the Ancient World" and "Modern Materialism", our statement begs some explanation. We have chosen to call this a discussion of the history of philosophy because, for Bogdanov's purposes, the history of materialism *was* the history of philosophy. Because he deemed materialism to be the more progressive of the two lines of philosophy at any given time, the progress of philosophy as a whole was the progress of materialism. Although Bogdanov would credit Hegel with advancing philosophy in important ways,[12] idealism contributed little else of substance to the progress of thought. His comments on idealism in these chapters are few, and in them the reader is not taken beyond the arguments of "What is Materialism?"

We have implied above that Bogdanov saw a certain progress apparent in the historical development of materialism. In "What is Materialism?" we are told that materialism is progressive because it deals with a greater portion of the world of resistance to human action. This suggests that Bogdanov saw in the historical development of materialism a tendency toward grasping an ever-greater portion and that over time materialism approached a proper understanding of the relation of "action" and "resistance". Such was not the case. The progressive tendency in the history of materialism was its ever more "active" character as philosophy. By this Bogdanov meant that successive materialisms, especially in the modern era, assigned an increasingly more "active" role to knowledge, which in its systematic form is philosophy, in the struggle to dominate nature. Although it gave man no active role in determining being and clung to matter as "thing-in-itself", materialism nonetheless advanced philosophy toward the active worldview that present and future conditions demanded. Of the lessons to be learned from the study of materialism, the increasingly active role it accorded philosophy in relation to life was perhaps the most important one for Bogdanov.

Before we turn to the material of these two chapters, we must make one additional comment. Bogdanov tells us that his intention in writing them was not to provide a history of materialism as such but, rather, "to explain its basic methods and their objective sources". [PLE, pp. 120–1] In effect, he meant to corroborate the arguments of "What is Materialism?" with illustrations. As there is little in the way of new arguments on the matter of the methods of materialism, one could easily summarize Bogdanov's assessment of its ancient and modern forms in a few paragraphs. We are not led to do so, however, because these chapters contain a number of interesting and important explanations of the "objective sources" of materialism's methods which Bogdanov has not given before. We find out here something of the extent to which cognition is influenced by social production in his view. As we shall see, models taken from social practice are carried over into consciousness as cognitive forms. Our thinker now begins to call cognitive forms "sociomorphisms", a term which reflects their sources.[13] The more this term is used in *The Philosophy of Living Experience,* the more important it becomes in Bogdanov's arguments. In the chapter on empiriomonism in particular, new "sociomorphisms" are produced by Bogdanov which permit him to solve the contemporary problem of philosophy. In addition, the derivation or generation of "sociomorphisms" becomes part of his philosophy's method.[14] Unfortunately, he gives us no clue as to his inspiration in this. The idea of cognitive forms taken from and reinforcing the real world was common currency in Bogdanov's time. Marx certainly professed it, but he was nowhere as specific as Bogdanov. We can only assume that our thinker simply "made good" on a familiar idea and that, perhaps, it was the general influence of Marx which set him to it.

1.   *The Materialism of the Ancient World*

The first of the two chapters on ancient and modern materialism, although lengthy, [PLE, pp. 86–125] contained little analysis which was really new. Aside from the matter of "sociomorphisms" and a discussion of those ancient philosophies which took individual sensations as their starting point, the chapter was primarily devoted to the career of materialist substitution and abstract causality in ancient thought. In relating its contents, we will treat in turn Bogdanov's discussions of Milesian hylozoism, Democritus' atomism and the ancient philosophies proceeding from individual sensation. His general assessment of ancient materialism should become apparent as we go along.

At the beginning of his discussion of ancient materialism, Bogdanov focused his attention on the Milesian school and, in particular, on Thales and Anaximander. Materialism, he said, was born together with philosophy. In fact, Milesian hylozoism, the doctrine which professed an animate view of matter, was probably the earliest form of both materialism and secular world-view. [PLE, p. 86; also p. 121] It was completely understandable to Bogdanov why this species of materialism arose in ancient Ionia. As we have seen, the rise of extra-religious thought was purportedly the result of the growth of exchange economy and, with that, the quickening of technical progress. "To this", Bogdanov said,

... the fact fully corresponds that the birthplace of materialism, as well as of philosophy in general, was the Greek trading colonies, where together with the force of exchange, the necessity of adaptation to new natural conditions accelerated the technical process. [PLE, p. 121; also p. 87]

Ionia was the birthplace of ancient exchange society, from the social practice of which secular thought could take its cognitive models. Bogdanov also noted that in Ionia religious tradition was weak compared to Hellas itself, and, therefore, resistance to secular thought was lower there. [PLE, p. 88; also p. 121]

Bogdanov asserted that Milesian hylozoism was the "naïve materialism" of sea-tradesmen and that this fact was clearly reflected in its basic schemes. In hylozoism, he said, the concept of matter did not achieve complete abstraction: materialist substitution had a more "concrete" character. [PLE, p. 88; also p. 121]

For all phenomena there was substituted a partial species of matter which played a particular role in the life of the social groups promoting the first philosophers: water and air. [PLE, p. 121; also p. 88]

Bogdanov contended that, for example, Thales' supposition that water was the explanation of all being was induced by the role of water in the social lives of the Ionian Greeks. He argued that this "concrete" form of materialist substitution was understandable, because a truly abstract form of causality had not been developed by the hylozoists. For them, he said, all matter exhibited "living strivings" and, consequently, matter's first cause was to be found in its own natural properties. Thales, then, had no need for a more abstract concept of matter; his substitute, water, was elemental, living being. [PLE, pp. 89–90] For Bogdanov, hylozoist causality was a hold-over from the authoritarian-religious worldview, and hylozoism on the whole appeared very close to the older system of knowledge. [PLE, p. 90]

Nonetheless, Bogdanov saw hylozoism as a step toward a proper secular worldview, because it attempted a form of materialist substitution. [PLE, p. 91] He also noted that it exhibited another sort of progressive sign. As with all post-authoritarian philosophy, said Bogdanov, hylozoism showed a concern for the relation of matter and action. "[In its] active understanding of matter, one might see [sic,] perhaps, echoes of that 'primordial dialectic', for which nature was the realm of action." [PLE, pp. 91–2] The reader should not be confused by these statements. The "concern for the relation of matter and action" in this instance does not mean the proper one described in "What is Materialism?" Bogdanov is referring here to the vague sort of recognition by materialists of the fact that physical nature resists human labor nature. [PLE, p. 90]

If there is any doubt that the Milesian school was on the track of a complete and proper materialism, said Bogdanov, one need only look at Anaximander's concept of the "Infinite" to see the refinement of the materialist substitute. He suggested that Anaximander had attempted to produce a more abstract understanding of the material essence of being. For this Ionian, water did not explain enough; it was too limited a substitute. Therefore, Anaximander posited that the beginning and essence of being was a chaos of eternal and undefined "matter", i.e., the "Infinite", from which all the elements of the world were formed. [PLE, p. 93] This, said Bogdanov, was the beginning of abstract materialist substitution. However, because Anaximander's primordial "matter" was qualitatively and quantitatively indefinite, it could not have become the basis for a complete and proper materialist worldview. According to Bogdanov, the materialist substitute had to be not only abstract but well defined. [PLE, p. 93] As we shall see directly, Democritus' material atoms met both requirements.

If hylozoism and Anaximander's "Infinite" were the first steps toward a complete and proper materialism, in Bogdanov's view, the atomistic materialism of Democritus marked the culmination of that process. Democritus' work, he said, represented the most progressive type of world-view for early exchange society, at least for one in which "no new forms of collectivism" had arisen. [PLE, p. 122; also p. 94] According to Bogdanov, the concept of matter reached the fullest abstract formulation in atomism. Similarly, he found in Democritus' notion of causality the full expression of abstract necessity. [PLE, p. 122; also p. 94] Bogdanov's notions about Democritus are particularly important. If one takes them together with the contents of his introductory chapters, one sees that Bogdanov's phrase "the most progressive type of worldview for early exchange society" means that the atomistic materialism of Democritus corresponded to the "scientific point of view", and that atomism was based on the "whole of collective experience" of its time. [PLE, p. 122, also p. 94] Thus, Bogdanov was not simply noting that Democritus had an abstract and well-defined concept of matter and causality. It was clear that he considered Democritus' concepts of atomism and causal necessity to be the "sociomorphic forms" most appropriate to ancient exchange society. All of ancient thought would be measured against that of Democritus.

Not concerning himself with the development of Democritus' thought per se, Bogdanov went on to discuss the sociomorphic character of atomistic materialism. In the thought of Democritus, he said, one finds two principal instances of the "unconscious application of models taken from social practice". [PLE, p. 122; also p. 95] Atomism created a picture of the world "by means of mentally breaking it up into elements and subsequently mentally unifying these elements into a structured whole". [PLE, p. 122; also p. 95] This method was a copy of the basic social forms of exchange society: "labor technique" and "general organizational activity". [PLE, p. 95; also p. 122] In social practice, said Bogdanov, the same activity occurs; various social groups are broken into parts, and these parts are "organizationally combined" into new relationships. [PLE, p. 95; also p. 122] The second instance of sociomorphism which Bogdanov saw in atomistic materialism was an obvious one. The elements of atomism, he said, were considered exclusive of and different from one another. Their only possible relation to one another was purely "external", that is, their relation was thrust upon them by the "mental unification" process. [PLE, pp. 96–7] Bogdanov argued that one need only look at non-materialist forms of atomism to see what was afoot here. For Leibniz, the "formal atom" was seen as an individual personality in extreme opposition to other personalities. [PLE, p. 98] Such was the case with atomistic materialism. The material atom reflected the individual personality in exchange society and was given a relationship to other atoms by a unifying force akin to that of the "organizer" who obeys the strictures of economic necessity. [PLE, p. 99]

Bogdanov felt that the "closed system of individualism" accounted for the attractiveness of atomistic materialism for the progressive minds of ancient exchange society. [PLE, pp. 100–2] While asserting that individualism and atomism were certainly progressive when compared to their predecessors in authoritarian society and thought, Bogdanov claimed that the most progressive feature of atomistic materialism was its concept of abstract causality. [PLE, p. 103] Again, he stressed that abstract causality was cognitively progressive; permitting an infinite number of steps of cause and effect, the notion of abstract necessity encouraged an endless search for explanation. [PLE, pp. 104–5] Bogdanov noted that the majority of ancient materialists did not hold exclusively to the abstract notion of causality: they were wont to look for willful causes. The reason for this, he said, was that the structure of society itself was hardly uniform: "its various relations, giving models for contradictory forms and schemes of thought, always pressed systematists toward unconscious eclecticism." [PLE, p. 124; also pp. 110–12 *passim*]

With these remarks, Bogdanov ended his discussion of ancient materialism as such. Before going on to the modern materialists, however, he was compelled to deal with another aspect of ancient thought. It was an aspect, we submit, which he could not safely ignore. As we have seen, Bogdanov's central argument was that ancient materialism reflected the individualism and economic necessity of exchange society. More specifically, he argued that the atomistic materialism of Democritus was the most advanced worldview of its time. That is, it best reflected and reinforced the individualism and economic necessity of exchange society. It must have occurred to Bogdanov that some explanation had to be given for those ancient philosophies which appeared to be more "individualistic" than atomistic materialism. Otherwise, his readers might contend that, for example, solipsism had to be considered a more advanced worldview for exchange society according to Bogdanov's own reasoning. Accordingly, he set out to explain "the basic methods and sources" of philosophies which took individual experience as their starting point. [PLE, p. 113] His object was two-fold. First, he wished to show that these philosophies were simply unable to provide as complete a worldview as atomistic materialism, because they were based on something less than the collective experience of mankind in their time. Secondly, Bogdanov wished to assert that solipsism, pan-psychism and, in particular, sensualism were actually only extreme forms of idealism and materialism, because they employed either idealistic or materialist substitution. He did not deny that such philosophies comprised a "third line" in the history of thought. However, he considered that "third line" to be dependent on the other two and hardly viable in its own right. [PLE, p. 114]

In his discussion, Bogdanov chose to focus on the sensualism of Protagoras, that philosophy of individual experience which he considered closest to materialism. Before he dealt with the thought of Protagoras as such, however, Bogdanov set the stage by explaining the rise and development of the entire "third line" trend. The "third line" philosophers, he asserted, took as their basis a view of matter cut off from action, matter as thing-in-itself. Once this was assumed, Bogdanov said, it was easy enough for them to see action in the form of purely individual activity. Individual activity naturally seemed weak in the face of the world it acted against. Because of that, individual activity was seen as "passive", "reflective". [PLE, p. 114] Bogdanov noted that

This sounds very strange, activity relating to its object passively: but it is no more strange than matter existing for itself or, in other words, resistance not dependent upon or bound up with that which it resists. [PLE, p. 114]

Passive individual activity, Bogdanov said, came to be signified by the concepts "psychics", or "personal sensations", or "personal consciousness", all of which set individual activity apart from the rest of existence. [PLE, pp. 114–15] Psychic sensation was seen as that which is most familiar and directly accessible to man; to the individual only his sensations are directly given. This, said Bogdanov, became the first formula of the "third line" worldview. [PLE, p. 115]

From this perspective, Bogdanov asserted, a universal picture of the world was attempted, and various forms of substitution were employed to fill it out. The simplest method was that employed by solipsists, i.e., substituting individual psychical experience for the whole world. [PLE, pp. 115–16] Another broader and less naïve form of "psychical substitution", he said, was that employed by pan-psychism. From its perspective, being amounts to psychical complexes of varying degrees of complexity, from inanimate nature to the human mind. According to Bogdanov, pan-psychism was the most consistent, the most logical of all individualistic worldviews, because it eschewed "matter" altogether. [PLE, p. 116] For Bogdanov, both solipsism and pan-psychism were clearly inferior to atomistic materialism as systems of knowledge for exchange society, because they were based on and concerned with limited forms of experience. The solipsist ignored all but his own psychical sensations, and pan-psychicism ignored the whole material side of experience. In addition, Bogdanov judged solipsism and pan-psychism inferior, because they used forms of idealist substitution. [PLE, p. 117]

Sensualism Bogdanov considered both more interesting and more troublesome, since it was very close to materialism if not actually a species of it. [PLE, p. 118] In the work of Protagoras, he said, one could find a very clear example of materialist substitution. Protagoras, out of a concern for finding the origins of individual sensations, was led to posit material subjects and objects, the interaction of which produced sensation. This, said Bogdanov, amounted to materialist substitution in a particularly extreme form, since Protagoras' material subjects and objects not only stood apart from the sensations they produced, they were also deemed fundamentally unknowable. [PLE, p. 119] Sensualism, accordingly, was inferior to atomistic materialism; its substitute was abstract but undefined and undefinable. [PLE, p. 119] If this was not enough to establish its inferiority, said Bogdanov, one need only compare the Protagorian system of knowledge with that of atomistic materialism. For Protagoras, he noted, every subject was different from every other subject at any given time; and, therefore, no two subjects could be expected to generate the same sensations with regard to the same object. Every subject-object interaction, then, had to be considered equally valid. [PLE, p. 120] According to Bogdanov, Protagoras' conclusion that "man is the measure of all things" implied individual and not collective man as the subject. This not only contributed to the cause of philosophical relativism, it also implied the impossibility of knowledge. With that, Protagoras contributed to the rise of philosophical skepticism as well. [PLE, pp. 120–1] For Bogdanov, sensualism was clearly a "philosophy of individual experience", a "private philosophy". [PLE, p. 121] In spite of the fact that it employed materialist substitution and did not deny either mode of experience, sensualism failed to encompass the "accumulated experience of mankind" in its time and, on account of that, could present no real challenge to atomistic materialism. Its failure was a function of the "third line's" starting point, individual sensation or experience. [PLE, p. 121]

Although the two chapters on the history of philosophy are best considered together, we might make a few comments in summarizing the first of them. Bogdanov's discussion of the basic methods of ancient materialism and the sources of those methods give somewhat more substance to his perspective on the history of materialism. He attempted to show how materialism developed toward its atomistic species by advancing the concepts of matter and causality toward greater abstraction and definition. As the highest and most complete worldview of antiquity, atomistic materialism best reflected and reinforced the individualism and exchange character of ancient society. It had been "the scientific point of view" of its day.

In tracing the development of ancient materialism, Bogdanov expanded his view of the relationship of philosophy and life by suggesting that all of the concepts of ancient thought, substitutes and causal notions being the most basic of them, were cognitive forms taken from human practice. The best of these "sociomorphisms", Democritus' material atoms and notion of causal necessity, were purportedly based on the collective experience of mankind. This, in turn, rendered Democritus' worldview the most progressive of its time. Here, one begins to see another side of Bogdanov's view of philosophy. Implied in the above is the notion of philosophy as the systematic organization of sociomorphisms. It will become more and more clear that this is Bogdanov's view as we go along. The notion will receive its clearest explication in the chapter on Bogdanov's own worldview, where the taking of sociomorphisms becomes the method of "the philosophy of living experience".

Progressive or not, ancient materialisms were for Bogdanov the products of early exchange society. The truth in even the best of them was relative and of temporary significance. The lesson to be learned from studying them was obvious: man had passed ancient materialism by long since. The same lesson was to be learned from the study of "third line" philosophy in the ancient world. If such individualistic philosophies as solipsism, pan-psychism and sensualism had failed to compete with main-line materialism in the ancient world, they certainly had no value for the present.

2. Modern Materialism

In his discussion of modern materialism, [PLE, pp. 126–73] Bogdanov continued to employ the same sort of analysis of methods and sources which he had applied to ancient thought. Given his procedures in the previous chapter, one might have expected further comparisons of materialist philosophies and, perhaps, an attempt at finding a modern counterpart to Democritus. Such was not the case. Bogdanov chose, instead, to study tendencies of the whole. The result of this choice is a rather diffuse essay which, after its cogent initial arguments and a discussion of Bacon supporting them, deals with seventeenth-, eighteenth- and nineteenth-century materialist thought in a rapid and disjointed survey. The question arises as to why Bogdanov opted to treat modern materialism in this way. Several answers might be advanced. First, it is clear that our thinker viewed modern materialism to be essentially the same species of thought as its ancient counterpart. He had already spent two chapters discussing materialist thought; why should he do any more than hit the high points of the modern period? Secondly, it is clear that Bogdanov viewed Marx and Mach as the most progressive figures in modern materialist thought. He chose not to include either in this chapter, however. One might surmise that Bogdanov was principally interested in elaborating the contents of the "pre-Marxo-Machist" materialist inheritance. Modern materialism for Bogdanov, simply completed that inheritance by "scientifically refining the abstract concepts of matter and causality". [PLE, p. 126] Whichever (or some other) was the case, one is still inclined to examine this chapter carefully for evidence of the development of Bogdanov's own philosophy. Therefore, we will go through each of its sections in turn, as has been our practice thus far.

As we have said, Bogdanov considered ancient and modern materialism to be the same species of thought. He judged their basic methods to be identical, even though they exhibited certain different tendencies. Bogdanov's general argument implied that modern materialism presented a significantly more "active" worldview than its ancient predecessor. Just how active he considered modern materialism to be, and why, will be seen shortly.

Bogdanov asserted that the new materialism had been created under the influence of the old. [PLE, p. 127] This is not to say that he felt the former was simply a continuation of the latter. For Bogdanov, ancient thought could not have been the principal determining factor in the development of modern materialism; that place was reserved for contemporary social conditions. Nonetheless, it is interesting to note that he did not minimize the influence of classical culture. Ancient "science", he said, gave its modern successor support in the struggle with nature and obsolete social forms; that support came from the legacy of "complete, general schemes for individualistic consciousness". [PLE, p. 128] The suggestion here was simply that modern exchange man learned from his exchange past. In addition, Bogdanov felt that the thought of ancient exchange society contained many unsurpassed expressions of individual consciousness which might serve man in modern exchange society. [PLE, p. 128]

On the whole, however, he considered modern materialism to be more complete as an individualistic system of knowledge, and he held that new historical circumstances played the principal role in its formation. Modern society, he said, was more completely an exchange society than its ancient forerunner. The latter had been "two-sided"; while its thought and culture corresponded to the exchange character of its upper levels, ancient society's productive basis remained slave labor. This "two-sidedness" was the chief cause of the decline of classical society and culture. [PLE, p. 129] Bogdanov implied that materialist philosophies could not be handed down unchanged from one exchange society to another when such gross differences in productive base were involved. While the difference in base was important for him, Bogdanov saw the main difference between ancient and modern exchange society in the fact that the modern was "technically progressive". [PLE, p. 130] By this he meant that the labor relations and organization of the new society developed at an increasingly more rapid pace. Along with this, he said, the struggle with nature became increasingly more successful. Technical advances and the victories over nature served to expand "human experience" at a rate unknown in the ancient world. [PLE, p. 130] As models of thought were taken from human experience, they had to correspond to and serve it. Thus, said Bogdanov, the accelerated struggle with nature necessitated and produced a more "active" materialistic system of knowledge. [PLE, p. 131]

Bogdanov noted that in ancient materialism, the question of "system" predominated. He implied that such thinkers as Epicurus and Lucretius merely sought to explain the essence of things in order to satisfy man's need to feel comfortable in his world. This emphasis on "system" made ancient materialism ineluctably passive. [PLE, p. 131] From the very beginning, that is, from Bacon, he said, the new materialism was an active philosophy, a philosophy of struggle. Bogdanov found that the "spirit of *practical research* was the basic structure of modern times". [PLE, p. 131] The goal of modern science and materialist philosophy, he said, was not simply to know nature, but to dominate it. Thus, for materialistic philosophy, the questions of "practice" and "methodology" predominated over the question of "system". This concern for practice and method was the single most important tendency of modern materialism and the feature which made it "active" and progressive. [PLE, p. 131] Bogdanov summed up his thoughts in the first paragraph of the chapter's conclusion.

The new materialism was not simply a continuation of the old. It was, of course, created under its influence but in different historical circumstances [and] subject to other social demands. Reflecting the technical progress of modern times, [with] its numerous victories over nature [and] its continuous series of discoveries and inventions, materialism acquired a predominantly "methodological" character. Adopting from its ancient teachers a general point of view and basic schemes, it strove to apply all of this to the tasks of further research. [PLE, p. 169]

Bogdanov found the thought of Francis Bacon "unusually typical in this regard". [PLE, p. 169] As we have said, he found no modern counterpart to Democritus; however, it is clear that Bogdanov accorded Bacon favored status among modern materialists. For Bogdanov, it was Bacon who, more than anyone else, exhibited the new concern for method. Furthermore, he argued, Bacon had acted upon this concern to render an enormously significant service to modern materialist thought. According to Bogdanov, Bacon possessed a fully materialistic understanding of the aim of knowledge. Because he took the aim of knowledge to be the conquest of nature, Bacon was able to draw the proper and progressive conclusion that knowledge must begin with actual human experience and serve actual human needs. Such was his explanation of how Bacon arrived at the inductive method. [PLE, p. 132] Bogdanov criticized Bacon for lacking a truly modern notion of matter (he judged it to be akin to that of hylozoism) and for not appreciating the value of the experimental method. [PLE, pp. 133–4] However, these things were insignificant to Bogdanov when compared with Bacon's contributions in the realm of inductive explanation. One gets the impression that Bogdanov considered induction to be the appropriate method of all philosophies based directly on human experience. Bacon's contribution, then, was more than simply the predominant methodology of modern materialism for Bogdanov. He asserted that Bacon gave modern man the "highest degree of induction",

the "abstract-analytical method". [PLE, p. 135] Bogdanov's description of
the "abstract-analytical method" is interesting and we shall find references to
it later in *The Philosophy of Living Experience.*

The essence of this [abstract-analytical method] is that *tendencies* are established
subject to the study of facts in union with their conditions; the formulation of the basic
tendency of a series of phenomena is their abstract law. In order to establish it, it is
necessary to simplify phenomena, to eliminate from them the secondary, complicating
tendencies along with those partial conditions on which they depend. In the experiment
this is achieved by real, technical simplification of the research process; when experiment
is inapplicable, it is replaced by the mental [stripping away] of complicating elements.
[PLE, pp. 169–70]

One might surmise here that, for Bogdanov, all philosophies based
directly on actual human experience properly formulate laws in the inductive
manner. Bacon allowed human experience to speak for itself, and this must
have been part of his attractiveness for Bogdanov. However, we shall see that
it is more probable that our thinker favored Bacon because the "abstract-
analytical method" accorded man an active role in simplifying human
experience. Bogdanov said nothing at this point about the character of or
justification for the process of simplifying experience. Later, he would credit
Marx with employing the "abstract-analytical method" in the study of
society to formulate "scientific laws" in an area where experiment is
inapplicable.[15] Like substitution, the "abstract-analytical method" was seen
by Bogdanov as a fundamental practice which, although it had had several
socially and historically relative forms, was nonetheless vital to the
formulation of any system of knowledge. Again like substitution, it was
apparently a procedure that proletarian philosophers were bound to employ.
[PLE, p. 135]

Bogdanov also noted Bacon's broad program of inductive research in the
most varied realms of experience. That Bacon considered it possible and
necessary to apply his method to the study of man and society, Bogdanov felt
was only consistent with his progressive appreciation of the aim of knowledge
and the universal applicability of the "abstract-analytical method". [PLE,
p. 136]

From Bacon, Bogdanov moved on to the English empiricists. As we
have suggested, his treatment was rather disjointed. It appeared to be
without a central focus, save for his intention to show the progressive
characteristics of their thought. Bogdanov chose to deal with the materialist
substitution of Hobbes and Locke to show both the influence of the "spirit
of the times" and the refinement of the concept of matter. Hobbes, he held,

showed the progressive concern with method in his attempt to formulate abstract laws governing matter. Like Bacon, he did this by stripping away its secondary qualities. His method, said Bogdanov, was not inductive but the opposite. Proceeding from the assumption that extension, form and movement were the primary qualities of matter, Hobbes practiced a form of materialist substitution which learned towards geometrical constructions and mathematics. [PLE, p. 137] According to Bogdanov, this leaning reflected the spirit of a time when new practical techniques arose operating on more exact measurement and numerical calculation. This, he said, was the same spirit which produced modern higher mathematics and, most especially, the calculus. [PLE, p. 138] For Bogdanov, then, Hobbes gave the modern concept of matter its quantitative characteristics of extension, form and movement. He saw this contribution limited, however, by the fact that Hobbes judged the other qualities of matter, i.e., hardness, weight, impenetrability to be only sensations produced by its movement. [PLE, p. 139]

For Bogdanov, Locke exhibited the same sort of concern with method as Hobbes, for he, too, was out to define the primary qualities of matter. Bogdanov devoted a good deal of space to tracing the logic behind Locke's concept of "substance", which he judged an inferior concept of matter because Locke had begun his inquiry with individual psychic experience. [PLE, pp. 140–5] More important to Bogdanov than the limitations of Locke's sensualism, however, was the contribution he had made to defining matter's primary qualities. Locke's concept of "substance", said he, was used to supplement his sensualism and, as such, amounted to indefinite materialist substitution. [PLE, p. 145] But in so doing, Locke added the primary quality of mass to Hobbes's spatial forms and movement. This important addition to the concept of matter, Bogdanov asserted, was a reflection of the progress and systematization of mechanics and especially the work of Newton. [PLE, p. 147] It appears that for Bogdanov, Hobbes and Locke had been the chief modern contributors to the concept of matter as thing-in-itself. Democritus' individual atoms had been given qualities which could be measured and quantitatively related by abstract mathematical and geometric laws.

Bogdanov's interest in Hume was somewhat different. He was concerned to show that Hume had exhibited a progressive interest in methodology and that Hume's sensualism involved a form of materialist substitution. Bogdanov was most interested, however, in Hume's attack on the concept of matter and abstract causality. He elaborated in detail Hume's claim that matter constituted bundles of sensations and that causal bonds were conventional associations of sequences of facts. [PLE, pp. 148–54] What did that attack

mean to Bogdanov? At this point in *The Philosophy of Living Experience* it is
difficult to say. Two answers come to mind, however. First, it may have
meant that the modern concepts of matter and abstract causality had been
sufficiently well-established to permit such an attack. Secondly, it may have
meant that the "living instability of the bourgeois world" [PLE, p. 155]
would not permit its own progressive worldview a stable, quiet career. To
be sure, Bogdanov intended in part to make a comment about the "sociomorphic" character of modern sensualism. On the whole, however, it appears that he wished to show that even at the time when materialism was
most progressive, its basis was being undermined. Clearly, Bogdanov approved
of Hume's attack; but, he implied that because it had been made from a
sensualist perspective, the attack had its limitations. It is our guess that
Bogdanov brought up Hume to emphasize the impossibility of overcoming
the concept of matter as thing-in-itself in the eighteenth century. He hinted in
his discussion of hylozoism and Protagoras that partially true concepts of
matter, i.e., matter seen in some relation with action, had indeed been
formulated. The individualism of ancient exchange society, however,
rendered them incomplete. One might assume that he was saying the same
sort of thing about modern concepts of matter.

Summing up the thought of the French Enlightenment, Bogdanov argued
that its materialism was not differentiated from its forerunners by dint of
originality but, rather, by dint of the breadth of its propagandization. [PLE,
p. 160] He wished to show that the modern materialist concern for method
was blunted somewhat by a new sort of concern for "system". The Enlightenment systematization of materialist thought, Bogdanov said, "flowed
out of the necessity for simple and strict ideological organization of progressive forces." [PLE, p. 160] Apparently, he believed that modern materialism had to be systematized in order to pursue the struggle with social
and political reaction. Bogdanov noted that the basis of this new system was
the concept of "natural order" which posited the "free and individualistic
structure" of the natural world and society. [PLE, p. 161] For Bogdanov, the
appearance of the concept of natural order added enormous breadth to the
materialistic worldview and brought it to completion. As we shall see directly,
Bogdanov considered Enlightenment materialism to be the culmination of the
formulation process and, in its way, unsurpassed in breadth and completeness.
He felt that the application of the concept of natural order to society was
progressive, because it implied that abstract law governed society rather than
the will of individual men. [PLE, pp. 162–3] Nonetheless, said Bogdanov,
the concept was fetishistic; natural order was, after all, a doctrine which

professed an individualistic and absolute view of human nature. The proponents of natural order considered man apart from social relations. [PLE, pp. 164–5]

If Bogdanov's treatment of seventeenth- and eighteenth-century materialist thought was cursory, it was extensive compared to his treatment of nineteenth-century materialism. He had little specific to say of its character, except that it was more narrow and less original than the materialism of the Enlightenment. [PLE, pp. 166–7] Focusing for all of seventeen lines on Moleschott and Büchner, Bogdanov concluded that nineteenth-century materialism was closely tied to certain specific advances in the sciences (particularly in physiology) and, thus, "it was the intellectual course, by and large, of the bourgeois intellectual who had the most narrow relationship to the progress of technique and natural science". [PLE, p. 167] Having "the most narrow relationship" implied that in the nineteenth century the "new materialism" was the worldview of bourgeois specialists.

With this, we are brought full-circle to the criticism of contemporary philosophy which Bogdanov advanced in his introductory essay. For him, nineteenth-century doctrines reflected the specialization of production in advanced exchange society. More than that, the thought of a Moleschott or a Büchner reflected the specialization and fragmentation of modern philosophy in general.

What may be concluded with regard to Bogdanov's perspective on the history of thought prior to Marx and Mach? We have seen that materialism, although always fundamentally the same, has become over time more sophisticated and complete. The concept of matter as thing-in-itself and the laws which rest on the concept of causal necessity, have become better defined and more extensive. As the progressive form of philosophy at any given time, materialism reflected and reinforced the progressive character of exchange society and production. On account of this, materialism has progressed along with exchange society and production. Modern materialism reflects and reinforces the accelerated and ever more victorious struggle with nature. Because of this, it has developed a trait which differentiates it in an important way from ancient materialism. We have seen this trait portrayed as the tendency to make philosophy ever more "active", that is, ever more a guide in the struggle with nature. Bogdanov tells us that ancient materialism, by contrast, was fundamentally passive. Its concern for "system" reflected the domination of man by nature. Now that man has hope of finally winning the struggle, his philosophy is no longer limited to the simple contemplation of the world; it may now, and indeed must, provide a program for action. It should be noted, although it is obvious, that an "active" role for philosophy vis-à-vis life is one of Bogdanov's demands for a philosophy which deals with human experience and serves human needs in the present. Because of this, it is clear that for Bogdanov the history of materialism presents man with definite directions as to what contemporary philosophy must be. Although materialism has become more "active" in character over time, it is not the answer to the problem of philosophy in the present. Because it affords man no active role in the determination of reality, that is, it continues to regard matter as thing-in-itself as primary being, it cannot seize the present reality and become, with that, a secular monism.

We have seen that Bogdanov's evidence for ascribing a more "active" character to modern materialism is the concern of its thinkers with method. In part, this concern amounts to giving matter as thing-in-itself a more definite form. In assigning to it characteristics which are mathematically expressible, modern materialists provide the means for man's greater mastery of it. The concern with method is also manifest in Bogdanov's view in the search for a more effective way in which to apprehend and organize human experience. This more effective way, the "abstract-analytical method", permits human experience to speak for itself, while at the same time according thinking man the active role of simplifier.

For Bogdanov, the career of materialism showed definite progress but not in an absolute sense. Because of its basic premise, it could only approach a complete monistic worldview. Although modern materialism showed an "active" tendency in its concern with method and the purpose it gave philosophy, it had to give way to a concern for system in order to consolidate its gains. For Bogdanov, materialism as a philosophical system appeared unchanged since the Enlightenment, although its nineteenth-century adherents were to advance some of its concepts. Justifiably, he said, materialism had become the philosophy of bourgeois speicalists, and little help could be expected from that quarter in solving the contemporary problem of philosophy.

CHAPTER II

EMPIRIOCRITICISM

We have advanced the thesis that the first half of *The Philosophy of Living Experience* is introductory in that it prepares the reader for the discussions of Marx and Mach and the exposition of Bogdanov's own worldview in the second. It could also be argued that the chapters on empiriocriticism and dialectical materialism are introductory as well. In them, Bogdanov's principal intent was to dispose of Marx and Mach in the manner of his treatment of earlier thinkers. For one reason or another, he deemed their philosophies unsuitable, obsolete solutions to the contemporary problem of philosophy.

Although these chapters are introductory in the sense alluded to above, we have chosen to treat them as separate aspects of *The Philosophy of Living Experience*. Our reasons for this are several. First, these chapters differ in scope of intentions from those of the first half of the work. While Bogdanov's discussions are primarily intended to place dialectical materialism and empiriocriticism alongside earlier philosophies as unsuited to the present, they were also intended to offer substantial internal criticisms. For Bogdanov, Marx and Mach were more than obsolete thinkers; they were serious competitors as well. Relegating their thought to unsuitability by means of the arguments raised in the first half of the work was obviously not enough for Bogdanov. Internal criticism was necessary to discredit fully Marx and Mach. Thus, although these chapters are introductory, they are not introductory in the same manner as those of the first half of the work. Bogdanov's handling of Marx and Mach as competitors must be considered, and the treatment of these chapters apart facilitates this. Secondly, considering the discussions of Marx and Mach in and for themselves facilitates our treatment of the relationship between dialectical materialism, empiriocritism and "the philosophy of living experience" as it appears in the work. As we shall see, this relationship is of a different sort than that of Bogdanov's worldview to earlier philosophies. Dialectical materialism and empiriocriticism were more than ordinary expressions of past thought for him. In fact, Bogdanov regarded them as attempts to break away from the legacy of the past in the interest of creating world-views more suited to the present. For our thinker, Marx and Mach failed at this; but inasmuch as they recognized the need to create something new, their failure offered vital sorts of lessons for the would-be "philosopher of living experience". Dealing with dialectical materialism and empiriocriticism to a certain extent outside the content of obsolete philosophies allowed his readers to see these lessons more clearly.

In this chapter, we will deal with the assessment and critique of empiriocriticism which precedes Bogdanov's discussion of Marx. Although we will treat the discussions separately, some introductory comments on the relationship between Bogdanov, Marx and Mach would not be out of order here. It has been suggested that Bogdanov sought to bring dialectical materialism and empiriocriticism together into some sort of philosophical amalgam.[1] Even the most superficial consideration of the second half of *The Philosophy of Living Experience* reveals that such was not the case. We find even before the exposition of Bogdanov's own worldview that his intention was to learn from the failings of Marx and Mach and to go beyond them. It is for this reason that we have chosen our title. *Beyond Marx and Mach* conveys better than any other, perhaps, what the worldview presented in the work was meant to be.

As we shall see in Chapter IV, Bogdanov's Empiriomonism purported to begin in some of the same places, with some of the same perspectives and inclinations as empiriocriticism and dialectical materialism. The end result, however, is so different as to make such labels as "Marxist" and "Machist" all but meaningless. For Bogdanov, Marx and Mach recognized the contemporary problems of philosophy in some basic ways. He implied, however, that they made what were but the barest beginnings at a solution. "The philosophy of living experience" would indeed be radically different from dialectical materialism and empiriocriticism both.

As we shall see, Bogdanov did not deny that his worldview was a development within the history of thought. This should not be taken to mean, however, that it had its origins in the thought of earlier times. Like Marx, Bogdanov held that philosophy reflects and reinforces reality and develops along with it. Present reality, therefore, is its principal determiner. Empiriocriticism and dialectical materialism were for him expressions of the arrival of the era of machine production and the beginning of proletarian society. That his own philosophy was also an expression of this he certainly did not deny, and it must have seemed only natural to him that it should have features in common with the thought of Marx and Mach. Bogdanov would not, however, permit his readers to think that his worldview proceeded directly out of dialectical materialism and empiriocriticism. Thus, we find Marx and Mach everywhere more criticized than acclaimed. Their philosophies were, in the final analysis, flawed solutions to the problem of philosophy which had to be exposed as such and got beyond.

More will be said, of course, with regard to the relationship between Bogdanov, Marx and Mach. For the moment, we must turn our attention to Bogdanov's assessment and critique of empiriocriticism. Therein, we will discover the substance of Bogdanov's regard for "Machism", after which we may conclude in a general way about the relationship between "the philosophy of living experience" and empiriocriticism as it appears in the work.

After careful consideration of the value of the alternative, we have decided not to give the reader an "objective" portrait of empiriocriticism as an introduction to this chapter. There are several reasons why this omission better serves our purposes. First, any such portrait would be out of tune with the one provided by Bogdanov himself. While he did not misrepresent the positions of empiriocriticism as far as I can discern, his perspective on the school is substantially different from that of its members and the view of contemporary scholarship as well.[2] For his purposes, empiriocriticism was a potential solution to the contemporary problem of philosophy. Bogdanov chose, therefore, not to meet it on its own ground. Instead of treating empiriocriticism as the epistemological position and philosophy of science that it was, our thinker dealt with "Machism" as a worldview, that is, as a potentially complete system of knowledge or entire philosophy. Secondly, any attempt to reconcile Bogdanov's view with one more objective would divert us from the study of the chapter's place in *The Philosophy of Living Experience*. It would almost certainly lead to an evaluation of Bogdanov's appreciation of "Machism" which cannot be done on the basis of the work at hand. Thirdly, Bogdanov's portrait of empiriocriticism is actually adequate for the purposes of his readers. As with ordinary materialism, he assumed that his audience knew little if anything about the school and devoted the first part of the chapter to a description of its major positions. While this description is not objective for the reasons mentioned above, neither is it substantially in error or obscure. If an appreciation of empiriocriticism is important to our comprehension of those positions Bogdanov sought to advance at the expense of the empiriocritics, then it is Bogdanov's appreciation as stated which will do us the most good. Finally, we have argued and will argue again that Bogdanov's empiriomonism was not intended to be either a refinement of or a legitimate successor to empiriocriticism. If they should not be regarded as doctrines of the same sort, an objective portrait of the former would not greatly enhance our understanding of what the latter is.

Bogdanov's essay on empiriocriticism has three aspects which, although they are not in fact separated, we will treat them separately in order to make his arguments clear. Although we do this, our exposition will follow the progress of the chapter rather closely. As we have noted, Bogdanov sought to introduce his readers to empiriocriticism. This comprises the chapter's first aspect. His depiction of empiriocriticism, however, begins with a brief critical assessment. This served to establish the intent of the chapter and the perspective which he wished his readers to have. After this assessment, the depiction proceeds largely without criticism. In the second segment of the chapter, Bogdanov passes on to his critique. There, he primarily sought to support his initial assessment but offered, as well, the substantial internal criticisms of which we have spoken above. Finally, our thinker completed his discussion with an assessment of the "social roots" of empiriocriticism or, if you will, of the "sociomorphic" character of its positions. These served to reinforce his assessment and critique with the sorts of social-historical arguments typical of the first half of the work and, with that, to bring the chapter into line with the rest of *The Philosophy of Living Experience.*

A.   EMPIRIOCRITICISM DEPICTED

Bogdanov introduced his discussion of empiriocriticism by letting the reader know straightway the outcome of his assessment and critique. In effect, he claimed that "Machism" was a species of materialism which did not perceive itself as such. This was put in the following manner. The appearance of empiriocriticism, he said, marked a new phase in the development of materialist substitution. In the first phase, the materialist substitute had a "living-concrete" character, as with the hylozoists. In the second, it had been "lifeless and abstract", as with Democritus and Hobbes. In the third phase, that is, with the appearance of Locke's concept of substance, it became "indefinite and vague". The fourth and newest phase, Bogdanov asserted, was characterized by open hostility to materialist substitution and the purported rejection of matter as a substitute. Nonetheless, materialist substitution was practiced in disguised form and matter as the substitute was unwittingly reaffirmed. The empiriocritics, said our thinker, showed the same sort of concern with "positive scientific methods" which characterized modern materialism and sought to develop and refine them. [PLE, p. 174] According to Bogdanov, there was a curious sort of irony in the empiriocritics' hostility to materialist substitution, since materialist substitution was the most basic of "positive scientific methods" and the one on which the rest depended. Thus, he said, the empiriocritics sought to advance these methods while at the same time attempting to disassociate them from the one in which they were grounded. [PLE, p. 174] As we shall see in the next section, Bogdanov doubted and, indeed, denied their success in this undertaking.

From this opening argument, our thinker went on to depict the tenets of empiriocriticism which purportedly allowed its adherents to claim that they eschewed materialist substitution and matter and, with them, the errors and inadequacies of past thought.

The empiriocritics, said Bogdanov, would have us believe that they have arrived at a proper concept of reality for contemporary man and an equally proper way of orienting him in that reality. The empiriocritical concept of reality holds that what is real, i.e., that which is given directly to man, is "experience". This "experience" has nothing whatever in common with the traditional concepts of reality, whether materialist, idealist or "third line". It replaces matter and idea as primary being. [PLE, pp. 174–5] While "experience" is comprised at once of things and mental representations, it is homogeneous. Both things and representations are composed of the same parts or "elements". "Experience" is not divided into separate realms, but is a homogeneous whole. Further, the Empiriocritics purport to reject all possibility of things-in-themselves either as the cause of "experience" or as that which "experience" reflects. Thus, "experience" is in no way "material" or "ideal" in the usual sense of these term. [PLE, p. 175]

Bogdanov noted that the empiriocritical "experience" should not be confused with the sensualist's concept of reality. The latter recognized only individual sensations and perceptions, while the empiriocritic envisioned a reality made up of things and mental facts. He said that those critics who associated the empiriocritics with "philosophers of individual experience" had misunderstood the basic positions of both. Our thinker judged the critiques of Lenin, Plekhanov and Ljubov' Aksel'rod in particular to be flawed by this misunderstanding. [PLE, p. 180] He noted that

... the elements of Mach and the Empirocritics exhibit a sensual character, of course, but for them the sensual world means real actuality, not sensations and representations begotten in us by the action of "things-in-themselves". [PLE, p. 180]

In comparison to the sensualist concept, Bogdanov asserted, empiriocritical "experience" was realistic. That the world was comprised of "things" and "mental facts" was something every "practical man" knew. [PLE, p. 181] Bogdanov asserted that

... the empiriocritics strove to overcome the duality of things and psychical facts, to advance philosophical thought toward realism, toward living experience, from which it has been separated. [PLE, p. 181]

Because it denied the import of individual experience, Empiriocriticism was an "impersonal realism". [PLE, p. 181]

The proper way in which man is oriented in reality, in "experience", is through the agency of "pure description". "Experience" exhibits characteristics, bonds and dependencies which can be described and to which man need add nothing in order to orient himself. With this, the empiriocritics reject all forms of substitution and all substitutes (especially matter and idea as things-in-themselves) except for "human expression", i.e., language. They also reject the truth and even the usefulness of all forms of explanation which they regard as the correlates of substitution. These include causal notions, natural laws and scientific theories. That is, they reject all statements which say "why" events occur. They claim that it is enough to say "how", to describe what occurs for man to be properly oriented in "experience". To do otherwise is to add things to "experience" which are not there. Such additions mislead, distort and obscure the true character of reality. Past world-views, in particular materialism and idealism, have accomplished nothing positive through explanation. Historical study of philosophy and science reveals the extent to which man has failed to create enduring explanations and how reality has been disfigured over time. [PLE, p. 175]

In accord with these positions, said Bogdanov, the empiriocritics claim the following things with regard to knowledge, the aspects of "experience" and its bonds and dependencies. First, they argue that the only material of knowledge is "experience" and that the goal of knowledge is the orientation of man therein. The empiriocritics, thus, accord knowledge an active role as a guide for man in the struggle for survival. [PLE, p. 176] For them, the value of knowledge and also the degree of its validity is determined by its effectiveness in practice. Success in practice can be predicted by the simplicity, the "economy" of the knowledge to be applied therein. [PLE, p. 176]

Secondly, in order to describe "experience" and achieve orientation in it, man must break it into its component parts and discover their bonds and relationships. Without this, "experience" would remain the unbroken stream, the undifferentiated whole which it is in its given form. This process also serves to eliminate spurious additions from "experience". [PLE, pp. 177–8] The breaking-up of "experience" is called "criticism". The "Machists" consider their criticism to be scientific although essentially the same as the process of everyday thought. The difference between the two for them lies in the fact that scientific criticism deals with a broader range of "experience" in a more systematic way and rejects all contradictions and "fictious cognitive additions". [PLE, p. 177] Criticism proceeds from the supposition that "experience" is man's environment and is made up of things and mental representations. Both things and representations may be broken up into their properties or elements, which are of the same material in both cases. Properties or elements may be further reduced to other properties and elements. There is, however, a limit, a boundary further than which the human ability to differentiate does not go. The ultimate, i.e., simplest, elements of experience reside at this limit. Once "experience" is so criticized, man knows its basic parts and may proceed to study their relationships. [PLE, pp. 177–8]

Thirdly, in contrast to other views of being, empiriocriticism considers all elements from the simplest to the most complex homogeneous. Because of this, no matter how diverse they appear, they all may be related to one another or, rather, they all have relationships to one another which may be discovered with time. This permits the empiriocritic to raise the prospect of depicting the character, bonds and dependencies of reality as an integrated whole without dividing it into separate realms such as matter, mind, inorganic nature, life, etc. With this, the empiriocritical doctrine of "experience" and its elements purports to be monistic and, as such, superior to other doctrines which regard reality as divided, hierarchical, of different orders, some primary and others manifestations of the primary. [PLE, p. 178]

Fourthly, the empiriocritic claims to have arrived at a proper concept of the physical and mental and, with that, to have surmounted all dualities. For him, a thing and its mental representation, while composed of the same elements and having a strict correspondence to one another, are not quite the same. They are different aspects of the same experience or, if you will, the same experience from two different points of view. To call something "physical", a thing, is not to imply that it is "material" in any usual sense. To call something "psychical", a mental fact, is not to say that its elements are "ideal", more abstract, or less real than those of the thing. For the empiriocritic, the difference between the thing and the mental fact is simply that the latter depends on the nervous system of the individual while the former does not. The elements of physical things are bound together independent of the nervous system, while psychical elements depend on it for their bonding. [PLE, p. 179] Thus, said Bogdanov, "experience" is homogeneous for the empiriocritic; only the *bonds* of experience are of different sorts. [PLE, p. 180]

Finally, the empiriocritic holds that all species of the bonds and dependencies of "experience", whether physical or psychical, are of one sort: they are functional dependencies. With this, they purport to have escaped the strictures of causality and, consequently, one of the most severe limitations of past thought. Instead of saying, for example, that friction causes heat, they say that there exists a functional dependency between the two such that one occurs in the presence of the other. They argue that attributing a causal role to friction amounts to adding a characteristic to friction, i.e., the ability and willingness to cause something, which it does not actually possess. [PLE, p. 184] Functional dependency is clearly the only sort of "explanation" appropriate to the act of pure description. Causality, like substitution, is an improper addition to "experience". As all forms of explanation depend on substitution and causality, they too are improper, false and distorting. From the empiriocritical perspective, said Bogdanov, the notion of one thing "causing" another was derived from the observation that the individual will causes the human body to act. Thanks to habit, they argued, man became accustomed to explaining all the relationships of phenomena in an analogous manner. [PLE, p. 183] Bogdanov noted approvingly that, like himself, the empiriocritics sought the source or model for causality in "practical, living relations". [PLE, p. 184] He criticized this perspective, however, because the source or model was not sought in living *social* relations. For the empiriocritic, causality was an example of "anthropomorphism", the taking of cognitive models from individual experience. Bogdanov explained that the bond between will and bodily movement was actually a case of authoritarian causality. It was a partial expression of the correlation of spirit and matter suggested by authoritarian labor cooperation. [PLE, p. 184]

Bogdanov concluded his depiction of empiriocriticism with the following summary of its picture of the world.

[The world is conceived as] an endless, uninterrupted fabric of elements, forming various complexes in various, changing relationships. Human individuals, complexes more coherent and rich [in elements], stand out in this fabric. Other complexes enter into various relations with these, and each network of similar relations is an individual system of experience, the center of which is the nerve apparatus of the individual. . . . The development of each individual network of experience proceeds toward the adaptation of the central part to its whole, that is, to its environment. All other complexes of this network, independent of the central apparatus, form physical experience; in as much as they are dependent on this apparatus, they comprise psychical experience, that is, "consciousness". Thanks to the "expressions" of individuals, a bond is created between the separate systems of experience, and among people a more general understanding of the *world* arises. . . . [PLE, p. 186]

B. EMPIRIOCRITICISM CRITICIZED

The thrust of Bogdanov's critique of empiriocriticism has been given at the beginning of the last section. He wished to associate its goals, methods and positions with those of modern materialism to the end of relegating empiriocriticism to similar obsolescence. As we shall see, Bogdanov was willing to grant that "Machism" was a step beyond ordinary materialism as an active, realistic and practical philosophy concerned with properly employing and refining "positive scientific methods". However, in all the crucial ways, he deemed empiriocriticism only "semantically different" from materialism. The several aspects of his critique are principally designed to support this assertion. His criticism, of course, goes beyond exposing empiriocriticism as a species of materialism to indicate in what other ways it could not reasonably be the solution to the contemporary problem of philosophy.

Bogdanov turned first to empiriocriticism's purported rejection of materialist substitution and matter. On the surface, he said empiriocriticism appeared to be free from materialist substitution, no less than from its idealist and sensualist counterparts. "Experience" was neither material nor ideal nor sensual in any usual sense. Human "expression" was acceptable as a substitute, but only because some medium was necessary for the communication between "individual systems of experience". "Expression" simply had to be lived with, and its acceptability should not lead us to generalize that other sorts of substitution were necessary or acceptable. [PLE, pp. 185–6]

If this was how things appeared on the surface, said Bogdanov, a look underneath revealed that they were otherwise than they seemed. He chose at this point to give, as an example of the empiriocritical attitude, the "Machist" aversion to defining psychical processes as movements of parts of the brain. [PLE, p. 187] If one examined the empiriocritic's definition of psychical experience closely, said Bogdanov, one would find that it was not actually different from the definition of the materialist. The rejection of the notion that psychical processes were movements of parts of the brain, he said, depended on the empiriocritical definition of psychical experience. He noted that the psychical was defined by the empiriocritics as that experience which depended on the structure of the nervous system. [PLE, p. 187] How, Bogdanov asked, could the "dependent series" of experience be known with any exactitude without the study of the "independent series", i.e., the physical nervous system, upon which it depends? [PLE, p. 187] He asserted that the empiriocritics effectively answered "It could not" and stated that Richard

Avenarius actually constructed his entire *Critique of Pure Experience* on the basis of this position. [PLE, p. 187]

Bogdanov then asked how this position differed from materialist substitution. If one thought about it, he said, one could only conclude that the difference was merely semantic. [PLE, p. 187] For Bogdanov, the honest materialist statement that the psychical or mental *is* natural nerve processes and the dishonest empiriocritical statement that psychical experience *depends on* natural nerve processes amounted to the same thing, i.e., materialist substitution. All that the latter statement did, he said, was to replace the phrase "the psychical is" with another not really so different, "they depend on". [PLE, p. 187] He chided "the newest empiricists" for not openly admitting what they actually believed, i.e., that the scientific and exact way of studying psychical experience involved the investigation of nerve processes. [PLE, p. 188] At the same time, however, Bogdanov praised them for eschewing such concepts as "idea" and "matter". [PLE, p. 187] He obviously saw nothing whatever wrong with rejecting the ambiguities of "idea" and "matter" as things-in-themselves, even if the empiriocritics failed to exorcise those ambiguities altogether.

As it turned out, said Bogdanov, the veiled empiriocritical form was

... the purest and most refined sort of materialist substitution; ... the new school, in its methods, completed that substitution on which the old operated in its "explanation" of the world. [PLE, pp. 187–8]

He noted that the notion of matter advanced by honest materialists in the nineteenth century had no real, sensual character. Like Locke, these materialists tended to view matter as "indefinite substance". [PLE, p. 187] "Indefinite substance" was not the material for an active worldview in Bogdanov's opinion. The empiriocritics, he said, while they rejected the concept "matter", restored it as a definite, knowable substance in their notion of "physical complexes given in experience". [PLE, pp. 187–8] For our thinker, the empiriocritics not only restored "matter" as a knowable substance, they also partially freed it from some of the superfluities and indefiniteness of older concepts. At least for them, the physical was not the sum of things-in-themselves. Obviously, Bogdanov considered the empiriocritical view of the physical a step toward his own and, therefore, toward a "philosophy of living experience".

From the matter of materialist substitution, Bogdanov moved on to make a critique of the empiriocritical position on explanation and causality. He began with his own perspective on explanation, posing the question as to whether it was possible to pursue exact science without its use and answering with the statement that "explanation, not description, is the highest goal of science". [PLE, p. 189] Bogdanov noted that explanation was so necessary to a scientific worldview that even the empiriocritics had to give it a place in their schemes. The latter, he said, employed abstract scientific theories to explain phenomena with the qualification that those theories are not part of knowledge per se, are not *true*, but are merely heuristic constructions. [PLE, p. 189] The empiriocritics, Bogdanov added, employed "as if" statements (such as light behaves "as if" it were matter) to get around the direct use of explanation. [PLE, p. 189] He considered that all this made for "strange caricatures" of great scientific theories. [PLE, p. 193] He reminded the empiriocritics that there were no "as ifs" in experience, only real facts. [PLE, p. 184]

If the heuristic use of theories were not enough to convince one that the empiriocritics actually employed forms of explanation, Bogdanov asserted, all one had to do was to investigate their concept of functional dependency. He held that the empiriocritical rejection of causality which "functional dependency" implied was far from complete, and he made a case for considering "functional dependency" as a form of causal necessity. [PLE, p. 189]

Bogdanov asserted that the empiriocritical aversion to causality only applied to one historically conditioned form of causal bond – the authoritarian. [PLE, p. 189] He noted that the principal empiriocritical argument for considering functional dependency as something other than causality was the fact that it only explained "how" and not "why". Bogdanov said that if we ask "why" a rapid chemical reaction follows the bringing together of gunpowder and a spark, the empiriocritic answers in terms of "how", i.e., the reaction happens when both conditions for it (gunpowder and spark) exist. [PLE, p. 189] Bogdanov asked whether such an answer could be considered a step beyond abstract causality. His answer was, "Clearly, no." [PLE, p. 191] He noted that the empiriocritic called the bond between such conditions as the presence of gunpowder and spark and the chemical reaction a "synonymous" bond. This term, Bogdanov said, had been coined by Petzoldt and meant that in definite conditions, fully definite events occurred and could not be otherwise. [PLE, p. 191] Our thinker held that this was the same as saying that certain causes necessarily lead to certain effects. Here, he said, was a scheme of causal necessity: "it is apparent that the functional bond of conditionality is only abstract causality in a disguised formulation". [PLE, p. 191]

Bogdanov argued that the empiriocritics were, therefore, further from "pure description" than David Hume, who would not have stood for such statements as "definite events occur under certain conditions". [PLE, p. 191] Accordingly, Bogdanov considered the empiriocritical claim to being a philosophy of pure experience to be, at best, dubious.

Bogdanov returned to the issue of pure description versus explanation to argue that the former was a "utopian" idea. By utopian Bogdanov meant that pure description bore a passive, "reflective" relation to experience, a usage he admitted to taking directly from Marx. [PLE, p. 192]

Knowledge organizes experience. Pure description is a slave to it. Knowledge must form and fulfill it, otherwise it may not prevail over it. Truth is not a copy of facts but a tool for dominance over them. [PLE, p. 192]

Bogdanov noted that the empiriocritical notion of knowledge and its relation to experience was dualistic. The "newest empiricists", he said, held the view that knowledge had a practical role in life while at the same time maintaining that its relation to experience was only descriptive. [PLE, p. 192]

Thus, Mach repeatedly asserts that knowledge comes from labor demands, "from technique," he [says] directly in one instance. But all this regards the application of knowledge [and] not its methods. [PLE, p. 192]

Bogdanov went on to conclude that for Mach and the others knowledge served human activity, but human activity was not permitted to determine its methods. This, he argued, amounted to saying that knowledge should not change human activity but be limited to its description; [PLE, p. 192] Bogdanov asserted that scientific thought is an "organizer" which binds facts and things together which were originally separated in experience. [PLE, p. 193] In this regard, Bogdanov asserted, the notion of "economy of thought" had to be considered carefully. It was obviously a valuable notion; however, if one were to follow the empiriocritics, it meant only the conservation of effort in making passive descriptions. [PLE, p. 194] Bogdanov noted that "victory over nature demands not the parsimonious doling-out of effort but the fullest utilization of it." [PLE, p. 194] Knowledge was no different from other realms of human labor. It was the realm of "economical" creation and struggle but not the realm of the economical "registration" of facts. [PLE, p. 194]

Turning again to the problem of the physical and the psychical, Bogdanov asserted that the empiriocritical view of elements of "experience" was too static. While he did not undertake a complete discussion of the problem, Bogdanov implied that such elements as "green", "red", "hard", "cold", etc., were taken by the empiriocritics to be unchanging absolutes and the same irrespective of their interaction with other elements of "experience". It was, he said, as if the empiriocritics were positing "greeness" or "hardness" as things-in-themselves. [PLE, p. 198] Bogdanov's own perspective was that the elements of "experience" had to have a dynamic, "sensually active" character, where "sensually active" meant "determined by collective human activity". They could not be static, "sensually passive", if all changes and flows in experience. [PLE, p. 198] He held that the empiriocritics exhibited the long-standing inadequacy of all philosophical lines in this regard: "Even though elements are not [material] atoms, they are similar in that they are too dead a sort of material to form the tissue of living experience." [PLE, p. 198]

For Bogdanov, the empiriocritical worldview not only suffered from a "dead" concept of experience but also from a fatal sort of dualism. He found that the empiriocritics did not achieve the unity of "experience" they professed. If the physical and psychical are two types of bonds of elements, he asked, how were they bound together themselves for the empiriocritics? He replied that they clearly were not. [PLE, p. 198] Bogdanov saw little difference if "the newest empiricists" said that elements of "experience" were uniform, if they maintained a dualistic view regarding their bonds. For Bogdanov, empiriocriticism suffered equally with older thought from a view of the world as separate "physical" and "psychical" realms. [PLE, p. 199]

Returning to "pure description" and "economy of thought", this time with the intent of relating these concepts to the general passive character of empiriocriticism, Bogdanov again noted that these principles had real value in chipping away the superfluities, distortions and useless cognitive additions from knowledge. He noted that empiriocritics understood well that those philosophical and scientific ideas which could not be verified in experience had no application in practice. They correctly realized that in knowledge there should be nothing superfluous "as there should not be anything super-fluous in a tool". [PLE, p. 200] However, Bogdanov asserted, the empirio-critic did not pursue the logic of this perspective to reach the conclusion that knowledge's relation to experience is active.

When one reasons . . . that knowledge should be only an adequate copy of experience, then it is like demanding that a tool is only a copy of that material from which it is made. [PLE, p. 200]

Building on his earlier remarks, Bogdanov made yet another attack on the empiriocritical division of experience into physical and psychical series. He held the supposition that the physical series is not dependent on any nervous system to be untrue. His argument in this had two aspects. The first regarded the relationship of collective physical experience and collective human action. For Bogdanov, the physical was all that which resisted collective human action, and, therefore, it must be tied directly to, and be dependent upon, collective human perception. [PLE, pp. 200–1] If, for example, he said, all men were blind, then physical experience would obviously lack those visual elements or properties it now has. [PLE, pp. 200–1] Thus, according to Bogdanov, the empiriocritical perspective denied the true relationship of the physical and the psychical. The physical was indeed dependent upon a nervous system, i.e., the collective nerve apparatus of mankind. [PLE, pp. 200–1] His second argument was made on a more individualistic basis. Bogdanov agreed with the empiriocritical notion that the psychical depended on the individual nervous system. However, he said, this perspective is rendered meaningless by the fact that the physical is also found in a dependent relationship with it. He argued that the empiriocritics had overlooked the obvious fact that the tissues and organs of the human body depend directly on the nerve apparatus. Clearly, then, the physical and psychical, whatever else they actually were, could not be defined as "dependent" and "independent" series of elements of experience after the fashion of the empiriocritics. [PLE, p. 202] Bogdanov would shortly give his readers another sort of definition of physical and psychical which reflected their mutual dependency as elements of "living" experience.

Bogdanov concluded that the only possible perspective one could maintain on the empiriocritical point of view was that its "psychical bond" had the character of substitution while its "physical bond" did not. [PLE, p. 202] Accordingly, he said, if the empiriocritics practiced substitution, then, try as they might, they could not avoid "that correlate of substitution as a method of knowledge", explanation. [PLE, p. 202] To avoid explanation, said Bogdanov, was to place an obstacle in the way of the scientific understanding of the psychical bonds of experience. It should also be apparent, he said, that an inadequate understanding of the psychical bonds of experience must necessarily impede the study of the physical. [PLE, p. 202]

Bogdanov concluded his critique with the following general statement.

We may say that on some points it [empiriocriticism] represents progress in comparison with the old materialism and sensualism; on others it is only semantically different from them . . . and in general continues their [philosophical] line. Its main mistakes arise from the reflective-passive point of view on cognitive tasks which is peculiar to this whole line [of thought]. [PLE, p. 203]

C. THE SOCIAL ROOTS OF EMPIRIOCRITICISM

In line with the discussion and critiques of the first half of the work, Bogdanov sought to establish the "sociomorphic" character of empiriocritical notions. As before, he reasoned that such notions reflect and support the interests of a definite group in society. It is interesting that Bogdanov found the social group which spawned empiriocriticism outside the boundaries of the bourgeois-proletarian class struggle. He held that modern machine production had produced a "technical intelligentsia" which occupied an "intermediate" position between the capitalist and working classes. [PLE, p. 204] The bourgeoisie, he argued, had initiated the new mode of production but had been cut off from direct participation in it thereafter. The proletariat, on the other hand, implemented the new mode without either directing or controlling it. The real technical organizational leadership, said Bogdanov, came from an entirely new social group, the technical intelligentsia, the *raison d'être* of which was the creation and refinement of technique and organization. [PLE, p. 204]

Unfortunately, Bogdanov did not expatiate on what he meant by the group's "intermediate" position in society. He limited himself to the comment that the technical intelligentsia was socially and cognitively more progressive than the bourgeoisie but less progressive than the proletariat. [PLE, p. 204] There is no indication in the text that he considered the group a "transitional class" in the Marxist sense, nor is there any evidence that Bogdanov saw the technical intellectual sharing the class interests of either the bourgeoisie or the proletariat. Bogdanov's object in this section of the chapter, however, was not to investigate the role of the technical intellectual in the class struggle. Thus, while one is tempted to advanced some tentative conclusions on the subject,[3] it would be best for our immediate purposes to proceed with Bogdanov's arguments.

For Bogdanov, empiriocriticism reflected and even epitomized the thought of the technical intelligentsia. In fact, he did not always make the distinction between the empiriocritic and the technical intellectual clear. His intention was to show that the roots of empiriocritical notions could be found in the practical life of this new social group. For Bogdanov, Mach, Avenarius, Petzoldt and the rest were technical intellectuals, even though their work was accomplished on institutions other than the factory. He considered universities, research institutes and laboratories adjunct to the factory in bourgeois society. [PLE, p. 206]

According to our thinker, two principal facts about the technical intelligentsia needed to be set down in order to proceed with the search for the social roots of empiriocritical notions. The first of these we have already mentioned, i.e., the organizational role of the intellectual in production. The second was the basic character of the intellectual's labor activity. Its character, he said, was almost wholly mental; it involved technical planning and the supervision and control of its fulfillment. From these two facts, he argued, one could go on to fully explain the sociomorphic character of empiriocriticism. [PLE, p. 205]

Bogdanov held that the empiriocritic's passive attitude toward knowledge was obviously a function of the intellectual character of his labor. As the technical intellectual had no direct dealing with "resisting nature", the impetus to create a completely active philosophy was missing. [PLE, p. 208] The position of the intellectual in production also explained the character of the empiriocritical view that the methods of knowledge were properly passive while its purposes were properly active. [PLE, p. 208] The intellectual's work did not by itself change nature, said Bogdanov; it did so only by means of employing the labor effort of the proletariat. [PLE, p. 208]

From the general empiriocritical attitude toward knowledge, Bogdanov turned to a sociomorphic explanation of its "impersonal-realistic" view of experience. He argued that, in his role as organizer of production, the intellectual's fundamental materials were physical objects and the "psychical" labor nature of men. His task was to combine them in productive ways. Obviously, said Bogdanov, neither one nor the other could be dismissed as "unreal", that is, outside the direct experience and concern of the organizer-intellectual. Furthermore, he noted, the relationship of men and physical material made it easy enough to see experience as essentially unified. [PLE, p. 207] Bogdanov went on to argue that all members of the new technical intelligentsia dealt with a largely homogeneous body of physical and psychical tools and materials. Therefore, he said, they had so much in common that it was difficult for them to believe that variations in individual systems of experience could be anything but inconsequential. [PLE, p. 207] According to Bogdanov, these conditions "made the view of experience as individual sensation too difficult to maintain". [PLE, p. 297] It was too difficult to view the world of experience in anything but realistic and "impersonal" terms. [PLE, p. 207]

Our philosopher continued this analysis with a series of discussions on the "economy of thought", the empiriocritical attitude toward causality, and the notion of "pure experience". Bogdanov asserted that the concept of "economy of thought" had its origins in the intellectual's attempt to economize in his own work activity. [PLE, p. 209] He noted that the progress of production had been paralleled by both an increase in the division of scientific labor and by "the colossal accumulation of materials and the complication of methods in each special science". [PLE, p. 209] To study one or another area of science, said Bogdanov, required enormous effort; the success of the individual depended on the complete mastery of a specialty. [PLE, p. 209] It was, therefore, wholly natural that the intellectual sought to economize effort with regard to knowledge; mastery of a specialty depended upon his ability to eliminate the superfluous and to seek out the simplest organization of material. [PLE, p. 209] Bogdanov, who obviously appreciated the principle of economy, also found it natural that this notion should have had the narrow character given it by the likes of Ernst Mach. The intellectual, he said, was concerned with mastering a specialty and not with forging the unity of science. His concern with economy was limited, therefore, to conserving the expenditure of effort rather than with achieving its fullest and most fruitful employment. [PLE, p. 209]

The empiriocritical attitude toward causality was also traced to the intellectual's position in the system of production. Bogdanov reiterated his argument that the empiriocritics were hostile to only one form of causality, the authoritarian. He argued further that the reason for this was not a lack of vision but, rather, the influence of exchange relations. [PLE, p. 209] The intellectual, he said, sold his labor effort on the open market, competing with his colleagues and dealing with capitalists. Exchange relations, therefore, held a central place in the intellectual's life. This, in turn, made him susceptible to schemes of causal necessity which reflected and supported the social and economic relations of exchange society. [PLE, p. 209]

For Bogdanov, the "sociomorphic" character of the empiriocritical notion of "pure experience" was clear. He called it a "fetishistic abstraction" and asserted that it had been formulated in the same way as other concepts, such as "matter", which had no real character. [PLE, p. 209] While he did not bother to state that such fetishism was characteristic of the thought of exchange society, the point was clearly implied. In making this criticism of "pure experience". Bogdanov made a pitch for his own conception. According to our thinker, the empiriocritic denied the collective nature of experience and labor in denying man the right to make cognitive additions to the "given". [PLE, p. 210] Returning to an argument advanced in the first chapter on materialism, Bogdanov asserted that the essence of experience is labor. Work, he said, is the interaction of human activity and nature, and human activity is not personal but collective in this interaction. He asked

whether collective activity was possible without speech or substitution, that
is, without other forms of explanation. Clearly, it was not. Men could not
understand one another, let alone pursue the collective struggle, without
these additions to experience. He implied that they were not additions at all,
but an integral part of collective experience itself. [PLE, p. 210] Bogdanov
stated that "pure experience" without additions was "as impossible as
resistance without the force to which it relates". [PLE, p. 210] Obviously,
experience could not exist apart from man's action for Bogdanov.

Bogdanov directed his final remarks on the "sociomorphic" character of
empiriocriticism to its tendency toward dualistic schemes. He suggested that
the direct labor relationships of the technical intelligentsia encouraged this
tendency. According to Bogdanov, those relationships were authoriarian
rather than exchange in character. He noted that the authoritarian mode of
labor collaboration was predominant in laboratories, institutes, universities
ana other enterprises that were the work places of intellectuals. [PLE,
p. 210] It is difficult to understand why Bogdanov did not find this fact
curious enough to warrant an explanation. The fact that authoritarian
collaboration was the mode of the times in a group "more progressive" than
the bourgeoisie apparently did not concern him. Bogdanov only wished to
argue that the technical intellectual, as epitomized by the empiriocritic, was
wont to see and maintain dualities analogous to the authority-subordinate
relationship of his own work experience. [PLE, p. 210]

In concluding the chapter, Bogdanov remarked that the empiriocritical
tendency toward dualism and other anachronistic models of thoughts
was greatly mitigated by the "impersonal-realistic" view of experience. [PLE,
p. 210] This perspective, he stated, had advantages over older views in that it
posited two forms of bonds of experience rather than two "essences" or
"substances". [PLE, p. 210] In his final sentences, Bogdanov concluded
that the progressive side of empiriocriticism continued and significantly
advanced the methodological and practical tendencies of modern materialism.
This side, he said, "mitigated its mistakes and contradictions in a whole series
of cases". [PLE, p. 210] According to Bogdanov, empiriocriticism was"the
highest step attained by the reflective philosophy of experience". [PLE,
p. 211]

Given the flow of *The Philosophy of Living Experience* from its introductory essays to this point, it should not be difficult to understand how and why
Bogdanov came to regard empiriocriticism as a species of materialism and, for
that, as yet another inappropriate solution to the contemporary problem of
philosophy. It is not yet possible, of course, to conclude fully on the relation-

ship between empiriocriticism and Bogdanov's notion of a worldview appropriate to the present. That requires consideration of Bogdanov's own philosophy. We may surmise with some assurance, however, that empiriomonism would be nearly as different from "the philosophy of living experience" as ordinary materialism, and the implication is that they would be very different, indeed. As this is the most we can say at this point with regard to the relationship of Bogdanov and Mach, we might do best to attempt another sort of conclusion for this chapter and summarize what the essay on empiriocriticism tells us about Bogdanov's search for a solution to the problem of philosophy.

The aspects, inclinations and perspectives of empiriocriticism with which Bogdanov was in sympathy suggest several things about that search. If we consider the contents of the essay in conjunction with positions taken earlier in the work, we may say the following. First, it is apparent that Bogdanov was in sympathy with the intent of the empiriocritics to formulate a new view of reality substantially different from any previous one. He tells us that the "impersonal realism" of the empiriocritical notion of "experience" was a step toward apprehending actual reality, toward bringing philosophy and the real world together after their long separation. That he found the "Machists" wanting, suggests that the solution to the problem of philosophy must include a view of reality transcending that of materialists, idealists, sensualists *and* empiriocritics.

Secondly, we see that Bogdanov was sympathetic to the empiriocritical suggestion that reality is something quite different from matter, idea and individual sensation. The empiriocritical concept of "experience", in which reality is depicted as homogeneous parts grouped into either things or mental facts, was a step beyond older concepts. As we have seen, Bogdanov's world was comprised of human activity and that which resisted it. For him, then, the empiriocritics at least gave a realistic view of that which resists activity. This suggests that the solution to the problem of philosophy, inasmuch as it was intended to bring philosophy and reality together in a proper relationship, might employ a concept of reality similar to empiriocritical "experience".

Thirdly, our thinker was in apparent sympathy with the attempt to define the homogeneous component parts so as to end the division of reality into various species of things and phenomena. With that, he also approved of the empiriocritical attempt to overcome physico-psychical dualism. As he tells us, the notion of two bonds of experience is a step beyond two "essences" or "substances". That the empiriocritics failed at conquering this most basic of dualities in his eyes, suggests that Bogdanov's solution would advance a concept of the physical and psychical which would.

Fourthly, since from the very beginning of *The Philosophy of Living Experience* he made the demand that philosophy must have an active relationship to the world, we can say that Bogdanov approved of the "Machist" goal for knowledge. The aim of "practical orientation in experience" gave knowledge an active role as guide. Similarly, the empirocritical notions of success in practice as the criterion of truth and economy in the application of knowledge were positive contributions to the progress of philosophy for Bogdanov. All this suggests that the solution to the problem of philosophy would be "active" in its goals. Because he criticized the empiriocritics for failing to give man an active role in determining the methods of knowledge, Bogdanov's solution would apparently be "active" in its methods as well. In several places in his critique, Bogdanov demands that knowledge explain, organize, and make possible the conquest of reality rather than simply describe it as the empiriocritics demanded. We might also say that, given his attitude toward the "Machist" criterion of truth and the principle of economy of knowledge, Bogdanov's solution would have philosophy work toward the fullest, most fruitful expenditure of both cognitive and practical effort.

Finally, and most obviously, Bogdanov was sympathetic with the empirocritical attack on materialist substitution, primary being as things-in-themselves and causal necessity. That he regarded this attack to be vital to the progress of philosophy is clear; no really new worldview could stand on such positions. Bogdanov appreciated the empiriocritical effort to destroy both the concept of thing-in-itself and the notion that abstract laws govern reality. As we have seen, he approved of the "Machist" attempt to find the roots of abstract causal necessity in "practical living relations", since this was the key to getting beyond it. As the empiriocritics judged matter and materialist substitution inappropriate to contemporary philosophy and causal necessity a false absolute, Bogdanov could only applaud "the newest empiricists" even in failing to judge them so for the right reasons. This suggests, of course, that Bogdanov himself would carry the attack on these notions forward. Given the arguments of the first half of the work, we might suppose that substitution would be redefined as part of the solution to the problem of philosophy. Matter, as defined in the empiriocritical fashion, might give way through criticism to "that which resists activity". If we considered Bogdanov's arguments on explanation and organization, we may surmise that the critique of functional dependency would give way to a new formulation of causality in "the philosophy of living experience".

CHAPTER III

DIALECTICAL MATERIALISM

Upon reading the chapter entitled "Dialectical Materialism", [PLE, pp. 216–66] one is tempted to conclude that it is mistitled. Although its pages contain a lengthy discussion and critique of Marx's thought, the chapter is more a discussion and critique of dialectical philosophy in general. In addition, its ultimate argument appears to have little to do with either Marx or materialism. Therein, Bogdanov stated that the philosopher must recognize the limitations of dialectical schemes and go beyond them in search of a more universal method of explanation and view of world-process in order to solve the contemporary problem of philosophy. That he had to dispose of the dialectic of Marx along the way toward his demand for a more universal method was hardly incidental, however. Marxism was far more than a moment in the history of dialectical thinking for Bogdanov. As we shall see, it was an important, if not the most important, step toward the solution to the problem of philosophy. Although he was compelled to criticize Marx's method, Bogdanov did so while affirming his contributions to a "truly active" view of man and the world. As in other parts of *The Philosophy of Living Experience*, one gets the impression in this chapter that Marx was actually very close to being Bogdanov's philosopher-for-the-present. His critique of Marx may be reduced to the single accusation that the latter's method of explanation and view of process was inappropriate to his otherwise genuinely active worldview. If Marx's dialectic was all that kept him from succeeding in Bogdanov's eyes, then it was reasonable for our thinker to concentrate on the matter of dialectics in general, with the intent of looking for another explanation compatible with Marx's worldview. Thus, while the chapter is a critique of dialectics, its further intent and effect is to remind the reader of the strengths of Marx's philosophy and to suggest a way of surmounting its limitations. The chapter serves, then, to take *The Philosophy of Living Experience* beyond Marx, and we must conclude that its title is, indeed, *apropos.*

In many ways, this is the most interesting and provocative chapter in *The Philosophy of Living Experience*, for it is more than an attempt to "get beyond" a certain species of philosophy. In it, we see Bogdanov stride out into the arena of Marxist controversies and proceed very much as though he belonged there. While he considered himself beyond all of its disputes, Bogdanov

87

chose to deal with Marxism from the inside. There, he would behave variously as the defender of orthodoxy and the revisionist in giving his assessment of Marx. His reasons for doing this are easy to ascertain. "Going beyond" Marxism for Bogdanov was not a simple matter of delivering it part-and-parcel to the heap of obsolete worldviews. There were vital lessons to be learned and many more, and more significant ones, than might be had from the study of ordinary materialism or empiriocriticism. As we shall see, Bogdanov wished to credit Marx for many progressive ideas and to find fault with him for others not so progressive. Consequently, the master had to be interpreted correctly and, with that, defended from certain revisionist views, or the good he had done might be lost to posterity. On the other hand, Marxism had to be revised in certain ways to keep what was bad from spoiling the rest. Thus, we find Bogdanov behaving as one or another sort of Marxist for the sake of putting "dialectical materialism" in the proper light. We find the chapter interesting and provocative for this very reason: it allows us to see the extent of his partisanship for Marx and what he made of his Marxist contemporaries. Also, we glimpse what sort of Marxist Bogdanov might have been had he not chosen to be his own man in philosophy. If lifted from the context of the work, the chapter makes for a controversial addition to revisionist literature of the pre-war years.

While the statements we made in introducing Chapter II regarding the relationship of Bogdanov, Marx and Mach are true enough, we must develop and qualify them a bit in introducing Bogdanov's discussion of dialectics and Marxist materialism. We have said that both Marx and Mach were thinkers to be put behind for the would-be "philosopher of living experience", since their attempts to detach philosophy from the legacy of materialism-idealism had not succeeded. Although both were obsolete in Bogdanov's eyes, they were by no means equally so. It will become clear how very differently he approached Marx and Mach in *The Philosophy of Living Experience*. Empiriocriticism is treated very much in the manner of ordinary materialism. For Bogdanov, the Machist attempt to create a new worldview was only a semantic exercise. Dialectical materialism, on the other hand, is regarded as a worldview significantly and substantially new. Marx's attempt to break away from past philosophy is portrayed as successful in so many respects as to place dialectical materialism close to the solution to the problem of philosophy. It is Bogdanov's notion that a complete break is necessary in searching out the solution which requires him to set Marx behind with Mach. Where empiriocriticism is but a refinement of ordinary materialism, dialectical materialism is a step beyond both materialism in particular and past thought in general. Marx is approached, then, in a very different manner from Mach.

It is, of course, curious that, while Bogdanov is clearly more the partisan of Marx than of Mach in *The Philosophy of Living Experience,* he should take a title for his own philosophy akin to empiriocriticism. We hope to show in the next chapter that Bogdanov's "empiriomonism" proceeds primarily from what he considered starting points and perspectives shared with Marx rather than Mach. In the final chapter of *The Philosophy of Living Experience,* empiriomonism was called variously "proletarian philosophy", "the labor world-view" and "philosophy from the labor point of view", but never "the new critical empiricism" or anything similar.[1] In the chapter on Marx, we have every indication that Bogdanov's worldview would be more reminiscent of Marxian materialism than of empiriocriticism. If one considers only the evidence there, one might be tempted to guess that "Bogdanovism" would turn out to be Marxism without Marx's dialectic. Of course, this would be incorrect, but there are such strong indications of Bogdanov's broad sympathy for Marx that this guess is quite a reasonable one. As we shall see later, empiriomonism is actually no more a species of Marxist materialism than it is a refinement of Machist critical positivism or an amalgam of both.

By way of further introduction, we might make several general comments on how Bogdanov regarded dialectical materialism and Marx. Much of what we note below has been implied above. First, and most importantly, Bogdanov regarded dialectical materialism as a "truly active worldview" and, for that, distinct from any before it. In other words, Marx met one of the most important criteria Bogdanov set down for the contemporary philosopher, that is, that he create a worldview which bore an active relationship to life. Similarly, our thinker found that this truly active worldview nonetheless had a serious flaw; its method of explanation and view of world-process (the materialist dialectic) was inappropriate to it. Bogdanov deemed Marx's dialectic "unreal" and, in important ways, "idealistic". The real dialectic, which Bogdanov defined early in his essay, was something far less than a process universal in reality. For Bogdanov, a truly active worldview must have a truly universal appreciation of process, a truly universal method of explanation, and its concept of dialectics must express the "logic of reality" only in those respects in which that logic is actually dialectical.

Secondly, and as we have implied, Bogdanov considered dialectical materialism as a worldview to be learned from and superseded. For our thinker, Marx said much that was true about the character of society, economics, philosophy and the flow of history which must be taken as part of the picture of present reality. Where he was wrong, said our thinker, he had to be challenged. "Getting beyond" Marx for Bogdanov meant beginning in those places where Marx had been correct about reality and proceeding in the search for a concept of process and universal explanation which those starting-points imply. The key to the search was a critique of Marx's dialectic.

Thirdly, Bogdanov considered Marx to be the sort of "materialist" with whom he could live, that is, no ordinary materialist at all. He found in dialectical materialism recognition that what is is comprised of human labor activity and that which resists it. He considered Marx's view of being a break from past views which held forth concepts of being as a thing-in-itself apart from human interaction with it. While Marx's concept of being was approved, his notion of process in reality was not. Since the two must coincide for Bogdanov, Marx's entire concept of reality could not be adopted as part of the solution to the problem of philosophy.

Having noted these general aspects of Bogdanov's assessment of Marx, we may pass on to the consideration of the chapter itself. The chapter may be broken into five segments, each of which forms something approaching a separate essay. In the first segment, Bogdanov formulated what he considered the real dialectic and suggested its proper scope as a method of explanation and notion of process. In the second, he went on to deal with the career of dialectics prior to Marx with the principal intent of showing "the real meaning" of the ultimate outcome of that career, the idealist dialectic. In this he argued that no dialectician prior to Marx had created a method of systematizing knowledge appropriate to a truly active worldview and, on account of that, no such worldview itself. In the third segment, Bogdanov sought to show how the struggle of Feuerbach and Marx against dialectical idealism had culminated in dialectical materialism. He credited Marx with having created a real philosophy of activity, in some sense a successor to materialism as the progressive worldview of its time, but one which fell short due to an inappropriate method of explanation. In the fourth, Bogdanov turned to other dialectical materialists, namely Joseph Dietzgen, Lenin, Plekhanov and Liubov' Aksel'rod. His intent was to show that their efforts had not served to take philosophy beyond Marx. In Bogdanov's eyes, the outcome of their labors was largely a catalog of old materialist errors. Finally, he drew some further conclusions as to the scope of the real dialectic and charged philosophy with the task of moving beyond it toward a more universal view of process and method of explanation.

A. BOGDANOV'S DIALECTIC

We have suggested that Bogdanov produced a definition of the term "dialectic" which he considered real in comparison to others. The way in which he arrived at that definition is both interesting and important. In contrast to his procedures in other chapters, Bogdanov began this one with an investigation of the social sources of the concept under consideration. He did not, however, attempt to evaluate the "sociomorphic" character of the term "dialectic" in any of its known forms. Rather, Bogdanov proposed to find a "sociomorphic" concept which could be considered real and fundamental, that is, the only one properly worthy of being called "the dialectic".

As Gustav Wetter notes in his brief but astute essay on our thinker, it was clear that Bogdanov wished to retain a form of the dialectic and to give it a notable place in his own philosophy.[2] Indeed, as Wetter does not note, the concluding chapter of the *Tektologiia* dealt in detail with what Bogdanov called "the organizational dialectic".[3] Thus, it is understandable why Bogdanov formulated his definition of the dialectic before going on to criticize the dialectics of others. He might have chosen to criticize the dialectics of Hegel and Marx without reference to some more proper concept. Instead, he chose to work that proper concept out for the sake of working it into his own schemes. Again pursuant to including the dialectic in his own thought, Bogdanov went on to establish the extent and limitations of his concept's applicability. He obviously believed that the "real" dialectic was a broadly applicable and an enormously useful type of explanation. At the same time, however, he denied that it could be the sort of universal method it had been for Hegel and Marx.

Bogdanov's argument regarding the real dialectic ran as follows. As with all other "real" and broadly useful concepts, he said, the dialectic must be a cognitive model taken from human experience. If the term was to be given its most fundamental meaning and broadest significance, its source must be sought in that broadest and most fundamental realm of experience, the collective labor process. Finding a clue in the meaning of the Greek word *dialektikē,* which he took wholly in the sense of dialogue, Bogdanov suggested that the real social model for the dialectical notion was the interaction of two workers attempting to fulfill a single task together. Bogdanov found this interaction to be the most basic sort in the labor process. Evaluating this interaction, Bogdanov asserted that it proceeded in three stages, the character and progress of which should be carried over to the concept which described it. In the first stage, he said, the two workers formulate their separate perspectives on how the task should be accomplished and resolve to accomplish it. In the second, their separate perspectives come into contact and, due to the particularistic nature of individual perceptions and the demand that the task be completed, into conflict or opposition. This conflict or opposition intensifies during the second stage in direct proportion to the workers' growing urge to fulfill the task. When the conflict reaches its fullest intensity, the third stage of the process begins. In it, the conflict is resolved in one of several ways; either one worker's perspective wins out over the other or some third perspective generated by the struggle of the other two is agreed upon. Bogdanov asserted that what goes on between the two workers here, and therefore in any properly dialectical relationship, is "*an organizational process, proceeding by way of opposites,* or, what comes to the same thing, by way of the struggle of various tendencies". [PLE, pp. 216–17][4]

The argument repeated above has been considered by Wetter and A. V. Ščeglov to be the principal source for the study of Bogdanov's dialectic.[5] Curiously, neither has attempted to analyze the concept as it appears in the *Tektologiia.* Wetter, who has obviously read this later work, limits his analysis to the argument above and several comments which appear later in the same chapter in Bogdanov's critique of Engels.[6] No proper or complete assessment of Bogdanov's dialectic can be made without considering its exposition in the *Tektologiia.* We are not concerned, however, with the matter outside the context of the work at hand. Our task is to explicate the argument above. In this, Wetter gives us considerable help. He concludes that Bogdanov's is a 'mechanistic'' dialectic, the essence of which "is an antagonism between distinct objects endowed with contrary forces".[7] Further, he states that Bogdanov found contradictoriness in the fact that everything is at war with its surroundings.[8]

A close look at Bogdanov's arguments bears out Wetter's conclusions and suggests several others. In the "sociomorphic" argument above, one sees none of the familiar dialectical components such as "thesis–antithesis" or "negation of negation". Antagonism originates from the contact of "various" tendencies previously unrelated to one another. Looking at the social model from which it is taken, we can reasonably conclude that the "organizational process" which is Bogdanov's dialectic proceeds from a state of organization, i.e., order, to disorganization, i.e., disorder, and then on to a new, higher state of organization. In the first stage of his social model, order prevails since the two forces have not yet been brought into contact. In the second, disorder prevails on account of the antagonism between the forces. In the third, a *new* sort of order is achieved, first, because the conflict is resolved and, secondly, because the task is accomplished. This meaning of "organizational process" seems all the more reasonable if one considers the implications of the following lines taken from Bogdanov's critique of Engels. Wetter, incidentally, cites them as a source for his assessment of Bogdanov's dialectic, but makes no separate comment on them or, for that matter, on the term "organizational process" in his essay.[9]

If this process has a beginning of any sort, there can clearly have been no conflict *until then* between the two opposed forces involved in the process, and in this respect a certain *equilibrium* will have prevailed between them. If the process comes to an end in any way, then there is undoubtedly *no longer* any conflict between the two given forces and hence a *new equilibrium* will have been established between them both. We therefore have the complete triad: from equilibrium, *via* the conflict between the two forces which disturb it, to a new equilibrium. [PLE, pp. 252–3][10]

Wetter's conclusion on Bogdanov's view of contradictoriness was made on the basis of the following statement also made in the discussion of Engels.

The organism is at war with its environment, continuously transferring to it the energy it expends and equally continuously drawing energy from it; so long as these two processes continue more or less in balance it remains "the same", and becomes different, "something else", in-so-far as one of them gains predominance over the other. [PLE, p. 253]

If we look for the sources of contradiction in the social model above, we find that the demands of the cooperative labor process pit one worker's will and perspective against the other. The opposition which develops between them does not proceed from the fact that one pespective is revealed as an antithesis logically contained in the other. It proceeds from the fact that both are simply different and the circumstance that the difference must be eliminated. "Opposite" does not have the strict meaning for Bogdanov that it had for, say, Engels. Thus, our thinker can take "by way of various tedencies" to amount to the same thing as "by way of opposites".

From his "sociomorphic" definition, Bogdanov went on to argue that the use of this dialectic to explain organizational process was fundamental and of obvious practical benefit to man.

The notion of dialectic is related originally and fundamentally to definite social phenomena of an ideological-organizational character. But, in accord with the law of sociomorphism, . . . the scheme of the dialectic, created in one realm of social experience, may be applied beyond its limits to other realms of phenomena, social and extra-social. [PLE, p. 218]

While he would later argue that there were limits to its use, i.e., that not all organizational processes were dialectical in character, Bogdanov asserted at this point that it was permissible and desirable to extend dialectical explanation into all "extra-social" realms, including that of inorganic phenomena.

Here, he was apparently concerned that his readers might consider society alone as the realm of organization. [PLE, p. 218] He argued that the inorganic world exhibits many organizational processes which could be described dialectically. [PLE, p. 219] As Wetter points out, Bogdanov viewed the organizational process as fundamental and universal, characterizing all activity, human and natural. [PLE, p. 219] [11] In the organizational process, all parts were to be considered "forces" which might relate and be related in various ways, among them, dialectically. Thus, Bogdanov could not consider "dead" nature a passive, "forceless", realm. He viewed the struggle of the forces of inorganic nature to be describable in the same terms as the struggle of men or man's struggle with nature. [PLE, pp. 219–20]

This, then, is Bogdanov's dialectic: an "organizational process" which proceeds by means of the struggle of various or "opposite" tendencies. The struggle is that of two real forces vying for predominance, and the process goes on from a lower level of "organization" to a higher one. Later in the chapter, Bogdanov would set his concept against the dialectic of Marx and deem the latter "unreal" by comparison. This comparison would be, however, only part of Bogdanov's critique of the materialist dialectic.

B. DIALECTICS PRIOR TO MARX AND THE MEANING OF THE IDEALIST DIALECTIC

Bogdanov devoted a considerable portion of the chapter to a discussion of dialecticians prior to Marx. His main intent therein was neither to depict the career of dialectics nor to compare past notions with his own, although the section has both effects. Rather, Bogdanov was concerned with assessing the most important dialectical scheme prior to that of Marx, i.e., that of Hegel. To a large extent, Bogdanov's remarks on pre-modern dialectics serve mainly to familiarize the reader with dialectical worldviews in general. Similarly, his remarks on Hegel's fellow idealists, Fichte and Schelling, serve mainly to introduce and support his assessment of Hegel. The focus of Bogdanov's discussion was the question of whether or not pre-Marxian dialectical philosophies and, in particular, the dialectical idealism of Hegel, could be considered truly active views of the world. His standard of measure was characteristically Marxian; philosophy must change the world to be truly active.[12] In addition, Bogdanov required that a truly active worldview have a social perspective on the essence of man and a view of world activity as "the living activity of labor". [PLE, p. 219]

Bogdanov centered his remarks on pre-modern dialectics on Heraclitus. He wished to stress the inactive role accorded to man in the latter's dialectical scheme. Bogdanov presented that scheme in a straightforward manner, reiterating Heraclitus's view that the universe was an eternal stream of change proceeding by the struggle of opposites. Because the essence of the world for Heraclitus was fire, which is transformed dialectically into all other things and back into which all other things are transformed over time, said Bogdanov, this thinker's view of universal life had a cyclical character. Heraclitus's cyclical theory of development was decidedly non-progressive, since it held that the flow of dialectical change repeated itself infinitely. Where there is no notion of steady progress, Bogdanov said, there can be no truly active role for man. Accordingly, Bogdanov judged Heraclitus's understanding of the world to be fundamentally passive. It contained no practical program for changing the world and provided only "a useful and necessary orientation in the field of struggle". [PLE, pp. 220–4]

As we have suggested above, Bogdanov's ultimate interest was with measuring the schemes of past dialecticians against his own criteria for an active worldview. For Bogdanov, Heraclitus, although far inferior as a dialectician to his German idealist successors, shared the characteristic of passivity with them. Heraclitus fell short due to an historical theory of cycles which permitted no steady progress for man and the world. [PLE, pp. 232–3] Bogdanov considered the German idealists to have surmounted the limitations of a non-progressive theory of history; however, he found their worldviews passive for other reasons having to do with the nature of the idealist dialectic itself.

Bogdanov analyzed the idealist dialectic as to content and sources in order to discover what he considered "the real meaning" of this form. In this, his paramount interest was clearly in Hegel, whom he credited with having created the fullest expression of the idealist dialectic, and to whom he accorded great importance as a systematizer of knowledge.[13] Fichte and Schelling were not ignored by any means, for Bogdanov devoted considerable space to outlining their thought. It is clear that our thinker's intention in dealing at length with these two was largely to show that Hegel's was very much akin to other idealist schemes of the dialectic and, therefore, subject to the same fundamental criticisms. Bogdanov would argue that the Hegelian dialectic could not be a universal method of explanation and view of process nor the basis for a truly active worldview for the same reason that the dialectical schemes of Fichte and Schelling could not have succeeded, i.e., because theirs was a dialectic of ideas rather than a dialectic related to real phenomena [PLE, p. 224]

According to our thinker, Fichte, Schelling and Hegel all saw world activity in terms of self-developing thought. Each one, he said, took as his starting point some concept of "absolute idea". Bogdanov asked his readers to recognize this as a form of idealist substitution and to consider the ramifications of an idealist starting point. [PLE, p. 224] He argued that when idea is taken as primary reality, all cognitive models must necessarily be taken from the "life" of ideas. Accordingly, Bogdanov asserted, the idealist's attempt to formulate a dialectical method of explanation and view of process resulted in a cognitive model reflecting "the logic of ideas" rather than "the logic of living practice". [PLE, pp. 230–1] Citing Fichte's "I" and "not-I" argument as an example, our thinker noted that therein the "logic of ideas" produced a dialectic which described only the relationship of ideas and their logical opposites. [PLE, pp. 224–6] This, he said, indicated the true meaning of the idealist dialectic; it was a dialectic of ideas which excluded consideration of the real phenomena of human experience. [PLE, pp. 233–4]

Turning to Hegel's scheme, Bogdanov went on to consolidate and strengthen his argument by attempting to show that the former's laws of the dialectic in no way altered the fact that his dialectic was based on the "logic of ideas". In this, Bogdanov made no attempt to attack Hegel's laws in all of their implications but, rather, focused on the notion of "thesis-antithesis". [PLE, pp. 228–32] Citing Hegel's notion that nothing may exist which does not contain its opposite, Bogdanov argued that Hegel was saying nothing different than Fichte had in his "I"–"not-I" argument. To say that an idea is overturned when the logical opposite which is internal to it is revealed, he said, does not alter the fact that the opposite is ideal and only exists in thought. [PLE, p. 229] Bogdanov noted that Hegel's laws of the dialectic were as much "naïve sociomorphisms" as the less developed notions of Fichte and Schelling. [PLE, pp. 230–1] "Naïve" here meant simply that the Hegelian dialectic could only be applied to ideas rather than to the whole of human experience (i.e., the real world) and that it had a character and contents different from those of Bogdanov's own scheme. That the Hegelian dialectic was a "sociomorphism", a model taken from the social life of man, was not explained. In conclusion, Bogdanov admonished his readers, and by implication Marxists in particular, not to make the mistake of those who attempt to separate Hegel's dialectic from the rest of his idealist system, accepting the former and rejecting the latter. The Hegelian dialectic was idealist, he said, and could not be otherwise, for the laws of the dialectic were based on "the logic of ideas". [PLE, p. 232]

While he obviously found Hegel's dialectic limited with respect to his own scheme which dealt with the real instead of the ideal world, Bogdanov asserted the superiority of Hegel over all other thinkers prior to Marx. For our thinker, the appearance of Hegel marked an enormous advance in systematized knowledge. Bogdanov looked with favor on Hegel's attempt to work out the laws of the dialectic pursuant to establishing them as a universal method of explanation and view of process. On the basis of this new and broader method, he noted, Hegel was able to create "the fullest and most structured system of knowledge to his time". [PLE, pp. 231–2] "If knowledge is the organization of experience", Bogdanov said, "then . . . Hegel created the possibility of the more complete domination of accumulated experience". [PLE, p. 231] Our thinker did not go into any detail on how this possibility was created. One might be tempted to conclude from this that Bogdanov simply meant that Hegel's great system and search for a universal method were precedents from which the "philosopher of living experience" might learn the scope of his task. Several statements which followed those above, however, make one realize that the matter was not that simple for Bogdanov. First, he stated that Hegel had given many "deep and true explanations of phenomena in various realms". [PLE, p. 231] Secondly, he remarked that it was no accident that Marx was able to make great progress by simply "overturning Hegel's thought". [PLE, p. 231] Neither of these statements is supported with further explanation or evidence. One must conclude on the basis of this that Bogdanov considered Hegel's contributions to the advance of systematized knowledge to have some substantial content. What that content was is not ascertainable in *The Philosophy of Living Experience.*

Bogdanov ended his discussion with the argument that, in spite of Hegel's triumphs, dialecticians prior to Marx had not produced a single, truly active worldview. In the same manner as Marx in the theses on Feuerbach, he acknowledged the fact that idealist dialecticians had developed a principle of world-process where their materialist contemporaries had not. [PLE, pp. 233–4] Suspicious of that principle, however, he asked what gave the idealist schemes "their apparent active coloring" and whether they were, in fact, real philosophies of action. [PLE, p. 233]

If the world is interpreted as the self-development of the creative "I" or absolute spirit, then is this not a real theory of universal progress and does it not show the ways and means for human activity by investigating universal . . . activity, the manifestation of which it recognizes as man himself? [PLE, p. 233]

Bogdanov answered, in effect, that appearances deceive here. Taking his cue and a quotation from Marx's eleventh thesis on Feuerbach, he asserted that the idealist principle of activity was abstract, "because idealism by its nature does not know real, sensuous activity". [PLE, p. 233] It does not know it, Bogdanov said, because it is cut off from real activity by idealist substitution.

It sees the essence of the world in *thought* [and], therefore, world practice has a theoretical character for it. When the abstract activity of thought is substituted for the living activity of labor, it is impossible to arrive at a philosophy [which] actually changes the world. [PLE, pp. 233–4] [14]

Going further, Bogdanov stated that no philosophy could succeed in changing the world "which is an expression of the spirit of individualism". [PLE, p. 234] Reasserting the principle that human activity is social in essence, our thinker made the following comment on German idealism:

When one "I" opposes itself to the universe as infinite "not-I" (and this is the point of departure of German idealism), then it [i.e. the "I"] may stand either in a reflective or a speculatively-active relationship to the world process. [PLE, p. 234]

According to Bogdanov, "ideal", "speculative", "unreal" activity and a view of isolated, individual men unable to change the world by dint of their separation from others are what one sees in the schemes of dialectical idealism [PLE, p. 234]

C. THE MATERIALIST DIALECTIC AND MARX'S TRULY ACTIVE WORLDVIEW

In this part of the chapter, Bogdanov broadened the scope of his essay considerably. His concern was not only with the development of the dialectic beyond Hegel, but also with assessing dialectical materialism as a worldview. To fit this section into the rest of the chapter, Bogdanov structured his assessment around the contrast between dialectical materialism's strengths as a truly active philosophy and the vague and inadequate character of its dialectic. The result is a complicated and multi-faceted argument which disposes of Marx's dialectic and puts his philosophy in perspective as a stepping-stone to "the philosophy of living experience".

The essay began with remarks on Feuerbach and Marx as successful (in Feuerbach's case, semi-successful) opponents of idealist substitution and the individualistic view of man which lay at the base of dialectical idealism. Without coming across any argument as to why it was the case, we find shortly thereafter that the result of this opposition was more than the discrediting of the idealist perspective of man and the world; it ended in Marx's creation of a truly active philosophy. Apparently, Bogdanov wished to avoid discussing what had occurred as the "over-turning" of Hegel. The text suggests that Marx was set on the road toward an active worldview by dint of his attack on dialectical idealism. Bogdanov emphasized, however, the importance of another sort of starting-point in Marx's case, i.e., the view of man which saw his essence in the labor collective. After elaborating the basic tenets of Marx's thought, Bogdanov moved on to an extensive critique of his dialectic. The essay ended with conclusions which stressed the incompatibility of Marx's dialectic with the rest of his worldview.

Bogdanov contended that Ludwig Feuerbach and Karl Marx had understood the true meaning of the idealist dialectic and had seen the need to attack the individualism and idealist substitution of the German idealists. [PLE, p. 234] The result of their attempts to "over-turn" dialectical idealism, to take the dialectic and philosophy in general beyond Hegel, was not only a "materialistic" view of the dialectic but, most importantly, a truly active philosophy. Bogdanov judged Feuerbach's contribution to the advance of philosophy toward an active worldview to be of enormous importance, although certainly of far less magnitude than that of Marx. [PLE, pp. 234–8 *passim*] For Bogdanov, Feuerbach's thought represented an "intermediate" stage between dialectical idealism and dialectical materialism. He considered this young Hegelian a materialist and a dialectician who had not succeeded in combining the two. His materialism had been of the pre-Marxian variety, passive and reflective. His dialectic was that of Hegel, a dialectic of ideas, and the two could not be reconciled. [PLE, p. 238] For Bogdanov, Feuerbach's contribution was not the fact that he had attempted to create some sort of dialectical materialism. It lay, rather, in his attempt to turn philosophy away from self-developing idea toward a concern for self-developing social man. [PLE, pp. 234–5] According to Bogdanov, this attack on the idealist substitution and individualism of dialectical idealism was a crucial first step toward an active worldview. Feuerbach had begun the search for concepts of man and the world which Marx would later establish. [PLE, p. 238]

Bogdanov noted that Feuerbach had been profoundly disturbed by the "abstract dryness" of Hegelianism. Because he was a man of great feeling, said Bogdanov, Feuerbach sought to return philosophy from

... the cold heights of self-developing idea to spontaneous, sensually-concrete life, to take real human existence as the base and center of his constructs, [and] to create ... a philosophy of the self-realization of man. [PLE, pp. 234–5]

Doing this required more than the rejection of self-developing idea as primary reality, said Bogdanov. Feuerbach had also to attack the individualistic

concept of man held by the idealists. He noted that Feuerbach had accordingly rejected the isolated individual and sought the essence of man in social
relations. The outcome of his search for the ultimate social relationship and,
with that, man's essence was a concept of personal love between men as it
was found in the monogamous family. Bogdanov found this attempt to go
beyond the limits of individualism by seeking the essence of man in the
relations of the family a great advance which had not gone far enough.
Feuerbach had not recognized that the true source of man's essence lay in the
labor collective, and he had ignored the bond of social instinct as generated
by collective labor relations. [PLE, p. 235]

Bogdanov saw the reason for this shortcoming in Feuerbach's attack in the
fact that he represented the social interests of the *petite bourgeoisie*. This
class, he asserted, stood in between the individualistic bourgeoisie and the
collectivist proletariat. Oppressed by the former but unable to identify with
the latter, the petty-bourgeois thinker might recognize the need for a collectivist view of man; but, at the same time, he could not shake off entirely
the individualism of the bourgeoisie and arrive at a concept of man's fundamental labor nature. Thus, said Bogdanov, it was understandable why
Feuerbach, as a petty-bourgeois, looked to familial relations as an alternative
to individualism; the family was the only type of collective permitted in
exchange society. [PLE, p. 236]

Passing on, Bogdanov asserted that Hegel's system was as far as bourgeois
philosophy could go toward an active worldview. He believed that there was
no hope that a bourgeois thinker could ever make a wholly effective attack
on dialectical idealism, since that thinker was caught in a web of individualistic social relations. Bogdanov stated that a fully adequate attack could only
come from one who made use of the collective experience of the proletariat
to formulate a truly active view of man and the world. [PLE, p. 241]
Obviously, he considered Marx to have been such a thinker.

Bogdanov was willing to grant Marx's complete success at surmounting the
limitations of idealist substitution and individualism and at effecting a truly
active worldview. He denied, however, that Marx's efforts to overturn dialectical idealism had produced a new concept of the dialectic which was wholly
compatible with a philosophy of activity. [PLE, p. 241] At first glance,
Bogdanov's reason for saying this appears to center on the accusation that
Marx's dialectic was fundamentally idealist; it retained Hegel's laws of the
dialectic unchanged. Indeed, his long discussion of Engel's adaptation of the
laws which followed was meant to show that Marx's dialectic dealt in logical
rather than real opposites. Bogdanov indicated in several places, however, that

Marx's dialectic was indeed new and different by dint of his fundamental opposition to the idealistic view of man and the world. In order to decide the exact nature of Bogdanov's assessment of the materialist dialectic, we must follow out his general assessment of Marx's thought.

As Bogdanov had indicated in his critique of Feuerbach, one had to seek the essence of world activity and man in the labor collective in order to overcome fully the limitations of idealist substitution and individualism. Marx, he said, took the experience of the proletariat as his starting-point rather than that of the family or the individual. This taught him that the essence of world activity was human activity in the broadest sense, that is, "collective practice" or "living, collective labor". [PLE, p. 238] Bogdanov held that human activity was the center of Marx's thought rather than some sort of primary matter as the term dialectical materialism was usually taken to imply. [PLE, p. 238] If one uses the term "materialism" to designate Marx's thought, said Bogdanov, it must be understood as the opposite of "idealism". Where "idealism" deals with the activity of thought or ideas, Marx's "materialism" deals with concrete, human labor activity. [PLE, p. 238] "Matter" for Marx was not primary physical substance, but reality in all its aspects, both physical and psychical. It was an opposite of "idea" or "spirit" in this way. [PLE, p. 238] In addition, Bogdanov asked his readers to remember that Marx recognized "matter" and "activity" as correlative and inseparable concepts. [PLE, p. 238]

The central notion of concrete human practice, collective labor activity, made Marx's philosophy a truly active worldview in Bogdanov's eyes. The underpinnings which had made dialectical idealism passive were thoroughly disposed of. Choosing human practice as a starting point, he said, Marx could not reject self-developing idea in favor of a concept of self-developing matter divorced from human activity. Positing the social-labor nature of man, Marx consequently made any individualistic perspective of human nature impossible. [PLE, p. 238]

From the above, Bogdanov went on to summarize the basic tenets of Marx's social and economic thought, suggesting that all of it was the direct outcome of his proper view of man and world activity. We will not repeat that summary here, since there is nothing exceptional about it. Suffice it to say that, therein, Bogdanov indicated his approval of Marx's positions on such matters as man's active relationship to nature and his ability to change it and himself, the relationship of social being and social consciousness, the role of classes in history, the active purpose of philosophy, etc. [PLE, pp. 239–40] All this is implicit in earlier parts of *The Philosophy of Living Experience*.

Moving on to the more immediately important matter of Marx's dialectic, Bogdanov suggested that it, too, was fundamentally determined by his view of social man and the world process as human labor activity. Marx's dialectic was "materialistic" in the same manner as the rest of his thought; it was antithetical to its "idealist" predecessors. [PLE, p. 241] Both Hegel and Marx defined the dialectic as "development through opposition". [PLE, p. 241] But whereas Hegel had focused on the struggle of ideal contradictions, Marx concerned himself wholly with the struggle of such real concrete opposites as man and nature, the bourgeoisie and proletariat, etc. [PLE, p. 241] In his dialectic, said Bogdanov, Marx dealt with processes "not logical but 'material,' i.e., real". [PLE, p. 241]

Bogdanov's critique of Marx's dialectic began with a statement which appears to go directly against the conclusions just mentioned. Marx, he said, retained unchanged "many aspects of the old [idealist] dialectic, most notably, the laws of the 'triad'." [PLE, pp. 241–2] The statement above and the long discussion of Engels' adaptation of Hegel's laws which followed soon thereafter encourages one to suspect that Bogdanov actually considered Marx's dialectic to be idealist. One is prepared to suspect this, since Bogdanov had made such a point of the fact that the idealist contents of Hegel's dialectic had made its laws idealist as well. If the form of Marx's dialectic is idealist, then its content should be idealist as well, that is, if Bogdanov is consistent in his reasoning. However, such consistency is not forthcoming. As we shall see, Bogdanov did not argue that the form and content of Marx's dialectic coincide. In fact, he clearly felt that they did not. In spite of the charge that Marx's dialectic was idealist in many respects, Bogdanov's intent was not to force it into one category or another. His actual intent was two-fold. First, Bogdanov wished to affirm the presence of a dialectic among real phenomena, i.e., the possibility of a "real" dialectic. Secondly, he wished to show the impossibility of applying idealist laws to the relationships of the real world and, thereby to discredit them as improper forms for Marx's thought and, for that matter, for his own. For Bogdanov, the result of Marx's efforts was neither a "materialist" nor an "idealist" dialectic, but one which simply did not make much sense attached to what was, in almost all other respects, a truly active worldview dealing with concrete realities.

In pursuing the matter of idealist "pollutants" carried over into the Marxist dialect, Bogdanov dealt not with Marx but with Friedrich Engels. While he was willing to admit that the features and emphases of Engels' "materialism" differed in some ways from Marx's scheme, [PLE, p. 255] Bogdanov made no effort to separate their views on the dialectic. Clearly, our thinker considered Engels a "lawful" expositor of Marx's notions in this regard.[15] Thus, we can assume that Bogdanov placed the blame for adapting Hegel's laws of the dialectic squarely on Marx's shoulders.

Before embarking on his critique of Engels, however, Bogdanov chose to describe the difference between Marx's notion of the dialectic and his own. This brought out another sort of criticism of dialectics, one which had little or nothing to do with Bogdanov's assessment of Marx vis-à-vis the idealist dialectic. Restating his definition of the dialectic as an organizational process proceeding by way of the struggle of opposite tendencies, Bogdanov asked whether Marx's notion corresponded to it. His answer was, "apparently, not quite." [PLE, p. 242] Bogdanov accused Marx of dealing in "developmental" rather than "organizational" processes, stating that the first term was indefinite and relatively "unscientific" compared to the second. [PLE, p. 242] "Development", he said, was usually applied "in the sense of complicating some kind of complex, real or abstract". [PLE, p. 242] For example, he said, one might speak of the development of organisms, machines, illnesses or contradictions. In the first two of these, "development" implies the growth of order or organization. In the second, it implies the opposite. "Development", then, may be applied to all processes (and is so applied by Marx) without regard to progress or regress in organization. [PLE, p. 242] Bogdanov argued that the dialectic should properly apply only to processes moving from lower to higher forms of organization. The dialectical process was also progressive in character. [PLE, p. 242] Since he gave no concrete examples of the inferiority of the "developmental dialectic" to the "organizational" as a useful form of explanation, we must assume that Bogdanov based his argument on the fact that "development" was not implied in his social model. He stated in conclusion that the application of the "developmental dialectic" was inexact and without proper limits; in other words, it was so broad as to be useless. [PLE, p. 242] If one understood the dialectic properly, said Bogdanov, one must conclude that it was something less than a universal method of explanation and view of process. Its application was limited to explaining only those organizational processes which proceeded by means of the struggle of opposites. [PLE, p. 242] That the Marxian dialectic fell short of being a universal method, Bogdanov considered obvious, if only because it was indefinite. It failed to prove valuable as a partial method of systematizing knowledge for the same reason. [PLE, p. 242]

This, then, was the first aspect of Bogdanov's critique. The real dialectic dealt with the relationships of real phenomena in a particular sort of organizational process, i.e., one proceeding by the struggle of opposite tendencies to a higher level of organization. Marx's scheme, in contrast, dealt with the relationships of real phenomena in every instance of change, in every sort of process.

Turning to the matter of idealist pollutants, Bogdanov embarked upon his long discussion of Engels. [PLE, pp. 243–5] In the discussion, Bogdanov concerned himself wholly with the dialectic as it appeared in the *Anti-Dühring*.[16] His point was to show that Engels had indeed applied Hegel's laws of the dialectic to real phenomena and that the result was a series of misrepresentations of fact. The discussion focused on Engels' adaptation and application of the three Hegelian notions of "contradiction", "negation" and "transformation of quantity into quality".[17]

Bogdanov reminded his readers that real contradiction meant only one thing, the struggle of real forces working in opposite directions. Engels, he said, had nothing to say about this in the *Anti-Dühring*. [PLE, p. 243] Taking up his dialectical explanation of mechanical movement, Bogdanov showed that Engels saw contradiction, the source of mechanical movement, in the fact that a body is found and is not found in a given place at a given time. [PLE, p. 243] He noted that this was the same sort of thing Zeno had done when he attempted to prove the impossibility of movement.

In this matter Engels, like Zeno, observed only the contradiction of two ideas applied to movement, the ideas "found" and "not found", and not the contradiction of real forces or tendencies. [PLE, pp. 243–4]

The contradiction of these two notions, said Bogdanov, is ideal, since it only exists in thought. Properly, neither notion could be applied to a moving body. [PLE, p. 244] The best one can do using the notion "to be found" in conjunction with movement is to say that "a body is not found in some definite place but *moves*". [PLE, p. 244] According to Bogdanov, the contradiction in a process of mechanical movement exists between a body and its environment. Both are forces bearing some relation to one another. Movement is a type of organizational process which begins when the body and its environment cease to be in a state of rest ("equilibrium") vis-à-vis one another, which proceeds in the form of a struggle of the two forces, and which ends when a new state of rest is achieved. [PLE, p. 244]

Going on to Engels' notion of negation, Bogdanov again saw a clear manifestation of the dialectic of ideas. For Engels as for Hegel, Bogdanov charged, "negation" meant the development of antitheses out of theses. [PLE, p. 245] A real negation, a real "antithesis", is something which stands outside of and in opposition to something else. Here, Bogdanov resolutely rejected the notion that a single, definite negation could be assigned to, let alone be found within, each component of the real world. The logic of the real world simply did not correspond to the logic of ideas in this regard. [PLE, p. 245] Bogdanov noted further that Engels had not been logically consistent in the application of ideal negation. [PLE, p. 250] Taking up one of the latter's well-known examples of the dialectic in mathematics, Bogdanov sought to show that ideal negation could be arbitrarily applied and, indeed, was by Engels in that instance. Engels had stated in the *Anti-Dühring* that the antithesis or negation of the quantity +2 is −2. The negation of negation, that is, the outcome of the dialectical struggle of thesis and antithesis, he held to be $(-2)^2$ or +4. [PLE, p. 250] Bogdanov argued that −2 was only ideally the negation of +2. In the real world, a force designated by the number +2 was not by any means bound to be opposed by another force of equal magnitude working in the opposite direction. [PLE, p. 250] Furthermore, he said, the choice of the square of the negation as its negation was wholly arbitrary; it was neither ideal nor real. True, the interaction of real forces designated by +2 and −2 might result in a new force designated by +4 in certain circumstances, but by no means in all of them. [PLE, p. 250]

According to Bogdanov, Engels had lost the possibility of explaining "the transformation of quantity into quality" by his insistence on considering change in ideal terms. [PLE, p. 248] He explained that real changes in quality occurred in the following manner:

If one or another process — the movement of a body, the life of an organism, the development of a society — is defined as the struggle of two opposed forces, then as long as one force predominates, the process goes in that direction. When the other force grows and becomes equal to the first, then the whole character of the process changes, its quality changes. [PLE, p. 248]

Bogdanov's position here is simple enough; the quality of a process changes when the one force which gives the process its character ceases to predominate. Change in quality occurs at the point of equality of forces, and the forces may then take on a new relationship. We see that there is no notion here of change in the form of a "leap" from one quality to another. For Bogdanov, in effect, a process changes in quality before any new quality appears.

Citing Engels' example of the qualitative transformation of water into steam by the quantitative addition of heat, [PLE, p. 248] Bogdanov argued that the former's concept of change had a "mystical" character. For Engels, he said, 100 degrees of heat produce a revolutionary transformation of water into something else, i.e., steam. Real forces and their real dialectical relationship are ignored here, because Engels is again dealing in ideas; steam is the ideal negation of water and must always appear in a qualitative leap at the critical temperature of 100 degrees. [PLE, p. 248] According to our thinker, the transformation of water to steam had a *real* dialectical character, since it was the outcome of the struggle between two opposed forces: the pressure of water vapor and the pressure of the atmosphere. At 100 degrees and at sea level, the pressures of the two are equal and water vapor may escape where it could not before. If one lowers the atmospheric pressure on the surface of the water, the possibility of the water vapor's escape takes place at a lower temperature but always at the point of the equality of pressures. [PLE, p. 249]

Bogdanov concluded that organization or equilibrium exists when one force in a process predominates, disorganization or the disturbance of equilibrium (and the transformation of quantity to quality) occurs when the two forces are equal, and a new organization or equilibrium comes into being when one or the other force comes to predominate. [PLE, p. 249] In the boiling of water, Bogdanov saw the change in quality occurring when the possibility of the vapor's escape occurred. For Engels, he said, the change in quality came later, when the pressure of the vapor actually predominated. The reality of the struggle of forces and the change resulting from their equality could not be ignored or "leapt over"; to do so was to ignore the real nature of the process. [PLE, p. 249]

Bogdanov saw the basic flaw of the Marxian dialectic in its attempt to apply laws governing ideal processes to real phenomena. In so doing, the logic of ideas obscured the logic of reality. Bogdanov did not deny the usefulness of such notions as "contradiction", "negation" and "transformation of quantity to quality"; but, as with the notion of the dialectic itself, he felt that these notions had a real character which could not be reconciled with the logic of ideas. [PLE, pp. 252–4] According to Bogdanov, the result of applying idealist laws of the dialectic to the real world was not another form of dialectical idealism. It was, rather, a "materialist" philosophy which failed to find for itself an appropriate universal method of explanation. [PLE, p. 254] As we shall see, the appropriate method was not dialectical at all, and the only sort of dialectic possible given Marx's view of man and the world was the partial method of explanation which Bogdanov defined in his own dialectic.

D. JOSEPH DIETZGEN AND THE RUSSIAN DIALECTICAL MATERIALISTS

As we have seen, Bogdanov held that Marx had failed to create a concept of the dialectic compatible with his active worldview. It is also clear that he considered his own "organizational dialectic" to be compatible with Marx's invaluable "materialist" view of man and the world and, yet, not the most basic or universal method of explanation and view of process for it. In wrapping up his assessment of dialectical materialism, Bogdanov wished to show why prominent figures such as the German worker-philosopher Joseph Dietzgen and the Russian social-democrats – Lenin, Plekhanov and Liubov' Aksel'rod – had not succeeded in improving on Marx's worldview. His object was to argue that the only improvement on Marx could come from a critique of his dialectic. There was nothing wrong with Marx's view of reality, of "matter" vis-à-vis human activity. An adequate critique of Marx's dialectic leads to a proper perspective on his contributions to the advance of philosophy, provides a true notion of the dialectic itself, and points toward the universal method of explanation and view of process compatible with a truly active worldview. For Bogdanov, the result of the efforts of Dietzgen and the Russian Marxists was, for the most part, a repetition of old errors.

In dealing with these dialectical materialists, Bogdanov chose not to discuss their thought in any detail but concentrated, instead, on certain of their arguments. While this has no effect on his arguments regarding the Russian Marxists, it creates certain problems for understanding his assessment of Joseph Dietzgen.[18] Bogdanov asserted that Dietzgen moved toward the "materialist" dialectic independent of Marx and Engels by attempting to unite the dialectic with an idea of "universal monistic being" taken largely from Spinoza. [PLE, p. 256] In this, said Bogdanov, Dietzgen produced a worldview free from dualism and eclecticism. [PLE, p. 256] It occurs to the reader to ask whether he is to assume that Dietzgen's notion of "monistic universal being" is akin to Marx's concept of reality. Here, Bogdanov gives no clear indication. For our thinker, Dietzgen's concept of being, although progressive in its monism, is "abstract and contentless". [PLE, p. 258] This suggests that it was not akin to Marx's view at all; however, Bogdanov never tells us how and why this is the case. How Dietzgen can be considered a dialectical materialist is not revealed by Bogdanov. It may strike the reader that this is a relatively unimportant matter, given the main purpose of Bogdanov's dicussion. However, Bogdanov had several very positive things to say about Dietzgen. The importance to the advance of philosophy accorded to Dietzgen by Bogdanov would indicate that our thinker regarded him as a forerunner of sorts. We would like to know then exactly how and why Dietzgen's worldview diverged from that of Marx in Bogdanov's eyes. Unfortunately, this is impossible to discern here.[19]

What did Bogdanov say about Dietzgen? First, as regards Dietzgen's monism, Bogdanov noted that he had adopted Spinoza's idea of the universal unity of reality, that is, the idea that the material and spiritual worlds were one unified reality, "universal monistic being". [PLE, p. 256] Dietzgen, he said, also accepted Spinoza's idea that man and man's thought are part of that being. But whereas for Spinoza materiality and spirituality were two different but parallel attributes of being, for Dietzgen they existed in phenomena together and inseparably. [PLE, p. 256] In this, said Bogdanov, Dietzgen was similar to Schelling, since Schelling found the ideal and the real simultaneously in all phenomena. [PLE, pp. 257–8] Our thinker noted that Dietzgen, however, leaned away from idealism toward materialism. Matter predominated in his world-picture, Bogdanov said, and sometimes Dietzgen characterized general being as "material". [PLE, p. 258] From this brief assessment, Bogdanov moved directly to the conclusion that Dietzgen's "monism of being" was as abstract and contentless as Spinoza's "monism of substance". [PLE, p. 258] We can only conjecture here that this conclusion was made on the assumption that Dietzgen identified "universal monistic being" with ordinary matter rather than with "matter" in the sense given it by Bogdanov and, in Bogdanov's view, by Marx. If this is the case, then in spite of his monistic inclinations, Dietzgen could not improve upon Marx, let alone measure up to him in Bogdanov's estimation.

Bogdanov noted that Dietzgen's view of the method of knowledge was, like his notion of matter, also an old error. He found the worker-philosopher to be very near the Empiriocritics in this matter, since Dietzgen proposed that knowledge was the registration of phenomena, the classification of facts. [PLE, p. 258] Leaning thus toward pure description, said Bogdanov, Dietzgen moved away from Marx's perspective toward a reflective understanding of the relationship between knowledge and life. [PLE, p. 258] Curiously, Bogdanov was willing to forgive Dietzgen for this. It is necessary to remember, he said, that in Dietzgen's time the notion of pure description was a weapon against metaphysical constructs, and, therefore, progressive. [PLE, p. 258] Bogdanov had not let the empiriocritics off so easily.

In spite of the "abstract-contentless" character of Dietzgen's concept of being, Bogdanov found that his philosophy showed

... an extraordinarily progressive tendency in its demand for strict monism, forcing our every duality and eclecticism from his world-understanding and, with that, in asserting the possibility of monism. [PLE, p. 258]

Dietzgen's work was an important stage in the history of philosophy, said

Bogdanov, for other reasons besides his demand for a monistic view of reality. Dietzgen was the first true worker-philosopher in the nineteenth century. [PLE, p. 258] Furthermore, he was the first to express "the thought of the inevitability of working out basic, proletarian class-forms of knowledge: 'special proletarian logic', as he put it". [PLE, p. 258] Bogdanov noted that Dietzgen was even more decisive than Marx in this regard. [PLE, p. 258]

While he had a number of positive things to say about Dietzgen, Bogdanov assessed the Russian dialectical materialists in an entirely negative manner. Although a thorough-going evaluation of Lenin, Plekhanov and Aksel'rod was not within the scope of *The Philosophy of Living Experience,* the brief and summary fashion in which they were treated indicates their relative insignificance for Bogdanov. He virtually brushed them aside, if you will, as being unworthy of consideration alongside the likes of Joseph Dietzgen, let alone Marx and Engels. Bogdanov accused the Russian Marxists of seeking to replace Marx's perfectly fine notion of the material with a concept more appropriate to eighteenth-century materialism. [PLE, p. 258] The result, he said, was a "very original position" which amounted to the attempted reconciliation of Marx's teachings with a view of matter as thing-in-itself. [PLE, pp. 258–9] Here, the word "original" strongly implied "improbable".

To establish the fact that Lenin, Plekhanov and Aksel'rod regarded matter as thing-in-itself, Bogdanov produced a quotation from Plekhanov (without citation) to that effect. The following is a paraphrase of Plekhanov's argument. That which acts on our sense organs and causes sensation is called "matter". In this, "matter" is the opposite of "spirit" which, as defined by idealists, does not act on our sense organs. Kant was right in saying that that which acts on our senses is a thing-in-itself. "Matter" is the totality of things-in-themselves. [PLE, p. 259] Bogdanov made no attempt to demonstrate unanimity among the three Russian Marxists in this. He supplemented Plekhanov's argument with a brief quotation from Aksel'rod which said no more than that we know matter by means of its action on us. [PLE, p. 259]

Bogdanov gives us the following in critical response to Plekhanov's argument:

As we see, here man and his consciousness are posited as the passive product of external matter. This is that reflective relationship to reality which was characteristic of all old materialisms and against which Marx asserted himself. Matter is the object of human activity; and here, on the contrary, man is viewed wholly as the object of the action of matter. This is a direct contradiction of the social-historical theory of Marx, where production, labor, human activity, serves as the starting-point. [PLE, p. 259]

Thus, Bogdanov made Plekhanov's position out to be a denial of Marx's notion that the essence of the world process is human activity. For our thinker, the assertion that matter acts on man undermined the possibility of a truly active philosophy. [PLE, p. 259] Continuing his critique, Bogdanov stated that the Russian Marxists were satisfied with only an "external bond" between their view of matter and Marx's social thought. Ignoring or not understanding that the adjective "materialist" has two different senses, they used it to bind their view of matter as thing-in-itself and Marx's social thought together in supposed unity. [PLE, p. 260]

Bogdanov reminded his readers that a view of matter as thing-in-itself places matter outside of human experience. Because they took this view, he said, it was easy enough for the Russian Marxists to believe in absolute and eternal truths. This was the second of their "old errors" and another way in which they had moved away from Marx toward eighteenth-century materialism. [PLE, p. 260] While he accused Plekhanov, Lenin and Aksel'rod of this, Bogdanov gave no evidence that such was the case. Apparently, he felt that their position was well-known. Going on, he noted that absolute and eternal truths were simply impossible in Marx's view and that the Russian dialectical materialists could not consider themselves Marxists in that regard. [PLE, p. 260] As if this were not enough to condemn them as beneath serious consideration as thinkers, Bogdanov went on to state that the Russian Marxists were also at odds with contemporary scientific thought in general "which demands an unlimited critique and rejects all absolutes in knowledge". [PLE, p. 260]

In conclusion, Bogdanov argued that the Russian Marxists were no more dialectical materialists than Ludwig Feuerbach had been. More than that, he denied that Lenin, Plekhanov and Aksel'rod had any worldview at all!

Recognition of [pre-Marxian] materialism on the one hand and dialectics on the other does not produce dialectical materialism. Together they lead to contradiction. When both are taken in contradiction, they not only do not form dialectical materialism but no definite worldview. [PLE, 0. 260]

In this manner, Aleksandr Bogdanov disposed of "the father of Russian Marxism", the mastermind of the Russian Revolution and an extraordinarily well-educated Marxist philosopher. He placed them alongside Joseph Dietzgen in their failure to improve upon Marx. Before concluding on the matter of dialectics in general, Bogdanov made his ultimate argument with regard to dialectical materialism. According to him, the main inadequacy of "present-day dialectical materialism" was that it did not criticize its own dialectic.

[PLE, p. 261] "But", he said, "if it would do this, it would cease to be as it is and would transform itself into another form of world-understanding." [PLE, p. 261] This other form of world-understanding was, of course, Bogdanov's own. Throughout his critique of dialectical materialism, Bogdanov continually implied that the way to the solution of the problem of philosophy ought to begin with the critique of Marx's method of explanation and view of process. Criticize the materialist dialectic, find the real one, contemplate the fact that world activity or process is not "developmental" but "organizational", and glimpse the direction that must be taken in the search for a universal method of explanation suitable to "a philosophy of living experience".

E. THE REAL DIALECTIC AND THE TASK OF PHILOSOPHY

Certain that he had properly disposed of all other dialectical schemes, Bogdanov returned to his own in making a final argument. Once again he stated that the real dialectic was an organizational process proceeding by means of the struggle of opposites. It could not be universal method of systematizing knowledge, since the dialectic was only a partial case of organizational processes in general "which may proceed in other ways". [PLE, p. 261] While Bogdanov had made this last point earlier on, he had not taken the trouble to provide illustrations. Now, however, he chose to give several examples of organizational processes which could not be explained in dialectical terms. There was no basis to assert, he said, that the initial unification of reproductive cells into an embryo is the result of a dialectical struggle between those cells. [PLE, p. 261] Similarly, he denied that the labor cooperation of primitive social groups could be seen as the outcome of the interaction of opposite tendencies. [PLE, p. 261] Bogdanov argued further that the scientific method, "a method of organizing the facts of experience", was not dialectical in its basic character. [PLE, p. 261]

One cannot help but wish that Bogdanov had made more of this part of the chapter. His case for the limited applicability of the dialectic would have been strengthened considerably by the suggestion of nondialectical methods of explanation appropriate to his examples. However, he apparently considered this sort of thing to be outside the scope of *The Philosophy of Living Experience*. Perhaps Bogdanov had no clear idea of other methods of explanation in 1910. He did, of course, find them eventually, since methods of organization were his primary concern in the *Tektologiia*.[20] The point of bringing up these examples was to give evidence against the universality of dialectical explanation, and Bogdanov must have felt that they were so clearly non-dialectical as to close the case:

In the closing paragraphs of the chapter, Bogdanov made his demand for a method of systematizing knowledge more universal than the dialectic. Establishing this as "the task of philosophy", [PLE, p. 261] he implied that the universal method must be comprised of all the partial methods of explaining organizational processes.

Elements of the dialectic may be found almost everywhere, but life and movement are not exhausted by them. Philosophy must, consequently, conceive of its task in the broadest and most general form: [it must be] to research the bonds of the world process in order to discover *all possible ways and means of organization*. Such is the basic notion of Empiriomonism. [PLE, p. 241]

In the final chapters of *The Philosophy of Living Experience*, we will see how Bogdanov attempted to fulfill this "task of philosophy".

On the assumption that our exposition has been clear, we need not summarize Bogdanov's positions on dialectics and dialectical materialism here.[21] Again, it would be premature to conclude on the relationship between Marx and Bogdanov, that is, beyond saying that in Bogdanov's eyes the two would apparently share common points of departure and certain perspectives which would show them closer to one another than Bogdanov and Mach. As in our exposition of the chapter on Mach, we would do best to conclude by noting what Bogdanov tells us about the search for the solution to the problem of philosophy.

As in the treatment of other thinkers in *The Philosophy of Living Experience*, Bogdanov's sympathetic statements on Marx suggest things about the character of the solution. As we have seen, dialectical materialism was deemed a truly active worldview, a real philosophy of activity, since it took the collective experience of the proletariat as a starting-point, found the essence of man in social relations (the collective labor process), exhibited a "realistic" view of the world as human activity and that which resists it, considered "matter" a correlate of activity and not being-in-itself, and attempted to find a universal method of explanation and a view of process corresponding to this "real" world. This suggests that the solution to the problem of philosophy would be similarly "active" by dint of a similar starting-point, concept of being and an attempt to find a universal method. Obviously, the attempt at the latter would succeed where dialecticians had failed, and the new method would go beyond the "materialist dialectic". With that, Bogdanov's worldview would be a view of reality, i.e., of being and process, transcending that of Marx and, by extension, all previous points of view as well.

In addition to what Bogdanov's sympathetic statements on Marx suggest, we find in this chapter several direct statements on the character of reality and the task of philosophy vis-à-vis that reality. Both of these have to do with the matter of process in reality and its explanation. The "larger" of them amounts to the following: the task of contemporary philosophy is to find a truly universal method of explanation or, as it might be better put, an explanation of the "real" processes of the world. Bogdanov suggests here that the process of the world, if you will, the "movement" of reality, has a universal character. This should be taken to mean that there is a real "law" or set of "laws" which, after the fashion of the "unreal" Hegelian and Marxian dialectics, govern and explain all processes. It is clear that Bogdanov's solution to the problem of philosophy would produce this. Already in the chapter on Marx, he tells us that the world process is organizational. While he says little about what this means, we know a) that an organizational process is one which moves from lower to higher degrees of complexity and order, and b) that such a process *may be* dialectical in character, but c) that the dialectical process is only a partial case. In what amounts to a restatement of this, Bogdanov suggests that the task of philosophy is to seek out "all possible ways and means of organization". This suggestion is a little troublesome, since it may be taken in either of two ways. First, it might be taken to mean that since the world process is organizational, man must discover the forms of organization that exist therein. Secondly, it might be taken in the more "active" sense that, since human activity is the appropriate starting point for "the philosopher of living experience", seeking ways and means of organization means creating them as tools for the manipulation of reality. Which of these perspectives is actually the case with Bogdanov we will see in the next two chapters. Suffice it to say at this point, that the solution to the problem of philosophy would involve a notion of world process as "organization".

Bogdanov's other direct statement in the chapter on Marx regards the dialectic. He tells us in effect that the solution to the problem of philosophy would involve a notion of the dialectic as a partial characteristic of the world process, and he demands that the would-be "philosopher of living experience" put the "real" dialectic in its proper place among other organizational forms. This suggests some things about Bogdanov's view of process and organizational forms in general. If the dialectic proceeds via the interaction of opposite forces, then there might be an organizational process which proceeds via the interaction of similar ones. For that matter, there may be organizational processes which proceed via other sorts of interactions. What these interactions and organizational processes may possibly have in common is (a) that they lead to higher levels of complexity and unity and (b) that they are, as Wetter says of Bogdanov's dialectic, "mechanistic", i.e., involve previously unrelated forces which are related to one another in various, purely mechanical ways. There is no point in pursuing that which Bogdanov's dialectic suggests here. As we shall see, *The Philosophy of Living Experience* is meant only as a prologue to Bogdanov's study of organization. In it, we find the organizational character of the world-process stated but not developed. The notion was part of his worldview in 1910 but was still incomplete. We know from the chapter on Marx that the "real" dialectic and a view of the world process as organizational must be considered part of Bogdanov's solution to the problem of philosophy. Although more will be said about these notions, the reader should not anticipate their complete development in the final chapters of *The Philosophy of Living Experience.*

CHAPTER IV

EMPIRIOMONISM

We now come to that part of *The Philosophy of Living Experience* where all introduction ceases, where Bogdanov at last elaborates the core of his own worldview. Since empiriomonism is "the philosophy of living experience" named in the title, one might expect the chapter devoted expressly to it to be the ultimate statement and crux of the work. [PLE, pp. 267–310] As we shall see, such is not the case. The chapter we are about to consider presents empiriomonism in two ways, first as the solution to the contemporary problem of philosophy and, secondly, as a worldview different from those of the past. Although the entire work moves toward this end, Bogdanov chose to take it further. For him, the presentation of empiriomonism could not be complete without an assessment of its relation to the thought of the future. What empiriomonism was in the present could only be fully understood in light of that which would displace it. Accordingly, Bogdanov devoted himself to this project in "The Science of the Future", the work's final chapter and conclusion. [PLE, pp. 310–27] The result of this is startling, for "The Science of the Future" is more than Bogdanov's statement on empiriomonism's place in the history of thought. It is, as well, an argument for the end of philosophy and the articulation of Bogdanov's vision of the future tasks of man and his thought. "The Science of the Future", thus, has the effect of taking *The Philosophy of Living Experience* substantially beyond the contemporary problem of philosophy. In it, the work as a whole takes on a broader character than its title suggests.

While we may not say "Here is what *The Philosophy of Living Experience* is *all* about" in dealing with the chapter on empiriomonism, we may conclude on the largest aspect of the work in unfolding Bogdanov's solution to the problem of philosophy. Here, at least, his search for a new and different worldview ends. If we consider its general scope and several tenets, we may discover what empiriomonism as the solution was intended to be and, with that, how Bogdanov's worldview relates to empiriocriticism and Marxist materialism as he apprehended them. The outcome of this consideration is, of course, of substantial importance to our appreciation of Bogdanov's self-conception and greater intentions in the work. From this, we may go on to "The Science of the Future" and see empiriomonism in the greater perspective set forth there.

Then, we may finally conclude on the intents and purposes, the full scope and meaning of *The Philosophy of Living Experience*.

Before discussing the chapter's contents, we would like to make several interpretative comments on how "empiriomonism" proceeds. This is an important matter in our view, since we believe that an appreciation of its process provides a key to what Bogdanov meant his worldview to be. More than this, we believe that the failure to consider this matter has kept past commentators from fully appreciating empiriomonism and has led them to misinterpret it in some important ways.

At the outset Bogdanov tells us that, as a whole, empiriomonism proceeds from a basic perspective of what contemporary philosophy should and should not be. [PLE, p. 261] It is what Bogdanov calls thereafter "the social-labor perspective", "the point of view of collective labor activity", "the proletarian perspective" and, most frequently, "the labor point of view". If one looks closely at the chapter on empiriomonism and Bogdanov's analysis of Marx,[1] the following definition of this perspective may be synthesized: "The labor point of view" is that which demands that a worldview and each of its tenets reflect and reinforce the needs and ambitions, the will and potential, of "collective labor activity", where "collective labor activity" implies the whole of human activity in the present. In light of Bogdanov's earlier statements on the demands which present reality makes on philosophy, one is tempted to consider "the labor point of view" a convenient designation for the sum of those statements and, for that, only a general perspective on the task of philosophy. It becomes clear in the chapter on empiriomonism, however, that "the labor point of view" is more than that. It is a philosophic principle as well and *the* philosophic principle from which Bogdanov's worldview proceeds. By this we mean that "the labor point of view" is not only meant to inform the philosopher as to the purpose of his enterprise but that it is also intended to determine how that enterprise should proceed in finding the tenets of a new worldview and collecting them into an integrated whole.

Evidence for this contention is to be found both in the chapter on empiriomonism and in earlier sections of *The Philosophy of Living Experience*. We remind the reader that because Marx took collective labor activity as his starting point, Bogdanov judged his "materialism" a truly active worldview, and, by implication, a great step beyond philosophies which "begin" elsewhere. We will see shortly that Marx's concern for "collective labor activity" makes him the first exponent of "the labor point of view" as well. In asserting the need to get beyond Marx, we find Bogdanov arguing that the key to creating a genuinely new worldview is a central concern with collective labor activity and the employment of "the labor point of view" in the basic ways demanded by the character of present reality.

It is apparent that for Bogdanov taking "the labor point of view" meant allowing insights into present reality to determine how philosophy must proceed and, with that, what it is. In every part of the chapter on empiriomonism, our thinker proceeds according to the demands of "the labor point of view". We submit, then, that Bogdanov's use of it is that which makes empiriomonism what it is for him, i.e., something new and different in philosophy and, therefore, the key which allows us to see empiriomonism as it was intended to be as the solution to the problem of philosophy.

The question arises as to why the role of "the labor point of view" has been summarily ignored in the scholarship on Bogdanov. While the primary source for the study of empiriomonism has been the three-volume work under that title, commentators have made almost as much use of its compact restatement in *The Philosophy of Living Experience.*[2] While it is easy to see why no one has considered the whole of this very complicated work, it is difficult to understand why the role of "the labor point of view" in Bogdanov's exposition of empiriomonism there has been ignored. The exposition begins with a clearly stated proposal to go beyond Marx in the employment of "the labor point of view" in order to find the basis for a new worldview. Thereafter, each subsequent section of the essay employs it, either directly or indirectly, in the generation of tenets and positions.

In some ways, it is really not so difficult to understand the lack of concern for "the labor point of view". First, the perspective is not fully articulated in the three volumes of *Empiriomonism.* To find it, one must look to Bogdanov's earlier works.[3] Because of this, past scholars may not have been willing to consider it important in *The Philosophy of Living Experience.* Secondly, if one has not studied the latter work as a whole and especially the chapter on Marx, one might easily take "the labor point of view" to be nothing more than a vague perspective and Bogdanov's reference to Marx as its exponent as a weak attempt to align himself with that thinker. In fact, one might even take it to be evidence of Bogdanov's confusion in attempting to proceed from Marx's point of view toward "Machist" conclusions.

Thirdly, and more ominously, all treatments of Bogdanov have considered empiriomonism either in relation to empiriocriticism or as part of the epistemological conflict between Bogdanov and his Russian Marxist contemporaries. With that, all regard it variously as a species of Machian "empiricism", a strange sort of Marxist materialism, or sometimes as an amalgam of both. If one is principally concerned with showing Bogdanov to be the heir of Mach and Avenarius or with making him out to be a revisionist or "Machian Marxist", then why confuse the issue by considering that Bogdanov believed himself to be the exponent of a point of view which was certainly not Machian and beyond that of Marx? Why suggest that he saw empirio-monism as an attempt to go beyond Marx and Mach initiated and shaped by the demands of the contemporary "labor point of view"? We are suggesting here that part of the reason "the labor point of view" and empiriomonism as "the labor worldview" have been ignored may be that consideration of this can only lead one to divorce Bogdanov from Marx and Mach and view empiriomonism as something new and different. Perhaps because it makes him more difficult to classify as a thinker, what Bogdanov considered himself and his worldview to be has been deemed either inconsequential or mis-leading. It cannot be argued, of course, that empiriomonism as something new and different was the chief legacy of Bogdanov.[4] However, neither the matter of its subsequent influence (or lack thereof) nor his partisanship for Marx and Mach should proscribe an attempt to find out what Bogdanov believed he was undertaking.

Whatever the reasons for not considering empiriomonism as it was intended to be taken, it is incumbent upon us in explicating *The Philosophy of Living Experience* to give the reader Bogdanov's worldview as it appears there. Accordingly, the role of "the labor point of view" will be emphasized and the tenets of empiriomonism will be given as positions generated and shaped by it. As a consequence, we will find that empiriomonism and its parts have meanings and implications different from those accorded them in past studies. By presenting empiriomonism as it was set forth in the chapter under consideration, we will also bring out several parts of this philosophy, such as "labor causality", which have been left out of previous expositions.[5] With this, we hope to provide the first complete picture of Bogdanov's worldview in the light of what he intended it to be.

We have said that, as a whole empiriomonism proceeds from "the labor point of view" toward "the labor worldview". A few words must be said in addition about the way in which it proceeds from part to part. As Bogdanov himself provides an explanation of why one section follows another, we need only focus on the point or tenet with which empiriomonism begins. Given the contents of previous chapters, one might expect Bogdanov to begin with and build upon the view of reality and its "organizational" processes expressed there. This does not occur. Instead, empiriomonism is developed from a concept of causality not found earlier in the work. Why is this? First, it is clear from Bogdanov's opening remarks in the chapter under consideration that a genuinely new worldview must begin with a new causal concept, since such a concept is any worldview's most basic part.[6] Causality, then, is deemed the foundation stone of empiriomonism and the most basic tenet generated by employment of "the labor point of view". Secondly, we would like to suggest that Bogdanov's statements on the character of reality and its processes were actually positions generated by the "empiriomonistic point of view". Unlike the "labor point of view" and "labor causality", they were not meant as foundations of his worldview but, rather, as parts or implications of it. In that case, they form parts of the solution to the problem of philosophy but not the parts most basic. That they were not so for Bogdanov is suggested by the fact that, while they are everywhere implied, they are not restated in the chapter. It is for these reasons, then, that empiriomonism begins elsewhere.

A. "LABOR CAUSALITY"

Bogdanov began the presentation of empiriomonism without any sort of introduction. There was no need to do so, since the chapter proceeded directly from all that had gone before. It might even be said that the earlier chapters of *The Philosophy of Living Experience* principally served to clear the stage for the triumphal entrance of Bogdanov's worldview. Of course, they did much more than that: what a worldview should and should not be in the proletarian era was established there.

The chapter's opening sentences take the reader back to the work's introduction and, at the same time, to its conclusions on Marx.

Each new class entering the arena of history goes through a long struggle in working out its culture [and] its particular world-understanding. Dialectical materialism was the first attempt to formulate the working-class point of view on life and the world. We have seen how strongly the . . . influence of the old ruling class weighed on its methods and ideas. [PLE, p. 267]

If dialectical materialism had been the first attempt at turning "the labor point of view" into a complete world-understanding in Bogdanov's eyes, empiriomonism was obviously the next and, as we shall see, the definitive one. While he reiterated his argument that the first attempt had failed because of idealist influences, Bogdanov now indicated that it came up short for another, even more basic, reason. According to our thinker, Marx had not employed "the labor point of view" in the most basic manner necessary for the establishment of a worldview. The construction of "the labor worldview", he said, must begin with the search for a "social-labor" notion of causality, since causality is the fundamental principle around which a system of thought is organized. [PLE, p. 264] While he said nothing about it, Bogdanov may well have considered Marx's notion of causality a form of "abstract causal necessity" and, therefore, "bourgeois" in the manner of his dialectic. Whether or not this was actually the case, he demanded a new causal notion based on proletarian labor experience, that is, causality from "the labor point of view". What Marx had not done, or could not do, Bogdanov proposed to accomplish himself. From this, empiriomonism as the proletarian worldview would proceed.

In a manner reminiscent of his contention that every proletarian understood the meaning and uses of philosophy, Bogdanov suggested that the working class was already in actual possession of the notion of "labor causality". The proletariat, he said, already rejects authoritarian and abstract causality as "fetishistic", because "in the life of the proletariat there exist new practical relations which differ from anything that went on before". [PLE, p. 268] Reiterating the argument that different practical relations give rise to different logics, Bogdanov asserted that the model for a new causality must be readily apparent in the relations of machine production to one holding "the labor point of view". [PLE, p. 268] He noted that the proletariat realizes the active relationship of man to the world in that he sees and acts on the possibility and necessity of changing it. This realization is a reflection of the way in which machine production itself changes the world. According to our thinker, the outcome and essence of machine production is "the systematic transformation of efforts, or, in scientific and exact terms, the transformation of energy". [PLE, pp. 268–9] Machine production changes the world by turning the physical, chemical, and electrical forces of nature into one another after the manner in which natural forces are turned into the mechanical forces of production. [PLE, p. 269] For Bogdanov, this feature of machine production generated a new perspective on the world and, subsequently, on causality; the new view was that, for the labor collective, "every process in the world is the possible source of every other process". [PLE, p. 269] "The practical bond of phenomena, the practical unity of nature", he said, "is expressed in this perspective". [PLE, p. 269]

More will be said shortly about Bogdanov's concept of "the transformation of energy". Before he himself explained that concept in full, Bogdanov delivered up the new notion of causality which grew out of the perspective that "every process was the possible source of every other". He argued that the relation of cause and effect must be seen in the following manner: if a phenomenon "B" results from another phenomenon "A", the latter is turned into the former in the same way that the energy of coal or falling water is transformed into the work of machines. "B" must not be seen as following "A" out of necessity but because man wills it and has the ability to effect the transformation. [PLE, p. 269] "An effect", said Bogdanov, "is received from a cause as in production a practical result is received from the energy expended to that end". [PLE, p. 270] It is apparent that, for our thinker, man can expect to make any phenomenon the cause or source of any other, since machine production shows the promise of unlimited advances in technique.

To make this notion of causality more clear, Bogdanov compared it to its authoritarian and abstract predecessors in the following manner. In the authoritarian view, he reminded the reader, cause predominated over effect as something strong and active. In the abstract view, effect followed cause out of some sort of natural or logical necessity. From "the labor point of view", cause is merely the "technical source" of effect and vice versa. Any "A" may potentially be turned into any "B", and back, through the will and "technique" of collective labor. [PLE, pp. 272–3] Furthermore, Bogdanov argued, "transformation" must be understood as a concept devoid of implications of creation or destruction. Effort or energy is neither created nor destroyed in machine production, it simply takes on different appearances and uses. Thus, in a view of cause and effect modeled on the transformation of energy, cause and effect must appear as "equal" in the sense that they are "different phases in a continuous series of changing and changeable phenomena". [PLE, p. 270]

The implications of "labor causality" were clearly considerable to Bogdanov. The above creates the impression that man enters the cause-effect sequence as its regulator. We get the sense that man may not only make anything the cause or source of anything else but also that he may interrupt cause-effect sequences which previously seemed necessary, i.e., outside of his control. It is as if Bogdanov sees man in the conventional role of cause and the unlimited manipulation of the world of phenomena to man's benefit to be the effect. Bogdanov's view permits him to ask man to act on the world of phenomena without fearing that his efforts may be proscribed by laws he himself has not made. He can ask man to find a useful effect for every possible cause and to turn every effect into yet another cause. The clear intent of "labor causality", then, is to grant man infinite power over the world which resists his activity. As we shall see in Bogdanov's doctrine of the "elements of experience",[7] the resistant world becomes infinitely malleable and useful to one holding "the labor point of view".

Before going on to argue the significance and effects of "labor causality", Bogdanov returned to his concept of transformation of energy. He obviously wished to avoid any confusion that might arise from his use of the phrase. Our thinker assumed that his readers would otherwise conclude that "labor causality" was actually based on the law of the conservation of energy produced by "bourgeois physics", [PLE, p. 270] Bogdanov would not deny the similarities between that law and his concept. He argued, however, that the law was unsuitable for inclusion in a "labor worldview", since it was based on an abstract and "fetishistic" concept of energy. According to Bogdanov, all exponents of the second law of thermodynamics saw "energy" either as primary substance, as "thing-in-itself", or as a pure but useful fiction. The first view, he said, considers energy as something apart from man and outside any direct relationship to labor activity. In the second, energy exists only in thought and not in fact. In both views, it is taken to be an absolute. This was not energy from "the labor point of view". [PLE, pp. 270–1]

For Bogdanov, energy represented the practical relationship of society to nature, of human activity to that which resists it. It was neither substance nor idea, but the factual outcome of the relationship between work and its object. [PLE, p. 271] The transformation of energy, he said, thus refers to the creation and change wrought by active, human effort on resisting nature; "to see 'energy' in the processes of nature means to look at those processes from the perspective of their possible labor exploitation by man". [PLE, pp. 271–2] While this definition seems a bit cryptic at first glance, it becomes apparent that what Bogdanov is attempting to say is that energy, like all other phenomena in human experience, has no existence apart from man. In other words, it is not something to be found *in*, say, coal or falling water, but is rather something resulting from man's interaction with them. [PLE, pp. 271–2]

From this, Bogdanov went on to describe the crucial effect "labor causality" had on "the labor worldview" proceeding from it. As a worldview is a system of knowledge, and as knowledge must be a program of world development as well as a program of description and explanation, he said, we must ask whether "labor causality" permits and encourages "the labor world-view" to be a truly active philosophy. [PLE, p. 272] His answer to this was, of course, affirmative.

Labor causality gives man a program and plan for the conquest of the world: to dominate phenomena, things, step-by-step so as to receive some from others and by means of some to dominate others. [PLE, p. 272]

By dint of its causal principle, then, empiriomonism could not help but be a truly active worldview in Bogdanov's eyes. In earlier stages in the history of causal notions, he said, working man had been ruled by nature and chaotic economic relations, his thought by authority and abstract, contentless necessity. [PLE, pp. 273–4] In the proletarian era, the stage of "labor causality", man overcomes the resistance of nature, the power of economic relations and, with that, the limitations of authority and causal necessity in thought. A truly active world-building philosophy may be formulated, since man himself is at last able to dominate the world outside him, to create the laws and principles to which it must conform. The most basic of these is the principle of "labor causality". [PLE, pp. 273–4]

Bogdanov tells us in conclusion that the stage of "labor causality" will be long and slow in developing, but that its completion as a stage is as inevitable as the complete success of machine production in the struggle against the forces of nature. [PLE, p. 274] Returning to Marx, he described dialectical materialism as a sure sign that the stage of "labor causality" had begun. Its "labor perspective" and central concern with collective labor activity had marked man's entry into that era, he said, since "labor causality" proceeded directly from it. It was now up to man to employ "labor causality" to construct "a complete, clear and scientific world-understanding". [PLE, p. 274]

It may seem curious that Bogdanov saw the stage of "labor causality" as long and slow to develop, since he obviously considered empiriomonism to be a complete world-understanding proceeding from "labor causality". If one takes account of the work's final chapter, however, it becomes clear that the stage of "labor causality" would produce more than a complete "labor world-view" or proletarian philosophy. In this stage, man would apparently move beyond philosophy altogether. Empiriomonism was for Bogdanov, then, but a sub-stage in which "the philosophy of living experience" drives out all others pursuant to the transcendence of philosophy itself.[8]

B. THE ELEMENTS OF EXPERIENCE

According to Bogdanov, the task of "the labor worldview" was to change the world, "to organize the world to man's benefit". [PLE, p. 274] This world with which man must work and which he is to change, the world from "the labor point of view", he called "experience" (*opyta*). Bogdanov tells us straightaway that this "experience" is the sum total of all human effort and resistance to that effort and that, in this form, it is a continuous unbroken stream. [PLE, p. 275] If, he continued, "experience" is organizable, and, of course, it is from "the labor point of view", it must be assumed to have component parts or "elements". As with experience as a whole, such elements must not be seen as existing apart from man. They are not *a priori* the component parts of experience; it is man who determines and defines them, who "separates them out". [PLE, p. 275] On the basis of this perspective, Bogdanov then asked what insights "the labor point of view" gives into experience as it is broken up by man. An answer to this question, he asserted, would lead to a definition of the elements of experience appropriate to "the labor worldview". [PLE, p. 275]

Here we see that Bogdanov approached the world as "experience" from, if you will, Marx's perspective rather than from Mach's. He proposed to proceed as an exponent of "the labor point of view" rather than as some sort of empiricist. While it may be in some ways correct and certainly useful to view him as part of the empiricist tradition,[9] to do so in the context of *The Philosophy of Living Experience* only serves to obscure the place of Bogdanov's notion of experience in "the labor worldview" he believed he was creating. Approaching Bogdanov's "experience" in relation to the concepts of empiriocriticism pushes the role of "the labor point of view" in its formulation into the distant background. We must, therefore, approach Bogdanov's "experience" and its "elements" as he himself proposed to, that is, as the product of human effort and resistance and not as some unusual species of sense-data.

If experience is broken up by man, Bogdanov asked, then how does this occur? His basic answer was that the elements of experience result from human practice. Man in his labor breaks up experience in accord with the needs of production. [PLE, p. 275] Returning to his arguments on the origins of speech and thought, Bogdanov was convinced that his readers must agree that the first elements of experience were man's own actions, from which the earliest "word-ideas" were derived. He reminded the reader that early word-ideas were the cries of labor which came to represent man's actions. In the next stage of development, word-ideas about *things* expressed their character "as tools and materials, as objects of production". Bogdanov argued that if the first elements had "a wholly active, social-practical character", then all other components of experience must be likewise. [PLE, p. 275] Because the demands of production define the separateness of this or that element and because one thing may have various relationships to labor, he said, the idea of properties developed. Things which were themselves "elements" were broken up into other elements. From "the labor point of view", the elements of experience must proliferate and be combined in new ways as production advances. [PLE, pp. 275–6]

From this, Bogdanov went on to give the following definition of the elements of experience. Each element, he said, expresses one or another sum of human effort directed against the world according to the needs of labor. It is a product of these efforts and, therefore, "a crystal of labor". In this crystal, that which resists effort or labor must have a part. Thus, each element is the result of a certain amount and type of effort directed against a certain amount and type of resistance, just as experience on the whole is the result of all human effort and resistance. [PLE, p. 276]

Bogdanov illustrated the concept of "element" as "labor-crystal" by choosing an obvious example. A brick, he said, is an element of experience. As a "physical" thing it is clearly the product of a particular sort of human effort and resistance. As a "mental" thing, the brick is similarly a "crystal of labor", since man must labor to create an idea which expresses its physical character. If man attempts to break the brick up into its component parts either physically or mentally, he produces still more labor crystals. New effort is directed against new resistance when, for instance, one attempts to detach "redness" from a brick. [PLE, pp. 276–7] "This", said Bogdanov,

is an application of the socio-economic principle of labor value to experience. An element of experience is the product of social labor embodied in consciousness; it is created on the basis of social demand in the delimitation of various parts of work in which consists, as Marx would say, its "demand value". [PLE, pp. 277–8]

Bogdanov argued next that labor is first physical and then mental. First one creates the brick as a physical element and then one forms the idea of it. Even if an element is created by mental operations alone, however, "technical-labor processes" serve as a model. If, he asserted, one splits the world into atoms in his mind, the model for this is the physical breaking up of things to get at their component parts. [PLE, p. 279] Bogdanov held that there were many ways to divide experience into elements, some seemingly more useful than others. While Mach's elements may seem superior in usefulness to the atoms of modern physics, he asserted, "it would be the greatest naïveté to give this or that division of experience a final, absolute character." [PLE, p. 280][10] According to our thinker, the labor perspective of the elements of experience guaranteed against such mistakes. From "the labor point of view" elements correspond to the task on hand, whether it be practical or cognitive. They are crystals of social activity, the product of effort and resistance. As components of experience, they make up the material for systematic grouping "according to the demands of the labor collective [which is] mankind". [PLE, p. 280]

Bogdanov concluded his discussion with the following statement. If Mach's elements are "sensual", he said, then those of "the labor worldview" are "sensual-labor".

They are the product of social effort in labor and thought; they are segregated out in dependence on practical demands, developing with the growth and complication of the system of labor. Experience as a whole and each of its elements is simultaneously . . . resistance and . . . activity, [i.e.,] sensual material in a crystal of labor. [PLE, p. 309]

From this it should be apparent that Bogdanov's elements are not the ordinary empiricist's components of sense-data. And yet, Karl Ballestrem suggests just that. While he goes so far as to say that Bogdanov "never dreamed of sensations without a human mind", Ballestrem takes no account of Bogdanov's insistence that experience is the product of labor and resistance.[11] For Bogdanov, experience had no existence independent of either man or the things on and among which he acts, since it is the product of social labor "embodied in consciousness". [PLE, pp. 277–8] It is not some epistemologically necessary and separate realm standing between man and that which is external to him but is the product of their interaction, a product which has no existence or character of its own apart from that which man willfully gives it. Bogdanov's elements are, thus, not "sensual" and certainly not "material." But, in a sense, they are both, if we take "sensual-labor elements" to mean the components of the physical world and consciousness created by labor activity in those realms in some relation with that which resists labor activity.

In the previous section we hinted at the implications of Bogdanov's view of experience. If its "elements" are generated by man's labor activity, then man is able to segregate out an unlimited number of them and, by extension, to combine them in an unlimited number of ways to meet his productive demands. As with the "labor view" of causality, the "labor view" of experience is an attempt to free man from external limitations. If man is to conceive of every phenomenon as the possible "source" of every other, then his view of the world must be such that the component parts of that world have no absolute and enduring character or order. There are no fundamental building-blocks in the world for Bogdanov. All of its elements are equally fundamental in that they are created for social-labor purposes. Thus, the element "atom" and the element "brick" are of the same order. Because elements are created to meet the demands of the task on hand, no single species of them can be considered more basic and, with that, ultimate.

C. OBJECTIVITY

Leaving the matter of experience and its parts, Bogdanov proposed to investigate "those methods by which the grouping of elements into a system of experience proceeds", again, in accord with "the labor point of view". [PLE, p. 280] For our thinker, this grouping of elements by man was a matter of "organization", that is, the systematic and purposeful structuring of experience into complexes for his own benefit. Organized experience had many "levels" for Bogdanov. These were man-created and were characterized by the *degree* of their organization. "The primal world environment", inorganic nature, life, the human individual and "the human collective" constitute levels in the organization of experience by man, the last being the highest. [PLE, pp. 307–9] We will have more to say about these levels below and then later, when we deal with them as components of the "empiriomonistic world-picture". For the moment, we must look at another feature of Bogdanov's view of the organization of experience, that is, his handling of the concepts "physical" and "psychical".

For Bogdanov, it was necessary to discover what sort of definition of physicality and psychicality was compatible with the view of experience as a hierarchy of organizational levels. His goal was to drive every sort of dualism out of his view of experience and, most especially, to overcome the sort of dualism he saw in the empiriocritical division of experience. As we have seen, Bogdanov portrayed the essence of the empiriocritical view to be that, although the elements of experience themselves are homogeneous, that is, neither physical nor psychical in character, the ways in which elements were bound together have the character of being either physical or psychical. In other words, for Mach and Avenarius, there existed sets of physical and psychical laws which were essentially different from one another. [PLE, p. 280] [12] For Bogdanov, this view was yet another dualistic view of the world, since in a true monistic view, not only its elements but also the ways in which they are related must be subject to the same laws, or to put it in Bogdanov's language, to the same "organizing activity". [PLE, p. 281] From "the labor point of view", man may create and has created laws, organizational relationships, which apply in similarly useful fashion to physics and psychology, biology and sociology. All laws which do not are "narrow and fetishistic". [PLE, p. 281] Thus, in Bogdanov's opinion, for the empiriocritic to say that man creates one set of laws which is physical and another which is psychical denies man the possibility of organizing the elements of experience into a single, monistic system. [PLE, p. 281]

What, then, are the physical and psychical for Bogdanov? We have seen above that these terms apply neither to the material or mental in any usual sense nor to species of laws as in the empiriocritical view. Gustav Wetter finds that Bogdanov's physical and psychical are experience organized in two different *ways*, the former by the human collective and the latter by individual men.[13] While most commentators on Bogdanov would agree with this, it is not entirely correct in light of what we find in *The Philosophy of Living Experience*. In Wetter's statement, the social and individual organization of experience are implied to proceed by different methods, according to different laws. If this is the case, then Bogdanov must by his own criteria remain a dualist after the fashion of the Empiriocritics. One can see, however, not only in *The Philosophy of Living Experience* but also in Wetter's own citations from *Empiriomonism*, that the physical and psychical refer not to different *methods* of organization for Bogdanov but, rather, to different degrees or *levels*.[14] To say that socially organized "physical" experience differs from individually organized "psychical" experience is to say that the former exhibits a higher *level* of organization than the latter, while implying that the organization of both proceeds according to the same methods.

Here is what Bogdanov gives the reader. Consider, he suggested, an axe. It may exist either as a real tool for use in production or as a mental representation. The axe is a physical or mental complex. Each resides on a different level of organized experience, although they may be made up of the same elements, exhibit the same properties in the same relation to one another. What gives the axe its physicality is the fact that it exists as a definite complex of elements related in definite ways in the experience of all men. [PLE, pp. 281–2] This is not to say that the psychical axe is *identical* for all men; after all, some are physicists and chemists and others are woodcutters. While the axe is not identical for all, the differences are complementary rather than contradictory. [PLE, p. 282] Thus, a physical complex belongs to "the socially agreed-upon experience of men" or to "socially organized experience". [PLE, p. 282]

Gustav Wetter tells us that the distinctive feature of Bogdanov's physical experience is its objectivity.[15] In fact, however, the physical and objective are one and the same thing for him; objectivity *is* physicality rather than an attribute or feature of it. What is objective is that experience which is socially agreed-to, socially organized. As Bogdanov himself put it, "The objectivity of physical experience is its social organization". [PLE, p. 282] Everything else is "subjective" and, as we shall see, "individually organized" or "psychical".

In Bogdanov's example we see further that what makes the mental image of an axe a psychical and, therefore, subjective complex is the fact that it exists in individual experience alone and apart from the experience of others. While the mental image may indeed conform to the physical regarding its elements and their relation and to other's mental images as well, said Bogdanov, we have no way of knowing either to be the case from our individual experience alone. Thus the mental "axe" cannot be objective; it belongs to the level of experience of the individual and is, therefore, subjective and the product of "individually organized experience". [PLE, p. 282]

Objectivity and subjectivity, physicality and psychicality in Bogdanov's usage correspond to the levels of organized experience which he designates as the level of the human collective and the level of the individual human psyche respectively. Bogdanov, however, cautioned his readers not to confuse experience socially organized with ordinary social experience. The latter, he asserted, refers to simple possession while the former indicates a degree or level of organization. [PLE, p. 283] The distinction being made here is a bit difficult to see. If the objective is that which is socially agreed-to, then is it not socially possessed? Bogdanov's answer to this was, in effect, "yes, but not always". "Social experience" for Bogdanov implies possession in the sense of sharing the same elements of experience but not necessarily in an organized form. He noted that society had been in actual possession of the elements of the Copernican model of the cosmos before those elements had been properly organized to form that view. Because of this, the Copernican view was not commonly accepted as true. There was, however, no reason to deny its objectivity because of this. The Copernican view was objective for two reasons. First, it had been arrived at by the use of methods, the objectivity of which had been established. Secondly, the possibility of refuting the Copernican view by means of those same methods did not exist; it could be verified by anyone choosing to do so. [PLE, pp. 284–5] For Bogdanov, socially organized, objective experience is socially agreed-to in the sense that it is either totally accepted or totally acceptable. "Social possession" does not connote this; what constitutes social experience is that which is generally accepted at any given time. Bogdanov concluded that objective and socially possessed experience may not necessarily correspond. In fact, he said, more often than not they diverge, as in the case of Copernicus. In general, social experience lags behind the objective as everyday thought lags behind the scientific. [PLE, p. 309] As we noted with regard to his discussion of the scientific point of view,[16] one gets the impression that such may not always be the case in light of the promise of the era of machine production.

For Bogdanov, the objective or physical has no existence apart from man; it is socially created and subject to continual renewal and re-creation in accord with the collective needs of man. Accordingly, he attacked Plekhanov for maintaining that an objective, physical world with its laws of inertia and gravity had existed prior to man. The two had clashed on the matter of objectivity prior to the writing of *The Philosophy of Living Experience.*[17] Now, Bogdanov renewed the polemic in order to show the contrast between his own perspective and that of a thinker claiming to be at one with Marx with regard to objectivity. [PLE, p. 286] While Bogdanov was willing to concede that man had come into existence rather late in the history of the planet, he denied that the physical world as we know it could have existed prior to man. That world and its laws were the result of human activity and could not be divorced from it. Nature was not something to be "read" to establish what is objective. Nature was that which resisted human activity and was by itself non-objective. The world described by the laws of physics was objective by dint of the fact that it was the social-labor creation of man. [PLE, pp. 289–90]

Another clear and important implication of the "labor view" of the physical was that social conditions determine objectivity. Because of this, he said, what is objective at one time under one set of social conditions may not be so at another under different social conditions. Bogdanov pointed out that spirits were part of the socially organized experience for our ancestors. Once upon a time they had indeed been objective. Now, of course, they are not. [PLE, pp. 287–8] He chided Plekhanov for insisting that we must be able to say that spirits were not objective for our ancestors, since they are not for us. To insist on this, said Bogdanov, was to demand that what is objective must be absolute and eternal. It was one step away from saying that something could not be objective in the future because it did not exist in the objective experience of the present or past. [PLE, p. 288] If Plekhanov does not believe in the objectivity of spirits for our ancestors, said Bogdanov, he certainly believes in their modern-day successors, i.e., "absolute truth, absolute objectivity and absolute matter". [PLE, p. 288] Furthermore, Plekhanov's denial of the social-conditionality of the objective made him "non-dialectical, non-historical and non-Marxist". [PLE, p. 287]

As we indicated, Bogdanov brought up Plekhanov because he considered "the father of Russian Marxism" to be typical of those of his critics who claimed to be at one with Marx on the matter of objectivity. Apparently, the consensus opinion had been that Bogdanov was no more than an isolated eccentric and certainly no decent representative of Marx. Our thinker found this assessment ridiculous, since he considered his view of objectivity to be thoroughly Marxist. He reminded his reader that in the theses on Feuerbach, Marx had referred to the objective world as "social practice". Does this mean, he asked in effect, that objectivity is in no way absolute and eternal but something socially produced and therefore dependent on social-labor conditions? [PLE, p. 285] With this attempt to associate himself with Marx and to thereby discredit his critics, Bogdanov ended his discussion of the physical and psychical organization of experience from "the labor point of view".

From all this it should be apparent why Bogdanov entitled this section of the chapter on empiriomonism "Objectivity". It is concerned with just that. Bogdanov did not attempt to establish a view of objective reality based on either physical substance or physical law. "Physicality" and "objectivity" are synonymous. The physical according to his definition is devoid of all of the customary meanings and connotations of the term. Bogdanov might have avoided its use altogether but for the need to exorcise it. For our thinker, man organizes experience into levels differentiable by the degree of their organization and, with that, by the extent to which they are objective. Gustav Wetter comments that Bogdanov "thinks himself able to preserve the primacy of the physical over the mental order which is incumbent on any form of materialism . . . by positing a hierarchy of experience with the physical at the top".[18] While there may be an element of truth in this,[19] by making it Wetter obscures Bogdanov's purpose in dealing with the physical and psychical. Bogdanov was not some sort of unwitting materialist touting the primacy of a strangely conceived matter called "socially organized experience". Rather, he was an exponent of "the labor point of view" seeking a criterion of objectivity compatible with the "labor view" of experience. The objective is not primary for Bogdanov as matter is for the materialist. He does not begin with it; his starting point is "collective labor activity".[20] The objective, the physical, is the highest and most useful product of human activity, the world "objectified" by collective labor effort. The "physical" is primary only in the sense of being superior to other levels in organization. Because it is the product of a continuing creative process, it must remain a product and never become some sort of fixed base.

Bogdanov apparently felt that this "labor view" of objectivity guaranteed further the active character of empiriomonism. For him, a view of the objective world as something existing apart from man denied the potential of collective labor activity. From "the labor point of view" the objective world, the real, is socially created; man as a whole makes and changes it without limitations placed on him by some reality other than that which he has created or may create in time. If you will, Bogdanov's objective world is made up of all phenomena traditionally named physical and mental, which are totally accepted or totally acceptable by the whole of mankind.

D. SOCIOMORPHISM

In discussing the problem of objectivity, Bogdanov dealt, then, with different levels of organization and not, as some have suggested, with different methods of organization. In proposing to discover "how the elements of experience are grouped", he meant to deal with the character of the products of organization rather than with the act itself. In line with this, we have argued that Bogdanov's physical and psychical levels of experience are organized by the same methods. From his perspective, the axe and its mental representation are complexes of the same elements organized in the same way, in spite of the fact that they exist on different levels of experience. The criterion of objectivity is not determined by method but, rather, by the degree to which experience is socially organized. If all this is the case, then what does Bogdanov tell us about the act or method of organization itself?

The section of the chapter on the act of organization is very short; no more than four pages are devoted to it. [PLE, pp. 290–3] Apparently, Bogdanov felt that describing the basic method of organizing experience was a simple matter. If in other parts of the chapter he proposed to give the reader distinctly new concepts of causality, experience and objectivity, here Bogdanov simply meant to uncover an eternal fact about thought. In his view, the method by which experience is organized, i.e., the basic act of thought, was as old as words and ideas themselves and, furthermore, a method to be carried over as an integral part of "the labor worldview". [PLE, p. 290]

According to Bogdanov, experience is organized by the use of cognitive models which included everything from words, concepts and notions to laws, systems of laws and scientific theories. Among them, words and concepts are the most basic, causal notions the most important and systems of scientific laws and theories the most complex and useful. [PLE, p. 290] The question of how experience is organized is answered, according to our thinker, when one answers the question "Where do these models come from?" [PLE, p.291] He tells us in response that almost all cognitive models have their source in collective labor practice. Thus, man organizes experience by means of cognitive models which reflect and reinforce collective labor practice or, what is the same thing, the activity of production. [PLE, p. 291] The role given the mind in this is not entirely clear. At times, Bogdanov seems to suggest that the production of cognitive models is an act of derivation accomplished in thought. At other times, he seems to suggest that cognitive models are a natural product of collective labor practice itself. Whichever was actually Bogdanov's view, it is clear that the relationship between mind and collective labor practice is reciprocal, that cognitive models which reflect practice also reinforce it.

Bogdanov has given us innumerable examples of the character of cognitive models in the discussion of the character of past thought and, most especially, in his own definition of the concepts of "labor causality" and the "elements of experience". Models so derived Bogdanov called "sociomorphisms" [PLE, p. 291] and the law according to which the process of their creation and employment proceeds, "the law of sociomorphism". [PLE, p. 293] If there was any doubt that cognitive models are sociomorphisms, Bogdanov asked his readers to consider again the character of "word-ideas", the first elements of consciousness and, therewith, the first cognitive models. [PLE, p. 291] He implied that what is true for the most basic parts of thought must be true for the rest. The first word-ideas, which in his view arose out of the cries of labor, were clearly the products of social-labor activity and, therefore, the reflections of that activity in consciousness. [PLE, p. 291] If it is the case that thought develops in accord with the growth of social-labor practice and corresponds to its demands, said Bogdanov,

it follows that action precedes thought [which, in turn,] seizes upon the forms of that action: the practical organization of labor effort precedes the mental organization of the elements of experience and produces it. If so, then where may the means of the organization of experience come from if not from the means of the organization of [practical] activity? [PLE, pp. 291–2]

Bogdanov did not, however, limit the source of cognitive models to simple social-labor practice, that is, to the direct action of man on nature. For him √ they might also find their source in the methods of "social-labor technique" and economic relations. Bogdanov tells us that methods of technique are those means by which society is organized in its labor. Both are directly created and conditioned by the collective labor processes and have no existence of their own apart from it. [PLE, p. 292] It is in these methods and relations, for instance, that causal models have their source. [PLE, p. 292] If we recall Bogdanov's depiction of the career of causality, we see that he gives productive and economic relations as the source for authoritarian and abstract causal notions and the "technical relations of machine production" as the source for "labor causality".

Bogdanov cautioned his readers not to view the carry-over of methods of organization from the practical to the cognitive as either simple or direct. Changes may occur which involve simplification, complication or combination. It should be clear, he said, that while atomism is ultimately derived from human individualism, it is a gross simplification. By contrast, the spirit-matter duality in thought is a greatly complicated reflection of the organizer-implementor practical socio-economic relationship. [PLE, pp. 292–3]

In Bogdanov's view, then, the "sociomorphism" is the necessary and universal means by which experience is organized. It is surprising that more space was not devoted to its elaboration. While the concept itself is simple enough, its implications are enormous. Bogdanov speaks of the great difficulties involved in finding the ultimate source of certain ideas. "Simplifications, complications and combinations" accompany the transfer from the practical to the cognitive. How and why does this occur? Bogdanov tells us only that it does and implies that an investigation of the matter would not alter the basic fact that man thinks by means of sociomorphisms. [PLE, p. 293]

The implications of the law of sociomorphism for the proponent of "the labor worldview" must be obvious to the reader. Bogdanov encourages him to take, or accept, cognitive models from the developing activity and relations of modern machine production. [PLE, p. 293] Implied in the concept of sociomorphism is the idea that cognitive models not only come from but also reinforce the practical methods on which they are based. The cognitive models of the proletarian era, beginning with the labor model of causality, although in a way inevitable, may be and, indeed, should be sought out. In addition, accepting the law of sociomorphism allows the proponent of the new worldview to jettison ways of thinking which conform to the activity and relationships of earlier modes of production, especially those conforming to capitalism and bourgeois socio-economic relations. For Bogdanov, the philosopher must be free to employ those methods of organizing experience which correspond to the productive, economic and social needs of his class. He must see himself as the ultimate creator of the tools of thought, because he is the ultimate source of the activity and relations of production on which thought depends. Accordingly, man is not subject to the demands of the methods of organization, they are subject to his will and needs.

E. SUBSTITUTION

Bogdanov held out the sociomorphism as the basic and universal tool employed in the organization of expereince. Its use constituted the method of organization itself. In the penultimate section of the chapter, he asked how experience is unified and systematized to form a whole free from discontinuity and contradiction. If the use of sociomorphisms is the method of organization, then how are "sociomorphisms" related to one another to form a continuous whole? [PLE, p.293] For Bogdanov, this sort of whole had been the goal of all philosophy and was to be the aim of the "labor worldview" as well.

He tells us that the method of systematizing experience into a whole is, like the method of organization itself, at once as old as speech and thought and as new as contemporary aspirations toward a monistic "labor worldview" [PLE, p. 293] All thought has employed it and a truly active philosophy must do so continuously and systematically. That method, said Bogdanov, is "universal substitution". [PLE, p. 293] In other places in *The Philosophy of Living Experience*, Bogdanov spoke of substitution as an elemental fact about thought. Again, he reiterated the argument that man began substituting when he uttered his first words, conceived his first ideas. The word "axe" is a sociomorphism, to be sure, but it is also something substituted for something else with which it has nothing whatever in common but which "corresponds to it, is bound with it in a strict, definite and continuous manner". The use of substitution in this way makes possible the greater manipulation of the world (experience), since man subjects to manipulation both the word and that thing or activity to which it is bound. The word is manipulated by the activity of consciousness, while the thing signified is subject to the activity of direct labor. [PLE, pp. 293–4] Substitution, then refers, to the replacement of one complex of elements of experience by another or, if you will, of one sociomorphism by another, for the greater understanding and usefulness, the greater manipulation of experience which is attained by doing so. [PLE, p. 294]

For Bogdanov, substitution is the basic way in which man brings various phenomena into relationships, the way in which he explains things. He tells us that to say the sun is a star, a conglomeration of gases in space which behaves in accord with the laws of motion, is to substitute something for the sun as it is visually apprehended by man. Here a visual phenomenon is related to a chemical and physical one. [PLE, p. 294] The process of relating according to Bogdanov actually amounts to replacing one complex of elements with another in thought. The sun as visual phenomenon is actually replaced by something else with which it has nothing in common but to which it certainly relates and corresponds. [PLE, p. 294] According to Bogdanov, substitution is employed on all levels of thought including those of philosophical and scientific explanation. These latter are merely the most sophisticated but differ in no basic way from early man's substitution of the word "sun" for a certain visual phenomenon. [PLE, p. 294]

According to Bogdanov, there is a law by which substitution proceeds, to wit:

We see that in place of complexes more simple, more defined and stable, it sets those more complicated, richer in elements but less defined, less [tightly] bound [together] : from simple and more organized contents it moves toward the more complex but less organized. [PLE, p. 300]

We will attempt a restatement and interpretation of this shortly, but for the moment we must give Bogdanov's explanation of why this law, this "tendency", exists. If one takes "the labor point of view", he said, knowledge may be seen as the product of effort and the result of the struggle with nature. If this is taken to be the case,

then it becomes clear to us that the production of knowledge, like the production of all other things, may be completed all the more successfully *when the material* with which it has to deal is *richer* and *the less resistance* it encounters. When we apply this conclusion to the method of substitution, it becomes apparent that substitution in *general* strives to replace lesser contents with greater [ones], permitting more combinations in consciousness such that the material for processing will be richer, and, at the same time, to replace complexes more simple and strictly organized with less structured, less organized complexes such that the resistance to the processing activity will be less. [PLE, pp. 300–1]

With this he gives us a concrete example of how substitution proceeds in accord with the law. Take, he suggested, a ray of light as it is directly perceived. This is a simple complex made up of a relatively small number of visual elements in simple, limited relationships. There is little we can do with it besides describe its path and explain the fact that something else may be illuminated by it. Suppose we observe that two such rays, combined in a certain way, cause darkness. Nothing about our simple complex makes this observation explainable. In order to do so, we must resort to substitution. We replace the light ray visually perceived by another complex richer in contents and less simply organized; we hold that the ray of light is wave-form movement in space, i.e., something outside of visual experience. If we say that light is a wave, i.e., something that has length, amplitude and frequency, then we may explain the observation that two rays of light cause darkness by saying that the two waves of the same length interfere with one another and cancel one another out. [PLE, p. 301]

What Bogdanov is saying here is quite simple, although it is not simply put.

For him, each substitution turns a simpler, less plastic complex with which man may do relatively little in consciousness or practice into one which is more complex, more plastic, and, therefore, more useful. It must occur to the reader that this is a particularly complex way of saying that man goes behind phenomena directly perceived to find out as much as he can about them, in order to relate them in some systematic way to one another. Of course, it is just that, but there is more to the matter. Bogdanov proposes that substitution is the basic method of bringing experience together into a continuous whole and that all such acts of unification amount to the same thing. The utility of this view is that it allows man the most important place in the structuring of experience, since he is the one who substitutes. For Bogdanov, calling a ray of light a wave is a human act. [PLE, p. 301] If light is a wave, it is a wave because man makes it so. One does not approach a phenomenon on the assumption that its elements are somehow natural to it and that most of them are hidden from direct perception. Man himself creates these elements in Bogdanov's view.

How does substitution fit into the "labor world view"? Bogdanov noted that his previous discussions hopefully convinced the reader that "the labor worldview" must be constructed on the basis of "labor causality"; that is, man should look at any phenomenon or process in nature as the source of every other for the labor collective in its practical and cognitive activity. [PLE, p. 303] Now we find, he said, that the structured and integral organization of experience may be achieved only by means of substitution. "Is this a contradiction?" he asked. "Are these two different methods of reaching the same goal?" [PLE, p. 303] Bogdanov answered, "No", to both questions; labor causality and substitution are two forms of the same thing, and "the new form of causal bond becomes the basis and explanation of substitution". [PLE, p. 303] Take for example, he said, the "scientific and technical substitution" which states that white light is the sum of the colored rays of the spectrum. This is at the same time a case of the new causality, since the sum of colored light is the technical source of white light and vice versa. [PLE, p. 303] Similarly, in optics, one meets two different expressions of what light is: "light *is* wave-form movement in ether," and "light phenomena *are caused by* wave-form movement in ether". The first is substitution, the second is causal explanation, but their objective sense is exactly the same. [PLE, pp. 303–4]

In the doctrine of substitution, as in the doctrine of labor causality, Bogdanov encourages man to deal with experience in all possible ways in accord with collective labor practice and its needs. To say that a certain phenomenon is "wave-form movement in space" instead of "a ray of light" makes that phenomenon more understandable and useful to man. One supposes that Bogdanov would countenance calling that same phenomenon "a codfish swimming in space" if doing so made it more rich in contents, more plastic, and with that more readily subject to integration with the rest of experience. In short, no sort of substitution is forbidden in his view as long as it advances the progress of knowledge. For him knowledge is experience manipulated in consciousness reflecting collective labor practice and conforming to its demands. If man may make one thing the cause or source of another, he may as well substitute one thing for another. What determines the possibility and propriety of this in Bogdanov's view is the collective will and need, along with collective practical and cognitive ability.

Apparently because he sees the tendency to substitute as having been fundamental and universal, Bogdanov encourages would-be exponents of "the labor worldview" to practice it systematically and continuously, i.e., universally and with the idea in mind that nothing outside of man proscribes that practice. [PLE, p. 310] The implications of this point of view are clear: man is permitted and encouraged to relate all the contents of experience in all possible ways. The boundaries between categories of phenomena vanish as man finds that sociomorphisms associated with one category serve to explain, to organize, those in another. This disappearance of boundaries had long since begun according to Bogdanov. After all, he said, had Marx not applied the biological notion of natural selection to society in order to better understand the class struggle? [PLE, p. 293] In conclusion, he asserted that the doctrine of "universal substitution" along with that of "labor causality" demands that man break down the boundaries and forge a monistic system of experience where "one method, one tendency reigns". [PLE, p. 293] That tendency was "universal substitution".

F. THE "EMPIRIOMONISTIC" WORLD-PICTURE

The ultimate segment of Bogdanov's presentation of empiriomonism begins with a statement to the effect that universal substitution proposes to work out a "strict, continuous and integral, monistic picture of the world". [PLE, p. 307] Now that we have been told what may be expected from the practice of universal substitution, Bogdanov tells us how that world-picture should appear, and we are shown the ultimate product of "the labor point of view".

According to Bogdanov, the world should appear in consciousness as "an endless stream of organizing activities", meaning an infinite series of levels of organized experience integrally and continuously related to one another. [PLE, p. 307] Since each successive level is more organized, it is "higher" than the one preceding it. At the highest level, that of "the human collective", the endless stream is pushed ever farther along by collective will acting in response to collective need. In spite of the fact that the stream is supposedly continuous, Bogdanov chose to break it into four major levels, those of "the primal world environment", inorganic nature, life, and "the collective organism of humanity". [PLE, pp. 307–9] As we proceed in describing these, the reader will undoubtedly wonder whether Bogdanov is not actually speaking of the progress of the world in conventional historical or, perhaps, in Comtean positivist terms, since each major level seems to correspond to a stage in the natural-historical development of the world and life. While Bogdanov may be a historical materialist and a positivist as well, his world as an "endless stream of organizing activities" is the world as it is now, that is, as it has become and promises to be. All levels of organized experience coexist with one another as they make up the total content of the world as we know it. Because they have been, are, and will continue to be the products of the same organizational method, each level is integrally related to those before and after, below and above, it. Indeed, all levels are complementary to one another. Bogdanov breaks up the endless stream in order to depict it as it is, that is, to show that, for example, what is conventionally called inorganic matter is not an isolated realm with its own laws, but a level of organized experience *among* other levels.

Here is how Bogdanov depicts the four major levels of experience. The lowest possible level of organization, he said, is that which we call variously "the primal world environment", "the elemental universe", and "ether with its electrical and light waves". On this level the world is a chaotic mass of elements with next to no organization at all. If organization is defined in terms of resistance to activity, then the chaos of elements offers infinitely little resistance. This level represents the lower limit of organized experience and man, of course, cannot possibly think about it in any real way. [PLE, p. 307] The second of the four levels is that of inorganic nature "with its internal atomic and inter-atomic energies". On this level, said Bogdanov, we find the elements of experience organized into stable complexes and those complexes organized in a relatively systematic way. [PLE, pp. 307–8] On the third level, that of life, we find a much higher degree of organization of complexes. What distinguishes the organization of life from that of inorganic nature is that its complexes, i.e., life forms, are self-perpetuating while inorganic complexes are not reconstituted by their own activity. In itself, life shows a series of varying degrees of organization, from the simplest cells to the human organism. Parallel to this series we find a series of psychical complexes from those peculiar to micro-organisms to the psyches of individual men. This is the level of subjective, individually organized experience. [PLE, p. 308] The fourth level is that of the human collective, "a multi-million part system composed of individuals in social relation to one another". On this level, life not only perpetuates itself but also expands and reconstructs the world. This socially constructed and still-to-be-constructed world, this realm of the conquering forces of labor and thought, this kingdom of socially organized elements of the universe, is the most grandiose and complete manifestation of life that we know. [PLE, p. 308] Bogdanov tells us that

such is our picture of the world: an uninterrupted series of forms of the organization of elements, developing in struggle and eternal action, without a beginning in the past, without an end in the future. [PLE, p. 309]

What was empiriomonism for Bogdanov? That is, what did he intend it to be? In advance of his ultimate statement on its role in the history of thought, we may say the following: first, and most importantly, empiriomonism was intended to be a philosophy which arose on the basis of insights into the realities of the machine age, the structure and tenets of which reflected and reinforced man's ability to make and remake the world at his convenience. This was Empiriomonism as "the labor worldview". Because it alone responded to the demands of "the labor point of view" in the age of "world-building" Bogdanov deemed empiriomonism new and different from all worldviews preceding it. Secondly, and in accord with the above, empiriomonism was meant to be a philosophy which gave man a totally active role vis-à-vis the world as creator and determiner of all things and the relation-ships between them. For Bogdanov, the empiriomonistic point of view allowed man to determine what may be a cause and what an effect. It made him the creator of reality ("experience") and its components (the "elements of experience") as entities arising from his need in line with his will and ability. Empiriomonism made man the sole determiner of what was objective and the organizer of reality via his labor activity, both physical and mental. It demanded that he weld reality into a unified whole through his labor practice, i.e., via "the transformation of effort or energy" and by devising a system of knowledge which related or made relatable every part of reality and every other part. Thirdly, and again in line with the above, empiriomonism was intended to be a worldview which freed man from all external limitations. According to its tenets, there were no "natural" laws, no necessary causal sequences. There was no "being" which man did not create and fashion according to the needs of his activity and, likewise, no absolute and eternal facts about the world. There were no ultimate building blocks to reality, no isolated worlds within the world. There were only building blocks and separate worlds which man created on a temporary basis at his own convenience for his own benefit. There was no bar to the creation of a world-picture comprised of homogeneous parts, fully related and infinitely relatable by man-created laws.

Of course, empiriomonism purported to be the solution to the contemporary problem of philosophy on account of the above. That it fulfilled the requirements Bogdanov set down for contemporary philosophy in the introductory part of the work is implied.[21] It is useful for us, however, to list those requirements and to show how Bogdanov appeared to fulfill them, since doing so illuminates the unity of the work.

1) That philosophy be "a tool of guidance in practice and thought". Empiriomonism purported to be such a tool since it was philosophy from "the labor point of view", and since it attempted to make philosophy a device aiding in the pursuit of, and integral to, every aspect of human activity.

2) That philsophy be "scientific", that is, based "on the collective experience of mankind controlled by collectively produced methods" Empiriomonism purported to be this on the strength of its central concern with "collective labor activity", its social-labor perspective on reality, and the breadth of its "objective" world-picture.

3) That contemporary philosophy not be the concern of specialists, "since specialization contradicts the task and sense of scientific philosophy". Empiriomonism purported to deal with all aspects of life inasmuch as the essence of life is "collective labor activity". Every man was its ultimate practitioner, the advancement of the life of mankind its purpose, a monistic world-picture and the concern of philosophy with all aspects of life its goal and predicted result.

4) That philosophy be viewed as a reflection of contemporary reality and no other, and that it make no claims to being absolute and eternal in the truths it imparts. Empiriomonism purported to be this in that it reflected present reality in its every tenet and as a whole, i.e., in its "labor perspective", in its causal notion, in its view of the world as "experience" and "elements of experience", in its view of the methods of knowledge, etc. That empiriomonism did not claim to apply to past realities is clear. That it did not claim to be the final form of thought will be seen in the next chapter.

5) That philosophy serve the progressive social class of its time, since that

class alone is in possession of the collected experience of mankind, and, with that, the scientific point of view. That empiriomonism purported to serve the proletariat in the present and future is not obvious in this chapter, but it is made clear elsewhere in *The Philosophy of Living Experience.* The "mankind" of which and to which Bogdanov speaks is either proletarian or soon to become so. His designation of the proletariat as the advanced segment of society and the progressive force which must needs develop a new world-view suggests this, as does Bogdanov's vision of the inevitable correspondence of the proletariat and mankind. In addition, we learn in the chapter on Marx that proceeding from "the labor point of view" meant capitalizing on the experience of the proletariat in the new era of machine production. As we shall see in the next chapter, Bogdanov's future world was one of men as the worker-organizers of automated production. Their prototype was the class-conscious proletarian of the present, and it was for these men that empirio-monism was intended.

6) That contemporary philosophy possess a causal notion suited to present reality. Empiriomonism purported to have such a notion in "labor causality". This notion was suited to the present because it makes man the determiner of all cause-effect sequences.

7) That philosophy understand the contents of consciousness as "socio-morphisms", i.e., cognitive devices derived from "living" social relations, and recognize or create those "sociomorphisms" which reflect and reinforce contemporary "living" social relations. Empiriomonism purported to do this in its rejections of "sociomorphisms" arising from past realities and by suggesting new ones, such as "labor causality", which reflected and reinforced present realities.

8) That philosophy understand "substitution" as the fundamental and eternal way of relating the parts of the world to one another and seek a notion of it most fitting for present thought. Empiriomonism accordingly purported to practice substitution, to reject its materialist, idealist and sensualist forms, and to possess the inclination to use substitution systematically, continuously and universally to build a monistic world-picture to coincide with the world as unified by contemporary labor practice.

It should be clear from all that has been said with regard to what empirio-monism was meant to be and how it purported to solve the problem of philosophy that Bogdanov considered himself the author of something genuinely new in philosophy. In a sentence, we might say that empirio-monism is new for Bogdanov because the reality apprehended from "the labor point of view" was itself new. In line with our earlier claims that empiriomonism was meant to be a philosophy beyond Marxism and Machian critical positivism, we would like now to suggest that Bogdanov's principal measure of its newness was how and the extent to which empiriomonism superseded them. Now that we have examined empiriomonism, we may finally conclude on the relationship of Bogdanov, Marx and Mach as it is expressed in *The Philosophy of Living Experience*. Doing this will permit as well a final statement regarding the uniqueness of empiriomonism for Bogdanov.

We have seen that Bogdanov considered himself to be at one with the empiriocritics on numerous issues. Principally, he claimed to share with them a view of primary reality as something different from traditional concepts of matter, idea or individual sensation. With this, he approved of the "impersonal realism" of empiriocriticism, that is, its notion that what is "given" to man (for Bogdanov the world of resistance to human action) is an environment filled with both things and mental facts which are the same order of thing for being comprised of homogeneous parts. Bogdanov claimed as well to share the empiriocritics' desire to end the false division of reality into separate realms, especially those usually designated "physical" and "psychical". Further, our thinker approved of their "active" goal for knowledge which demanded that it serve the struggle with nature, as well as the empiriocritics' practical criterion of truth and the principle of economy of thought. Most generally, Bogdanov claimed to share the Machist aversion to materialist substitution, the concept of being as matter, and causal necessity.

From Bogdanov's point of view, empiriomonism had gone beyond Mach in pursuit of the solution to the contemporary problem of philosophy for the principal reason that it presented a view of reality which fully eschewed the concept of being as matter and, with that, the practice of materialist substitution. Additionally, Bogdanov considered himself beyond the empiriocritics' "impersonal realism", because he had united that which resists human activity, i.e., things and mental facts, with human activity itself in the notion of "experience". With this, the separation of man and his environment ended and reality became fully the product of man's action on that which resists it. For Bogdanov, the "sensual-labor" nature of "experience" and its parts made the empiriomonistic view of reality a thing apart from, and a great advance over, the empiriocritical presentation of "the given".

Bogdanov believed he had superseded the Machists in finally overcoming physical-mental dualism by suggesting that there were only levels of organization in a world which was otherwise uniform in its parts and in the way in which those parts were connected. For him, not only were the parts of reality homogeneous but the methods by which reality was ordered were the same whether one dealt with things or with mental facts. That empiriomonism went beyond critical positivism was also suggested by the fact that it sought not only an active goal for knowledge as a "tool of guidance" for man but also an active role for man in determining both the contents and methods of knowledge. According to Bogdanov, where the empiriocritics had only permitted a description of that which resisted human effort, empiriomonism allowed man to create that which resisted and to explain the world pursuant to shaping it for his own benefit. Empiriomonism also purported to advance active knowledge by generating a criterion of objectivity which included but went beyond the empiriocritical notion of success in practical application and by expressing a belief not only in the "economic" expenditure of effort in the pursuit of knowledge but also a belief in that effort's fullest, most fruitful and most efficient utilization. Finally, and most obviously, Bogdanov considered himself to be beyond Mach in achieving notions of causality and substitution which were genuinely new in comparison to their Empiriocritical counterparts.

In the matter of detailing the relationship of empiriomonism and Marxist materialism, the process of comparison need be no different than the one above. While Bogdanov obviously considered himself closer to Marx in that the two shared "collective labor activity" as a central concern and "the labor point of view" as their point of departure in philosophy, empiriomonism was meant to stand nearly as much in advance of Marxist materialism as it was intended to be beyond Empiriocriticism.

We have seen that Bogdanov purported to share with Marx the notion that philosophy should be a means for changing the world as well as explaining it and, as we have noted, the notion that philosophy must accordingly take "collective labor activity" and the experience of the proletariat as a central concern. In Bogdanov's view, the essence of man for both himself and Marx was to be found in collective labor relations and the starting-point of philosophy was to be "the labor point of view". Additionally, we have seen that Bogdanov approved of Marx's view of "the material" as a correlate of activity, i.e., as resistance, and something different from matter as being-in-itself. It is also apparent that Bogdanov favored Marx's notion that there is a universal process to reality and his assertion that there is a "real" dialectical process as well.

In spite of the notions and perspectives shared with Marx, Bogdanov considered empiriomonism to have taken philosophy well beyond Marxist materialism. As the creator of "philosophy from the labor point of view", he purported to have proceeded in ways in advance of those of Marx. For Bogdanov, empiriomonism had taken shape in full accord with the demands of the contemporary "labor point of view" and, as a result, had proceeded step-by-step from the "labor" notion of causality, to the "labor" view of reality and on to new concepts of the method and unity of knowledge. By fully examining the character of labor activity as it appeared in the present and by bringing it into correlation with a concept of that which resists, Bogdanov considered that he had created a notion of reality of which Marx had had only partial knowledge.

By freeing considerations of the world process from idealistic influences and by setting forth a notion broader in scope than the dialectic, Bogdanov claimed to have uncovered the universal which Marx had failed to find. While Marx argued that universal process was dialectical, Bogdanov claimed that it was "organizational", i.e., an advance in orderliness proceeding in various ways, among them, dialectically. That Bogdanov considered the notion of "organization" to be in advance of Marx's concept was further suggested by the implication that even the universal organizational process was man-created, i.e., a feature of reality given to it by man. In formulating a view of the dialectic in contradistinction to that of Marx, Bogdanov made claim to uncovering the "real" dialectic with which contemporary philosophy had to be concerned.

That Bogdanov considered himself beyond Marx and Mach seems unquestionable. That he actually escaped their influence as well as that of all previous philosophers is, of course, more difficult to establish. Because it is our task to describe the relationship of Bogdanov, Marx and Mach as it appears in *The Philosophy of Living Experience,* we must conclude with Bogdanov that their influence on him was not considered to be a determining one. The most we can say regarding their direct influence is that empirio-criticism, on the one hand, gave Bogdanov a notion as to how he might supplant traditional concepts of being and reality. On the other hand, we can only claim that Marxist materialism gave him a notion of contemporary philosophy's purpose. If we consider what these contributions amount to, then we can only conclude that what Bogdanov took from Marx and Mach were a relatively few general notions and perspectives. While it is the case that he proceeded from these in creating empiriomonism, this process was procedure from shared perspectives rather than from shared principles. Even "the labor point of view" amounts to a shared perspective, since the philosophic principle Bogdanov made from it is one entirely his own. As it appears in *The Philosophy of Living Experience,* empiriomonism is something quite different from empiriocriticism and Marxist materialism. Its tenets, their sources and the manner of their succession, as well as the world-picture empiriomonism offers, can in no way be viewed as basically determined by the influence of Marxist or Machist principles. We are led to conclude with Bogdanov that empiriomonism was meant to be *in principle* a philosophy apart from empiriocriticism and Marxist materialism.

In bringing this chapter to a close, we would like to offer one further comment as to why Bogdanov considered empiriomonism a genuinely new worldview particularly in its relation to empiriocriticism and Marxist materialism. We have noted that Bogdanov judged his efforts original because empiriomonism purported to reflect and reinforce a new and different reality. While this is certainly the case, we would like to suggest further that what made empiriomonism a philosophy beyond all past philosophies for Bogdanov was its purported total response to the demand that a contemporary worldview be a tool of guidance. His notion of philosophy from "the labor point of view" suggests that the purpose of philosophy is to serve man's "world-building" activity. Accordingly, if man comes to successfully defy causal necessity in his labor practice, then philosophy must free consciousness from the notion of causal necessity and offer a new concept which encourages man to continue to defy causal necessity in practice. If man is principally the creator and determiner of reality rather than its passive contemplator, then philosophy must serve him first and foremost as a tool and only secondarily as a passive explanation of the world. Bogdanov's arguments regarding the inadequacy of past thought for present conditions make passivity its greatest flaw and weakness. As we have seen, he judged empiriocriticism to be merely the highest expression of contemplative philosophy. Marxism, of course, had escaped the tendency toward contemplation in Bogdanov's eyes. In spite of its active purpose, however, Marxism could not be the tool needed for the new "world-building". For Bogdanov, Marxism lacked those "active" notions of causality, reality and knowledge which had to accompany an "active" purpose in a worldview solving the contemporary problem of philosophy. Because empiriomonism was "active" both in purpose and tenets, Bogdanov considered it to be the first and only worldview fully conforming to the demands of the contemporary "labor point of view" for a completely active worldview.

With this, we leave behind the largest aspect of *The Philosophy of Living Experience.* The contemporary problem of philosophy has been posed, past worldviews have been judged unsuitable solutions to it, and, finally, the solution has been offered. With that, we also leave behind the matter of Bogdanov, Marx and Mach. As we have noted, Bogdanov's concern with the contemporary problem of philosophy is not his ultimate concern in the work. In the following chapter, we will see very clearly that Bogdanov considered empiriomonism to be but a step beyond all previous philosophies and, yet, not an end to human progress in thought. In "The Science of the Future", our thinker applied the notion that all thought is socially and historically conditioned in the generation of a perspective on empiriomonism's role in the progress of man as "world-builder". The outcome of this was an argument for empiriomonism as the *last* philosophy and a vision of the character of human practice and thought in the future beyond it. According to Bogdanov, empiriomonism would have to give way to something which was not philosophy at all but a form of practical and cognitive activity better suited to world-building as it promised to proceed in the future. As we shall see, the present was already giving way for Bogdanov. In closing *The Philosophy of Living Experience,* he tells us that

Philosophy is already living out its last days. Empiriomonism is already not wholly philosophy but a transitional form, because it knows where it is going and to what it will have to give place. [PLE, p. 327]

CHAPTER V

THE SCIENCE OF THE FUTURE

"The Science of the Future" is in many ways an essay standing apart from all the rest of *The Philosophy of Living Experience*. Because of this, we have suggested that it adds a dimension to the work which makes its broadest concern something other than the contemporary problem of philosophy. In it, Bogdanov takes the reader back to the matter of philosophy and life after the fashion of the introductory essays. This time, however, it is done with a view toward predicting the future of both and the outcome of the relationship between them. The basic effect which the chapter has on the rest of the work is the addition of an ultimate statement on the historical role of philosophy which is, by extension, a statement on the ultimate meaning and significance of empiriomonism as well. We find, however, that this effect arises from a discussion of something other than philosophy itself. The topic under consideration in "The Science of the Future" is actually the future of *knowledge,* and, at the bottom, the essay is an argument regarding the probable future relationship between *knowledge* and life. We find, then, that knowledge, which comprises both philosophy and science, is Bogdanov's greater concern and that, for him, the historical role of philosophy can only be known within the greater context of the future of knowledge. We are told, in effect, that while the problem of philosophy holds man's attention in the present, it will not always be so, for philosophy is not that form of knowledge with which man must ultimately be most concerned.

The above, we believe, is the view of "The Science of the Future" which Bogdanov wished his readers to take. It is clear that he intended to turn their attention and the flow of *The Philosophy of Living Experience* away from the problem of philosophy and toward the more important matter of the problem of knowledge. While we will discuss it from this perspective, we will emphasize its statement on the historical meaning and significance of philosophy in order to bring the chapter into line with the rest of the work. Previously, we described "The Science of the Future" as an argument for the end of philosophy and a vision of the future beyond it. If this is understood as a description of the effect the discussion of knowledge has on the rest of the work, then we have not misrepresented it.

Actually, "The Science of the Future" has several effects in addition to those mentioned above. For one thing, it provides a picture of the practice of science in the present which complements Bogdanov's depiction of the contemporary practice of philosophy in the work's introduction. While it advances a startling view of the ultimate form of knowledge, i.e., the science of the future, the chapter presents an equally startling view of the character of life (read: "collective labor activity") in the future. In these aspects, as well as in its statement on the future of philosophy, "The Science of the Future" enters into and completes the flow of *The Philosophy of Living Experience.*

"The Science of the Future" begins with an argument regarding the aspiration of knowledge toward unity and the reasonableness of struggling against its specialized practice. Bogdanov asserted that all knowledge, whether philosophical or scientific, is the organization (read: "ordering") of experience in consciousness. Because all organization strives to create an integral whole of that with which it deals, aspiration toward unity is a fundamental and enduring characteristic of knowledge. [PLE, p. 312] To dispel any doubts about this fact, Bogdanov reminded his readers that man had originally sought and actually achieved a complete monistic system of knowledge in the religious worldviews which lived out their careers prior to the appearance of exchange society. [PLE, p. 312] How and why, he asked, was a monistic system of knowledge possible in that era? It was so, he responded, because that era was one of slave labor and because slave labor was undifferentiated. As knowledge reflects and reinforces production, the system of knowledge in an era of uniform, undifferentiated labor must itself be uniform and undifferentiated. Without the division of labor, knowledge did not need to be broken up into various specialities. Bogdanov went on to argue that, of course, this condition did not and could not endure. Just as slave labor gave way to the specialized labor activity of exchange society, so did the monism of the religious worldview give way to fragmentation in knowledge: both trends were part of the progress of mankind. [PLE, pp. 312–13]

What, Bogdanov asked, are we to make of the fact that knowledge has moved steadily away from unity and that, in its present state, knowledge appears to contradict what we know to be its basic tendency? He argued in answer to this that the trend toward specialization was actually neither absolute nor a true representation of the progress and direction of knowledge in the present. In this era of accentuated specialization, he claimed, the need for unity was not forgotten. [PLE, p. 313] In fact, if one looked at the revolutions in contemporary science, one might see that modern science advances largely on account of its aspiration toward unity. Bogdanov noted that Darwin and Marx, for example, had broken down the boundaries of specialization to push scientific knowledge ahead. The former had applied Malthus's economic constructs in the solution of biological problems, while the latter had brought the dialectic out of philosophy into the study of history and society. All of this, he said, speaks to us of the possibility and even the necessity of surmounting specialization and unifying scientific methods. [PLE, pp. 314–15]

Although the above forms the introduction to an argument regarding the limitations of philosophy in the struggle for greater unity in human labor practice and knowledge, it sets the tone and establishes the subject-matter of "The Science of the Future". We are told, in effect, that the unity of knowledge has been lost to man on account of progress in labor practice and the growth of knowledge, its servant. Because knowledge exhibits a basic tendency toward unity, however, the specialization which typifies its current practice can only be a temporary condition. For Bogdanov the present, in spite of the appearance of machine production and the proletariat as the progressive class, is still part of the era of exchange society and, therefore, a time when specialized methods of knowledge predominate. This situation must be seen as masking the tendency of knowledge toward monism, and man must, accordingly, strive to end specialization. For Bogdanov, the question arises as to how this might be accomplished. As we shall see presently, philosophy itself cannot end specialization. According to Bogdanov, man must look elsewhere if he hopes to advance the unity of knowledge.

We must recognize, said our thinker, that philosophy is like all other forms of knowledge in that it is "the striving to organize experience into a unified whole". [PLE, p. 315] Unlike other forms of knowledge, of course, it attempts to organize *all* of experience into a complete and fully integrated world-picture. The creation of such a world-picture is its ultimate purpose and historical calling. [PLE p. 315] However, said Bogdanov, there is a basic inadequacy of philosophy which results from its very purpose. The best philosophy may do is to reflect and reinforce reality in a unified world-picture; it may not by itself create a greater unity than that which exists in actuality. [PLE, p. 315] At present, human labor practice and, with that, the social experience of man is fragmented. Is it possible for philosophy to unify that which is fragmented in actuality? Objectively, it is not, said Bogdanov, and it may be objectively possible . . .

only when actuality itself is changed, when practice ceases to be fragmented and specialization in knowledge no longer reigns. No effort of thought can gather and organize the parts of a shattered body into a living whole. Philosophy cannot work miracles. [PLE, pp. 315–16]

According to Bogdanov, this limitation did not mean that philosophy is a fruitless, meaningless activity. Philosophy still had an important role in the advance of unity, since man was ever in need of a unified world-picture reflecting the unity of actuality as it stood. [PLE, p. 316] At present, philosophy could not complete its task, said Bogdanov, because society and its experience were not organized in the whole. However, society is not an absolutely anarchical system and the division of labor does not signify the disintegration of the social whole into absolutely separated units.

Specialization *predominates* over the opposite tendency, the struggle between capitalists and other groups *predominates* over their unity: but intercourse exists, specialties are not so separated that there is no contact between them. The collective organization of experience proceeds .... [PLE, p. 316]

In actuality, Bogdanov asserted, specialization only obscures the growth of unity in practice and knowledge, and that growth continues apace. It follows from this, he argued, that philosophy may and must organize social experience to the extent that such experience is unifiable in actuality. Within this limit, it may be monistic and objective; beyond it, philosophy will be arbitrary and subjective. [PLE, p. 316] The practice of philosophy is hardly fruitless; it continuously prepares the way for the further unification of experience in labor practice and the pursuit of knowledge by bringing together what is unifiable at any given time. Without a sense of the unity of experience man cannot strive for greater unity. To accord philosophy the ability to change actuality is, of course, unreasonable, for "philosophy does not produce the experience it organizes". [PLE, p. 316]

According to Bogdanov, it is to man's practical labor activity that one must look in order to find the starting-point for the further unification of experience. Labor practice draws thought after it or, rather, gives the basis and possibility of thought. A more unified actuality gives rise to the greater unity of experience in consciousness. For Bogdanov, the task at hand for man was the unification and integration of practice itself and, with that, the merging of special methods of science, which directly serve production, into a single, universal scientific method. [PLE, pp. 317–18] Philosophy would have no direct role in the creation of these unities; the best it might (and must) do would be to bring new experience into its monistic world-picture. [PLE, p. 318]

What are we told here? First, we find that for Bogdanov all philosophy (and we can only assume that he includes Empiriomonism as well) has a limitation. He argues, in effect, that the historical calling of philosophy, i.e., to provide a complete and systematic understanding of actuality as it is, keeps it from being a direct agent in the process of changing the world. It may urge man to change actuality according to his needs, ability and will. It may be "active", that is, it may suggest a direction and a program for change in the sense that it encourages man to start from and then to go beyond what he has already accomplished in the organization of practice and knowledge. But, in itself, philosophy may not create a greater organization of experience than actually exists at any given time. Secondly, we are told that the process of changing actuality occurs fundamentally in the realm of labor practice. We are also told, however, that scientific knowledge, because of the way in which it serves production, must have a direct role in the advance of the unity of experience. It is as if science as a form of knowledge is accorded powers which philosophy as a form of knowledge lacks. Shortly, we will find this supposition further verified. Thirdly, Bogdanov's argument implies that the best philosophical knowledge might do is to provide a "monistic" and "objective" overview of the unity of actuality as it grows. For him, it is apparently limited to providing man with a sense of his practical and cognitive needs and abilities and, with that, encouragement to go on with his world-building.

What does this imply regarding the historical meaning and significance of philosophy? Apparently, a monistic and objective world-picture is the ultimate goal of philosophical activity for Bogdanov. Once a philosophy possesses the point of view, structure and tenets necessary to man in his aspiration to see the world as a unified whole, philosophy attains its final form and simply endures. One cannot help but get the impression that empiriomonism is that final philosophy for Bogdanov. In the chapter devoted to it, we found that empiriomonism reflects labor practice as it is in the present and promises to be in the future. Because of this, it seems reasonable to assume that for Bogdanov its point of view, structure and tenets are and will continue to be the ultimate characteristics of philosophy. If this is the case, then empiriomonism might adapt to any change in actuality and depict the increasing unification of practice and knowledge in its world-picture at any time in the future.

We have said that "The Science of the Future" presents an argument for the end of philosophy. What is better said, perhaps, is that Bogdanov argues the end of the search for the ultimate in philosophy. Philosophizing appears to go on in his scheme, but only in the sense of updating an already monistic world-picture. If philosophy is already "living out its last days" for Bogdanov,[1] it is doing so only in the sense that the focus of the pursuit of knowledge is changing from the search for adequate *philosophical* knowledge to the search for new labor practices and the *scientific* knowledge with which to effect the greater unity of actuality. Whether or not the analysis above is wholly the case, Bogdanov's arguments regarding the limitations of philosophy lead the reader toward the understanding that empiriomonism is philosophy in its ultimate form and that such a philosophy must know "to what it will have to give place" in the realm of human cognitive activity. The ultimate meaning and significance of empiriomonism, then, seems to lie in its role in pushing man beyond philosophy itself. For Bogdanov, the monistic world-picture of the post-religious era has been realized, and the religious world-view now has a proper secular successor in Empiriomonism. While practice and knowledge progressed to the detriment of the old monism, however, they would progress under the continued scrutiny of the new. [PLE. p. 318]

This is, perhaps, too grand a conclusion to draw at this point in our discussion of "The Science of the Future". The essay, however, shifts quickly away from the matter of philosophy's limitations toward matters of future labor practice and the progress of knowledge. Only briefly does it come back to philosophy and only then to make the contrast between its limited powers and those of the science of the future. The chapter's next argument proceeds as follows.

Bogdanov tells us that the growth of unity in practice and knowledge is already underway. After repeating his comments on the revolutions in contemporary science, [PLE, 319] he went on to argue that the facts and tendencies of modern machine production give positive indication of the possibility, if not the inevitability, of progress in the realm of practice. What does the career of machine production in the present show us regarding the future of practice, he asked? [PLE, p. 319] Principally, he replied, it shows us the following things. First, we see that the worker is no longer a "living machine". Direct labor is done by mechanisms which the worker guides. The basic human relationship with the machine is that of control and direction. As production moves toward complete automation, man's role of control and direction becomes ever more the order of things. [PLE, p. 319] Secondly, on the lower levels of machine production, there remains a difference between the "implementory" work of the simple worker and the "organizational" work of the engineer. As production advances, this difference will tend to disappear. Automatic mechanisms demand knowledge which transcends the limits of purely practical experience. All workers will become engineers out of necessity. [PLE, pp. 319–20] Thirdly, machine production appears to be approaching the time when the self-regulating machine will predominate. This type of mechanism will be the basis of collective labor technique in the future. When the supervision of such mechanisms becomes the worker's main occupation, "then every qualitative difference between worker and engineer will vanish, [and] there will remain only the quantitative difference in preparation and experience". [PLE, p. 320] At this time, the worker will be more than an engineer, he will be a scientist. Finally, it follows that alongside the development of machine production there exists a tendency toward uniformity in work activity. The division of labor will cease to be a division of men and methods; it will appear as the simple division of human labor effort directed toward various objects. [PLE, pp. 320–1]

We see here the sense which the phrase "greater unity of practice" has for Bogdanov. In his view, the men of the future will cease to be workers in the usual sense and will become, rather, the supervisors of production. We are reminded of Bogdanov's discussion of the "organizer-implementor" relationship of earlier times.[2] Apparently, the future would find human "implementors" everywhere replaced by mechanical ones. We are also informed that supervision of machines will become increasingly more uniform in character, to the extent that the division of labor into separate skills will end. The proletarian era for Bogdanov thus appears to share with the era of slave labor the feature of uniform and undifferentiated work activity. Because knowledge must reflect and reinforce collective labor activity, it, too, must of necessity become uniform and undifferentiated. Indeed, we are told subsequently that because scientific knowledge serves practice, it must progress along with it toward unity. In the future, said Bogdanov, specialties in knowledge will draw ever nearer to one another, and universal methods of science corresponding to the universality of undifferentiated labor practice will appear. [PLE, p. 321] All this will undoubtedly occur, according to our thinker, because the unification of knowledge, like the unification of production, is in the vital interest of the rising proletariat. Without it, proletarian society and culture cannot be created. [PLE, p. 321]

Bogdanov's vision of the future seems to have the advance of labor practice toward the end of the division of labor drawing scientific knowledge after it toward some inevitable universal method. Although it would seem that the progress of scientific knowledge toward methodological unity is inevitable in this scheme, Bogdanov nonetheless posited an active role for man. The advance of science toward the universal method – toward a science of sciences, if you will – was apparently to be man's principal cognitive concern in the future beyond philosophy. He asked, in effect, how universal methods of scientific knowledge would be gained and gave the following reply. We have seen, he noted, that the progress of machine production gives work activity an ever more organizational (read: "supervisory") character. This corresponds to the historical task of the proletariat which is to perform ever larger and more complicated organizational tasks. All this presupposes the unification of the organizational activity of work by man into a "universal science of organization". [PLE, p. 322] Apparently, to assure that "the universal science of organization" was understood as something more than a science of direct labor practice, Bogdanov asked his readers to remember that all activity or process in the world had the character of being organizational. "Technical activity organizes elements of external nature in society; cognitive and artistic [activity] the social experience of people". [PLE, p. 322] Even the elemental life of the universe is nothing but the struggle and development of various types and degrees of organization.

In this, human activity is not differentiated from world activity . . . . A science of methods of organization must, therefore, seize those means by which nature works out and completes its forms of organization. World methodology – here is the essence of the science of the future. [PLE, pp. 322–3]

Bogdanov went on to argue that each division of science as it stood in the present, whether technical or abstract, would become subordinated to the "universal organizational science". Their methods would be considered partial cases of the universal method. The division of science into branches would remain, but that division would be in no way absolute. All would be part of the greater whole, and each branch would continuously interact with every other, exchanging methods and points of view. [PLE, p. 323]

The argument above, which unfortunately lacks a great deal in the way of intermediate explanation, seems to present the following ideas. First, we are told that the active pursuit of unity in labor practice "presupposes" the active pursuit of unity in the knowledge of labor practice as "organizing activity". Bogdanov seemingly demands that, sooner or later, man must recognize all labor activity as a matter of organization and that the methods of organization of labor activity form a corpus of integrally related "organizational" laws not unlike, one would assume, Bogdanov's own "organizational dialectic".[3] Secondly, we are told without explanation that the study of organization in labor practice is the self-same thing as scientific knowledge itself. It is as if we are suddenly asked to leap forward to the realization that the activity of all scientific knowledge proceeds organizationally after the fashion of labor practice. Although Bogdanov informs us continually that all knowledge is organization, we are hardly prepared to make this leap. This revelation is supposed to suggest to us that the study of all activity, human or natural, is a matter of the study of forms of organization and that a science of sciences, comprehending the partial methods of the various disciplines and the methods of direct labor practice, can only be the study of "organization".

Without more in the way of explanation (and that cannot be found in *The Philosophy of Living Experience*), the reader is forced to accept the "universal organizational science" as the science of the future on faith. While there is some indication earlier in the work that science is an "organizing activity" and its methods "organizational", this is not enough to establish the reasonableness of Bogdanov's demand that the science of the future be organizational in character. In order to judge this, one must look beyond *The Philosophy of Living Experience* to the *Tektologiia* where complete explanations may be found. Since we cannot reasonably do this within the limits of the present study, we can only pass on to give the reader Bogdanov's vision of the "universal organizational science" as it appears in the work under consideration. Suffice it to say that for Bogdanov, then, the study of human labor activity and natural processes would eventually be subsumed in the greater study of the methods of organization. That the "universal organizational science" would bring these methods into a fully integrated whole is apparent to him, since "all knowledge aspires toward unity". Where man's principal task in the realm of thought had been the creation of a unified philosophical world-picture, his new task would be the creation of a unified science of sciences.

Following the argument outlined and discussed above, Bogdanov went on to a brief characterization of the "universal organizational science" in which its differentiation from philosophy was his principal concern. The general science of the methods of organization, he argued, would be exact and fully empirical. It would not be like philosophy in any way. In fact, it would be "the direct opposite of philosophy which is less empirical than any of the partial sciences". [PLE, p. 323] Philosophy is now necessary because of the incompatibility of the various realms of experience as organized by the partial sciences. Its purpose is to remove that incompatibility and, therefore, it does not have its special realm of experience. It may not rely on the "living experience" of all the separate realms because they do not comprise a unified whole. [PLE, p. 323] In contrast, Bogdanov asserted, the science of the future would have an experiential base as broad as all practice and knowledge taken together.

It will observe and strictly systematize all those methods of organization which are *factually* applied in society, life and nature. Regularities, which will be found and established in this manner, will give universal guidance to the total domination of the forces of nature. . . . From the most primitive cosmic connection of elements to artistic creation, to this time the highest and least rigid form of organizational activity, all will be illuminated, clearly and harmoniously bound, by the conclusions of the organized experience of the world of humanity. [PLE, pp. 323–4]

From these assertions, Bogdanov moved on to a characterization of the nature of the methods of the science of the future. We are told that the organizational science would be comprised of *"real world-formulae"*, that is, "practical formulae [which] will create the possibility of the systematic mastery of the totality of given elements in the world process". [PLE, pp. 325–6] While he gives no hint as to how these formulae would appear, he tells the reader that the "universal organizational science" does not have as its goal "a formula like Laplace's . . . which, in seizing the universe in all its complexity, would be as complicated as the universe itself. . . ." [PLE, p. 327]

According to Bogdanov, then, the universal organizational science was to be fully empirical, apparently because it would be science and not philosophy. The distinction between the two realms of knowledge is not clearly drawn here, but a little deliberation yields the differentiation Bogdanov attempted to make. We are told that the "universal organizational science" and philosophy are direct opposites, since the former is fully empirical while the latter is "less empirical than any of the partial sciences" and does not have its "special realm of experience". While one is tempted to take this as an argument denying philosophy any empirical base whatever, it appears that Bogdanov simply wished to point out that philosophy unified experience as it was organized by the various special sciences. As such, it was a step away from the direct organization of experience and, therefore, less empirical. The "universal organizational science", on the other hand, would apparently act directly on the empirical base in its pursuit of organizational methods for use in all of the various realms of knowledge. Perhaps the easiest way to put the distinction between science and philosophy for Bogdanov and, with that, the difference between the "universal organizational science" and empiriomonism, would be to say that science creates the experience it organizes while philosophy does not. Consequently, science, and the "universal organizational science" in particular, is for Bogdanov that tool most suitable for changing the world. Philosophy's role, while vital, is less direct.

Regarding the methods of the science of the future, we are told that practical formulae would be sought after instead of a single universal law. If we recall Bogdanov's remarks on universal process in the chapter on Marx,[4] we ought to understand this as a further attempt on his part to deny any affinity for notions of universal process which are so broad as to be meaningless. In speaking of practical formulae, it appears that Bogdanov meant to associate organizational methods with the laws of contemporary science. The "universal organizational science" would apparently be a diverse system bringing numerous methodological formulae into integral relation with one another in the manner of a science or science of sciences. The whole would be the sum of the practical formulae, and the concept of world process as organization would not be so much an initial assumption as it would be a conclusion arrived at inductively. Thus, Bogdanov's description of the world-process as "organizational" is meant to connote something quite different from, say, Engels' depiction of all process as "dialectical".

In conclusion, Bogdanov asserted the real possibility of the "universal organizational science" once again. If there were any further doubts as to the possibility of its creation, he argued, one need only consider the facts of human progress to dispel them. History has presented organizational tasks to man, all of which he has completed.

Man continuously organizes for himself the most strange and hostile forces of the universe. He organizes the very means of organization in knowledge. Never in the world, in experience, has there been something which has not been organized. [PLE, p. 324]

And so, for Bogdanov, not only the inevitable progress of practice and scientific knowledge but also man's fundamental ability to organize experience guaranteed the possibility of effecting the "universal organizational science". As for the question of whether all processes in labor practice, knowledge and nature were actually organizational in character, Bogdanov replied that past experience shows that the appearance of the same organizational processes in the most diverse realms cannot be accidental; they appear too often for that and are there to be discovered. In finding, for example, wave-form movement in inorganic nature, in the lower forms of life, in society, in art and music, man has discovered one of a large number of organizational processes which transcend the boundaries of all realms and levels of experience. [PLE, pp. 324–5] Consequently, said Bogdanov, the sole possible conclusion which may be reached is that "it is possible to establish general methods and regularities by which the most diverse elements of the universe are organized into complexes". [PLE, p. 327]

Finally, we are taken back to the matter of the future of philosophy in Bogdanov's prediction of the future of knowledge:

Philosophy is living out its last days. Empiriomonism is already not fully philosophy but a transitional form, because it knows where it is going and to what it will have to give place. The beginnings of the new universal science will come in the next few years. Its flowering will arise from that gigantic [and] feverish organizational work which will create a new society and complete the agonizing prologue of the history of mankind. That time is not far off.... [PLE, p. 327]

With this, both "The Science of the Future" and the work as a whole come to an end. In the final footnote of the 1923 edition, Bogdanov tells us that the "universal organizational science" had indeed come into being in the years following the writing of *The Philosophy of Living Experience*. [PLE, p. 327] In noting the appearance of the three volumes of his *Tektologiia* in 1913, 1917 and 1922, respectively, Bogdanov did nothing to efface the purposefulness and optimism he had shown in predicting the science of the future in 1910. The 1923 edition of *The Philosophy of Living Experience* remained unchanged save for the footnote above and the addition in appendix of "From Religious to Scientific Monism". [PLE, pp. 328–45] This would seem to indicate that Bogdanov still regarded man's primary task to be the advance of knowledge beyond philosophy and his own contribution of the universal organizational science to be of critical importance. The view of the future of practice and knowledge presented in *The Philosophy of Living Experience* apparently remained intact more than a decade later.

CONCLUSION

As we noted in our introduction, in the year following the creation of *The Philosophy of Living Experience* Bogdanov left politics in order to give his full attention to theoretical concerns.[1] It may be argued that not only the period from 1911 to 1917 but also the rest of his life reveal "organizational science" as Bogdanov's central concern. If one looks at his career in print after *The Philosophy of Living Experience* and before 1921, one sees, of course, a great flood of publications on proletarian culture.[2] Although the years of *Proletkul't*, they were also the years of the *Tektologiia*, the three volumes of that work appearing in 1913, 1917 and 1922. There is no evidence which suggests that Bogdanov's theoretical and organizational involvement with *Proletkul't* made organizational science a subordinate concern in those years. In fact, a review of his publications on both subjects suggests that they formed a single project in his mind. To take a single example, one finds the protagonist of his fantasy novel, *Engineer Menni* (1913) struggling to teach workers how to build their culture on the scientific organization of practice and thought.[3] "The Science of the Future" itself suggests the unity of Bogdanov's concerns after *The Philosophy of Living Experience*. We may read into it the argument that, if the universal organizational science was to be the science of the future, it was to be the science of the class of the future and, for that, a critically important part of proletarian culture. Judging from the proposed scope of the universal organizational science, Bogdanov must certainly have regarded it fundamental to the proletarian enterprise.

Between 1922 and 1928, Bogdanov's works were divided largely between new studies on or related to organizational science and new editions of older works, especially those on organizational science, economics and proletarian culture. Of the fifty works Dietrich Grille lists for this period, no less than 28 relate to organizational science, "organizational" studies of economics, and proletarian culture. Of the remainder, ten are new editions of works written prior to 1921. The rest comprehend a variety of subjects related to the affairs of the Socialist Academy, to early Social-Democratic Party history, to old associates, etc.[4] Bogdanov's only new intellectual concern was apparently relativity theory, on which he wrote two pieces in 1923–4.[5] He clearly showed no inclination to return to concerns predating *The Philosophy of Living Experience* save inasmuch as they related to his pursuit of organizational science.

160

That Bogdanov devoted the balance of his career to the reaffirmation and expansion of positions he had taken in *The Philosophy of Living Experience* is suggested not only by his career in print but also his involvement with the Socialist Academy and by the optimism he showed toward the end of his life regarding the future of organizational science. Michael Csizmas tells us that one of the principal tasks of that institution under Bogdanov's directorship was the application of "universal organizational methods" in "optimal economic planning".[6] While we have no evidence as to the extent of this project beyond the fact that Bogdanov and several other members of the Academy published articles regarding organization and economics between 1921 and 1923,[7] in 1926 Bogdanov was still encouraged about the future of his "science of sciences" in Soviet economic planning and other areas. In the introduction to the German edition of the *Tektologiia* in that same year, he wrote:

I note with great pleasure that my hopes for the cooperation of new colleagues have finally been fulfilled. Many scholars – both young and old – have entered the path of tektological investigation, in which they apply their method and proven conclusions to the living questions of praxis and science, to the state economic plan, to the progress and methods of education, to the analysis of economic transition, to [the study of] social and psychological types, etc.[8]

It must have seemed to Bogdanov that his earlier vision of the future of organizational science was coming true. The involvement of the members of the Socialist Academy and others with his methods must have suggested that universal acceptance was not far off.

All of the above suggests that Bogdanov's concern with organizational science was not only enduring but of the greatest importance to him as well. Accordingly, *The Philosophy of Living Experience* not only served notice that this study was underway as of 1910 but also gave an accurate projection regarding its importance for Bogdanov. The work's reappearance unchanged prior to the later editions of the *Tektologiia*[9] and the reaffirmation of its arguments in "From Religious to Scientific Monism" further commends the work as an enduring statement of Bogdanov's position and intentions after 1910.

The Philosophy of Living Experience ends, then, not only with an attempt to cast the problem of philosophy in the light of a broader concern with the future of labor practice and knowledge. It closes, as well, with a statement of self-direction. The personal character of the work's final chapter and conclusion further suggests the propriety of taking the whole of *The Philosophy of Living Experience* as a personal document. If the argument regarding organizational science implies a statement of self-direction, then Bogdanov's exposition of his worldview and his attempt to give it a place in the history of thought may reasonably be taken to imply a statement of self-assessment. Coming as it did on the heels of his dispute with Lenin, Plekhanov and Aksel'rod and prior to his departure from politics, *The Philosophy of Living Experience* met Bogdanov's interpreters fully in the open. It said, in effect, "Here is the entire corpus of Bogdanovism reduced to a statement of world-view; judge what I am by what my world-view amounts to."

To a certain extent, Bogdanov may have been revealed to himself in the writing of *The Philosophy of Living Experience.* While he made no comment to that effect either in the work or thereafter, several things about *The Philosophy of Living Experience* suggest it. First, it is clear that the work gathered together numerous and diverse notions arrived at between 1897 and 1910. Such a gathering process might well have brought Bogdanov a new perspective on himself and his work. Secondly, if we compare *The Philosophy of Living Experience* to *Belief and Science,* the defense of his epistemological positions written immediately prior to it, one finds that the latter reveals considerably less of Bogdanov to the reader.[10] *Belief and Science* was of substantial importance to him, as it answered the accusations made by Lenin in *Materialism and Empirio-Criticism.* Although limited to the defense of epistemological positions, the work nonetheless contained numerous summary statements regarding philosophy and knowledge in general. Taken together, they afford a view of Bogdanov and his worldview which is not out of line with the statements of *The Philosophy of Living Experience.* Bogdanov as the philosopher standing "beyond Marx and Mach", however, is not apparent there. In fact, one gets the impression that he wished to be considered no real adversary of either. At some point soon after the writing of *Belief and Science,* Bogdanov may well have found his position in need of reassessment and clarification. Inasmuch as *The Philosophy of Living Experience* stands in distinct contrast to *Belief and Science* as a personal document, it may well have been a self-revelation in the writing. Finally, and somewhat less conjecturally, Bogdanov may have come to the conclusion that his concern with philosophy *per se* was short-sighted while composing *The Philosophy of Living Experience.* The arguments and structure of "The Science of the Future" seem to indicate that Bogdanov had come to a point at which the segregation of knowledge into philosophy and science, which had not particularly preoccupied him before, was now necessary to effect. It could well be that he came to conclusions about the limitations of philosophy earlier, of course, as the concept of organizational science must have resided with him for some considerable time prior to 1910. It would seem, however, that his consideration of the end of philosophy and the function of knowledge beyond it is the very sort of concern which would lead one away from worldly affairs and back to the theoretical, as was the case with Bogdanov after the writing of *The Philosophy of Living Experience.* Also, one might argue that the vagueness, which one cannot help but notice in "The Science of the Future" with regard to the relationship of philosophy and science, may be an indication of a changing point of view.

It is unnecessary for us to conclude here on the substance of *The Philosophy of Living Experience,* since that has been done in moving from part to part in its explication. We began from the thesis that the work's primary purpose was to present a worldview. That such is the case is undoubtedly so. Even considering the numerous and diverse concerns of the work, one cannot help but conclude that the whole of it is involved in that presentation. Although the chapter revealing the core of that worldview, "Empiriomonism", comes rather late in the work, it may be said that all which precedes that chapter is discussed from the "empiriomonistic" point of view. In addition to noting the ubiquity of that point of view in its various discussions, one might say that the work reveals Bogdanov's worldview not only in positive statement and application but also by way of its deliberate attempt to contrast that worldview to others. In a sense, we come to know what Bogdanov's worldview is by way of a very ample statement of what it is not and, in contrast to organizational science, what it cannot be. In these ways, *The Philosophy of Living Experience* presents Bogdanov's worldview, to use expressions similar to his own, as a philosophy which knows what it is and is not, from whence it has come, where it is going and to what it will have to give place.

A corollary of our thesis was the argument that all of the various parts of the work were the frames or contexts into which Bogdanov's worldview was set and that, because of their ample development, these ought to be accorded some separate status and concluded upon as well. It is clear that in taking up the questions of the meaning of the history of philosophy, of the meaning of the career of labor practice and knowledge, and of the significance of Marx and Mach, Bogdanov meant not only to free his worldview of associations but to come to grips with all of these questions in a serious way. Thus, *The Philosophy of Living Experience* may be taken as a work which proposed to settle numerous questions which its author and many of his contemporaries considered of universal import. In its scope and intents, the work was as broad and ambitious an effort as one might expect from a thinker considering himself the creator of a new and universally significant worldview.

It seems very clear to this writer that *The Philosophy of Living Experience,* especially if read carefully, reveals a new or, at least, a rather different Bogdanov than has heretofore been glimpsed in scholarship. This, in turn, makes inevitable the conclusion that a new review of his life and works needs to be made and, with that, a review taking considerable account of what *The Philosophy of Living Experience* suggests about Bogdanov and his thought. Most obviously, of course, the work reveals Bogdanov in the self-styled role of creator of the genuinely new in philosophy and the extent to which the attempt to fulfill that role was his concern. If nothing else, *The Philosophy of Living Experience* suggests the narrowness of past scholarship's depiction of Bogdanov as Marxist, Machist or "Macho-Marxist". We are commended to approach Bogdanov in and for himself, that is, in accord with what he professed to be.

Again in contrast with the results of past scholarship, the study of *The Philosophy of Living Experience* suggests the unity and orderly progression of Bogdanov's intellectual concerns. For him, they were not a series of unconnected enthusiasms forced upon him by circumstance. If taken apart, *The Philosophy of Living Experience* leads the reader to conclude that Bogdanov's career as student of economics, history, and theory of knowledge gave him the tools and perspectives to make a social and historical investigation and critique of philosophy and then, in turn, to philosophize himself. Even were the study of the works prior to *The Philosophy of Living Experience* to reveal a lack of progression and unity, the progression and unity of Bogdanov's work as a whole ought still to be sought and established. It is clear that after 1910-11 he not only saw his earlier work in unity but also the direction in which it pointed for his future work. All this suggests that any new study of Bogdanov must take care to find the connections between his various works and concerns, to show the unity of the whole, and, of course, to measure the appearance of the whole against Bogdanov's self-assessment in *The Philosophy of Living Experience.* Regarding the study of sources and influences, *The Philosophy of Living Experience* clearly reveals that Bogdanov came to renounce the association of his thought with that of all other thinkers and especially his association with Marxist materialism and Machian critical positivism. Accordingly, this suggests that the study of the career of influences on Bogdanov ought to proceed from the supposition that Bogdanov was unlikely to consider any of them binding upon him. That is, the notion of Bogdanov being both under influences and striving to pass beyond them must be kept in mind.

Finally, we see in *The Philosophy of Living Experience* Bogdanov as a thinker of greater scope than past considerations of him as Lenin's rival or "Russian Machist" suggest. The number, diversity and, above all, the seriousness of all his concerns suggests that Bogdanov may reasonably be taken as an epitome of the sort of thinker who felt compelled to react broadly to the problems and possibilities of the world in those promising and disturbing years of war, revolution and the new Russian revolutionary regime. If Bogdanov considered himself "beyond Marx and Mach" it was not so much because he saw the need to refine their points of view, but because he believed himself to be reacting to the realities of his time in ways in which Marx and Mach had not and could not for being men of another generation. In drawing conclusions on the origins, meaning and ultimate effect of his thought, then, it seems that the student of Bogdanov must be willing to accord the general influence of the times a large role. He must be willing as well to deal with Bogdanov's works as attempts to respond to the condition of life and thought in their time. It is this writer's feeling that Bogdanov may eventually be considered more remarkable for the extent of his attempt to come to grips with the early twentieth-century world than for his effect on the development of Soviet Marxism or the outcome of that attempt which is his worldview.

Obviously, the study of *The Philosophy of Living Experience* leaves us a considerable distance removed from an appreciation of the Russian Machists as a group. It tells us that at least one of them considered himself and his thought unique (there is, of course no mention of Valentinov, Bazarov, Jushkevich and the rest in this work), and indicates the tenuous, if not transitory, nature of the influence of Marx and Mach. It also informs us that the central figure among the Machists was a thinker of universal concerns reacting broadly to reality as he found it. All of this suggests that what we asserted initially is probably true, i.e., that dealing with the Russian Machists may be very difficult under any approach save that of taking each in and for himself; for, if Bogdanov as the single most important representative of the group eschewed close association with Mach and other of Mach's Russian partisans, the whole may lack much of the unity that the appellation "the Russian Machists" implies. In the end, it may well be that the group can only be brought together by a comparative study of the influence of Marx and Mach upon each and a comparative assessment as to how the reaction of each to early twentieth-century realities was manifest in his work. Whatever difficulties the study of the Machists might present, *The Philosophy of Living*

Experience as a "Machist" document indicates the sort of rewards forth-coming for one willing to meet them.

To this point our study has been necessarily limited in scope and intentions by the structure and contents of the work under consideration. It may be appropriate in concluding, however, to cast the Bogdanov of *The Philosophy of Living Experience* in some broader light. One is, to a large extent, commended to this (or perhaps we ought to say "tempted to it") inasmuch as *The Philosophy of Living Experience* presents Bogdanov as a "large" intellectual figure living in an historically critical time. Whether or not he ought to be so considered, and how, is of course open to debate. It is not at all our intention either to be taken in by that presentation or to attempt to verify Bogdanov's self-perceptions. We simply wish to discover how that which we are ready to accept as true about Bogdanov on the basis of our study allows him to be placed in his time and within the broad trends of thought flowing through it. It goes without saying that we pursue this for what it might contribute to our better understanding of both the man and his times. If the proper role of concluding statements is the taking of the reader beyond the matter at hand on the basis of that matter itself, then we are not out of line in discussing, in this instance, Bogdanov in general respects, as suggested by *The Philosophy of Living Experience*. From what we have seen, any future consideration would be remiss in not regarding some of the sorts of things that will be said below as matters of some import to a proper understanding of Bogdanov.

It seems reasonable that Bogdanov might be placed among the most ambitious of those who regarded the late nineteenth and early twentieth centuries as the moment most proper for doing the new in thought. There are many from whom to choose, but let us suggest here the likes of Bergson, Georges Sorel and Freud with Nietzsche as perhaps the most generally representative. For these thinkers, reality seemed to press for dramatic changes in all forms of consciousness and, ultimately, in the general meaning and practice of philosophy. As with Bogdanov, the *fin de siècle* attempt to do the new was related both to a radical critique of past thought and to a critique of reality in most if not all of its parts. Whether reality and the way of apprehending it were approached from the perspective of psychology or social production, irrationalism or scientism, the intent was very similar: to reveal reality as hitherto misapprehended and to move beyond the limits of past methods of understanding and manipulating it. While Bogdanov was not comparable to the likes of, say, Nietzsche in the effect of his critique of contemporaneity and demand for the new in philosophy, it ought to be recognized that the two shared the same breadth of ambition.[11] What Bogdanov lacked in depth of criticism and understanding of philosophy, he more than made up for in their scope. It could scarcely be argued that Bogdanov meant to effect something less than the complete reform of consciousness and the wholesale transformation of the "material" to which it related as well as the fulfillment of human nature and the culmination of human history. As one passes from one "large" figure to the next in the *fin de siècle*, one is struck in turn by the presumptuousness, the intoxication, the ingenuousness and, quite often, by the genius and insight which Bogdanov may be taken to exemplify as much as anyone else.

Bogdanov may also be taken to represent well European thought in the late nineteenth and early twentieth centuries inasmuch as he was a thinker striving to end the division of knowledge into philosophy and science. Depending on the particular thinker, this was to be accomplished in a number of ways, from reconciling the one to the other, to elevating the one over the other in some final manner. Although philosophy and science were set apart according to their future functions in *The Philosophy of Living Experience*, it should be apparent that such was not possible before they were first brought into timely (and final) consonance. It may be argued that Bogdanov's thought was a landmark in the struggle to bring knowledge back to unity in that it strongly reflected one major outcome of that undertaking: the broad dominion of scientism in twentieth-century European philosophy. While, for instance, Bogdanov is not evaluated in *Knowledge and Human Interests,* Jürgen Habermas' complex critique of the effect of positivist scientism on the career of twentieth-century thought, it is certain that our thinker fits well among the figures discussed there.[12] In a way, it is useful to view Bogdanov not so much as an originator of the trend but as an indication of the momentum it had gained by his time. With this, Bogdanov's thought may also be taken as an indication of the trouble caused by positivist scientism among thinkers from early in the *fin de siècle* on into the 1920's. He was, of course, neither led to despair at the poverty of positivism nor moved to deny philosophy on the basis of it, as was the case with many. Bogdanov was rather compelled to join what the best of positivist notions suggested to him with what he considered philosophy to be so as to consolidate man's hard-won gains. Positivism was, nonetheless, something problematic for him: it had to be revealed for what it lacked and got beyond.

In contrast to many in his time but in line with its realities, Bogdanov was appreciative of the need for the study of general forms of system and organization as they were being revealed in society, thought and production. If he ran ahead of his contemporaries in this, the perspectives from which Bogdanov arrived at such conclusions were not entirely untypical of the *fin de siècle*. While many despaired at comprehending the complexities of mass industrial society in any rational way, Bogdanov, like many others still impressed by the transformation wrought by technology, regarded what he saw as the surest sign of coming human fulfilment. The way out of what seemed to others a malaise was simple enough for Bogdanov: one need only take a "social-theoretical" (or to use Bogdanov's term, "labor") point of view on reality and the rational "social" mind's relation to it. It may be said that Bogdanov represented a long enduring trend in this direction which had begun with Marx and continued in the undertakings of Georg Lukács, Karl Korsch, the Frankfort School and the humanistic socialists of present-day Eastern Europe. That the dialogue between "nature and society" did not yield for Bogdanov the same sort of questions which struck the humanistically-inclined and neo-Hegelian theorists is obvious. His tack was different but, again, not so peculiar in the *fin de siècle* and beyond among those radicals who still cleaved to the notion of the transformation of society via the transformation of its productive base. Bogdanov was looking out for the future good of society as might be achieved subsequent to mass industrialization and the "scientific" harmonization of social, intellectual and productive relations. If individual and society as a whole were aware of the need for and possibilities of this, one might say in Bogdanov's behalf, all things necessary to human dignity and fulfilling survival would be obtained. Such difficulties as the overcoming of alienation and the search for values required no more specific approaches.

Setting Bogdanov as he is glimpsed in *The Philosophy of Living Experience* into the context of the Russian *fin de siècle* once again suggests a broader significance for him than the limited confines of Marxism and Machism allow. For instance, were it not for the fact that Alexander Vucinich has all but done so just recently, we might go on here to argue at length the reasonableness of regarding Bogdanov as the culmination of the Russian search for a scientific social theory between 1861 and 1917.[13] Vucinich has made it abundantly clear, on the one hand, that many of the principal socially-concerned intellectuals in this period sought a *science* of society, that is, "an integrated system of scientific principles" for its study, which accompanied and grounded their social, historical, political or cultural analysis of the Russian condition.[14] On the other hand, Vucinich has shown that Bogdanov's thought, for all its seeming uniqueness and universalism, shows principal features which allow him to be set comfortably alongside the likes of Lavrov, Mikhailovsky, Danilevsky, Plekhanov, Tugan-Baranovsky and the rest. While Vucinich allows that Bogdanov is the culmination of the trend by dint of being the last such thinker independent of the Revolution, we would like to suggest that, in addition, his thought ought to be regarded as its fulfilment inasmuch as "the philosophy of living experience" and "organizational science" form the trend's most ambitious and highly original manifestation. We commend to the reader Professor Vucinich's book not alone for what it has to say of Bogdanov but also for its illumination of the search for a scientific approach as a principal feature of Russian social thought.

In addition to considering Bogdanov in the manner of Vucinich, there may be other ways in which to regard him as a Russian thinker. For instance, it might be said that Bogdanov, alongside Lenin and Vladimir Solov'ev, was the thinker most representative of the Russian *fin de siècle*, especially if one categorizes according to extremes. Almost any species of social, political or cultural thought in late nineteenth- and early twentieth-century Russia may be seen as an amalgam comprised in various parts of the spirituality and ethicism characterized by Solov'ev's views, the social-historicality and "toughness of mind" of Leninism, and the hopeful and aggressive scientism of Bogdanov's worldview. This is to suggest that scientism was an important strain in Russian thought in the *fin de siècle* and that Bogdanov was perhaps its most significant advocate. Professor Vucinich, we believe, has already done much to substantiate this.

As it is possible to set Bogdanov in the broad context of his own time both in Europe and Russia, so are we also able to set him in broad frames beyond it. If one were to study Bogdanov's positions carefully as they appear throughout the entire corpus of his work, undoubtedly a great deal could be noted about that which he anticipated in twentieth-century thought. Taking into account those made obvious from our limited study, we mention (as we did above) Bogdanov's clear anticipation of the need and search for the analysis of system, for one thing, and the pre-occupation with the concepts of positivist scientism in philosophy, for another. From what is said in *The Philosophy of Living Experience,* we might also see similarities between the efforts of Bogdanov, members of the Frankfort School and, most lately, Jürgen Habermas at finding a "social theory of knowledge" or, we might otherwise say, an epistemology derived from Marx. Additionally, it is perhaps not far-fetched to see Bogdanov as something akin to a pioneer in the search for formal principles of Marxist sociology. What he attempted shows affinities not only with the work of his near-contemporaries like Bukharin and the early Soviet "planners" but also with the present-day work of East-European socialist-humanists and those Soviet theoreticians seeking out the laws governing the transition from socialism to Communism.

The Philosophy of Living Experience, in that it reveals Bogdanov in self-conception as a historically-conditioned thinker, suggests that he be placed somewhere in the flow of nineteenth- and twentieth-century thought. If we cannot readily accord him the place of ultimate philosopher, then where to put him? It seems to us that one must either leave him where he perhaps fits most comfortably, that is, among the Russian social theorists or with the philosophic experimenters of his own time, or set him down as a transitional figure in the career of social theory and philosophy, standing somewhere between the *fin de siècle* and our own time. Given the fact that he participated in the career of a number of trends, one is almost compelled to place him in the flow, and any idea of shunting him aside as beneath serious consideration is forestalled by the importance of those trends themselves. It is most astonishing to find that the latter sort of assessment is still possible in scholarship. In a recent work by Adam Ulam Bogdanov is portrayed in just such a way. From what we have seen, what sense does it make (for Ulam) to call Bogdanov a New Left thrill-seeker anachronistically thrown into the first quarter of the twentieth century, whose thought exhibits the sort of voluntarism which the Chicago Seven would best appreciate?[15]

If it is to be argued, one might see Bogdanov as being transitional in two sorts of ways. First, he may be viewed as a link between radical social theorists in the *fin de siècle*, who were much taken with philosophical positivism and its scientism, and those Marxist-inclined thinkers, like Jürgen Habermas, more lately concerned with how positivist epistemology and scientism have interfered with the proper exercise of philosophy. We assert this inasmuch as Bogdanov's thought offered one of the alternative ways of relating positivist epistemology and scientism to radical social concerns, that is, the alternative in which the former (or notions similar to them, at least) were allowed to dominate. It may be argued that someone or other had to attempt a grand venture in this direction, as positivism, the new science and socialism of various sorts held such a large portion of the field of thought around World War I and, also, as there existed at the time a widespread demand to make the world at once more "scientific" and socially harmonious. It cannot be argued, of course, that Bogdanov's thought was crucial in precipitating the *Western* rejection of the sort of alternative he had advanced. He may be regarded as having something to do, however, with its rejection in Russia, inasmuch as he had a great deal to do with the coming into being of the "mechanistic Marxism" advocated and practiced in the Soviet twenties and later anathematized.

Bogdanov might also be deemed transitional as a link between the positivists and neo-Kantians among prewar radicals and the post-war Hegelians (such as Lukács and Korsch) in the sense that his thought so completely expressed the tack and ambitions of the former and was so very much at odds with the latter. It appears now that radical social theory had but two ways to go in the 'twenties, i.e., further toward positivism and other critical epistemological and scientistic stances or back toward Hegel. With the publication of *History and Class Consciousness* and *Marxism and Philosophy* in 1923, the latter direction showed itself to be the way of the future.[16] Positivist Marxism had its career in the 1920's with Bukharin and company in the Soviet Union but went no further, at least as an articulate competitor to the neo-Hegelian strain. It is difficult to know why the positivist strain lacked strong partisans. It may have been that positivist Marxism could only really appeal in the world of the Soviet experiment. As for the rest of Europe, and most especially for Germany and Central Europe, it is possible to say (with George Lichtheim) that what was wanted after World War I in radical social theory was a return to a more cautious and more contemplative mode. Certainly it is not accidental that Western radical theorists have come to be divided by and large between more or less respectable sociologists refining the critique of bourgeois society, on the one hand, and the formulators of proper understandings of philosophy, on the other. Lichtheim, of course, would like to suggest that Hegel could not be exorcised from social thought, especially among its most active practitioners, the Germans.[17] There are, undoubtedly, general historical reasons having to do with the dislocations caused by the war and disappointment with the new Soviet regime. At any rate, along with other sorts of thinking smacking of positivist influence and ingenuous scientism, Bogdanov's "active" philosophy was perhaps too "easy" and, certainly, it was very closely associated with other forms of thought discredited for their part in the creation of the way of life which had made a world war possible.

If we were to leave Bogdanov in the *fin de siècle* and deny the possibility of a career for his thought beyond it, we would not greatly narrow the number of ways in which he might be deemed significant. While that may have more than anything else to do with the nature of the times, it surely must have something to do with Bogdanov himself inasmuch as he was so much in consonance with them. Far from being simple obscurantism or confused wandering between Marxism and critical positivism, Bogdanov's thought seems much more like the natural meeting place of a variety of widely important *fin de siècle* trends. That he was compelled to respond broadly to the new science, the new technology, the new society, the new threat to philosophy, etc., makes him very much a man of his times. That he presumed to be able to make a new and unitary worldview out of the various strains of thought which met in him serves even more to locate him there. Again, Bogdanov may not be credited with "doing to philosophy" what a Nietzsche did. That he did not begin a strong autonomous trend is, however, largely a function of the fact that Bogdanov held to a number of characteristically *fin de siècle* notions which were severely challenged after the War and Revolution. Among these notions we might single out his views of the value of scientism for philosophy and social theory. Also, it is worth mentioning that, to the extent Bogdanov was perceived as a Marxist, his Marxism was the very sort most likely to come under the neo-Hegelian critique. Although we have implied the following again and again, we ought to say here especially that Bogdanov should be distinguished from all other Russian thinkers of his time for his attempt to set foot on the broad stage of European thought. It may be said that here is the most ambitious, wide-ranging and contemporary thinker of the Russian *fin de siècle*. So far as he may be taken to be the above, and that seems safe enough, it is not unreasonable to allow that Bogdanov be at least compared to some of the larger figures of European intellectual life in the late nineteenth and early twentieth centuries.

NOTES

INTRODUCTION

1 Dietrich Grille, *Lenins Rivale,* Cologne, Verlag Wissenschaft und Politik, 1966, p. 72.
2 *loc. cit.*
3 *loc. cit.*
4 A. A. Bogdanov, 'Autobiography', in Georges Haupt and Jean-Jacques Marie, *Makers of the Russian Revolution,* trans. C. I. P. Ferdinand, D. M. Bellos, Ithaca, Cornell U.P., 1974, p. 286.
5 *loc. cit.*
6 Georges Haupt, 'Aleksandr Aleksandrovich Bogdanov (Malinovsky)', in Georges Haupt and Jean-Jacques Marie, *Makers of the Russian Revolution,* trans. C. I. P. Ferdinand, D. M. Bellos, Ithaca, Cornell University Press, 1974, p. 289.
7 Grille, *op. cit.* pp. 42–3.
8 Karl G. Ballestrem, 'Lenin and Bogdanov', *Studies in Soviet Thought* 9 (December 1969) p. 283.
9 *loc. cit.*
10 Haupt, *op. cit.* p. 290; Ballestrem, *op. cit.* p. 286.
11 Haupt, *op. cit.* p. 290.
12 *loc. cit.*
13 *Ibid.* p. 291.
14 *loc. cit.*
15 Ballestrem, *op. cit.* p. 288.
16 For a study of Bolshevik Duma politics see Leonard Schapiro, *The Communist Party of the Soviet Union,* New York, Vintage Books, 1960, pp. 86–141 *passim.*
17 Bogdanov, 'Autobiography', p. 287.
18 Schapiro, *op. cit.* p. 105.
19 *Ibid.* p. 107.
20 *Ibid.* p. 105.
21 *loc. cit.*
22 The fullest and most accurate account of Lenin's dispute with Bogdanov may be found in David Joravsky, *Soviet Marxism and Natural Science,* London, Routledge and Kegan Paul, 1961, pp. 24–46.
23 Ballestrem, *op. cit.* p. 291.
24 *loc. cit.*
25 Bogdanov, 'Autobiography', p. 287.
26 See Schapiro, *op. cit.* p. 111; Adam B. Ulam, *The Bolsheviks,* New York, Collier Books, 1965, pp. 275–76; S. Livshits, 'Partijnaja škola v Bolon'e (1910–1911 gg.)', *Proletarskaja revoljucija,* no. 3 (1926), pp. 27–34.
27 Ulam, *op. cit.* p. 276.
28 The best account on the development of *partijnost'* may be found in Joravsky, *op. cit.,* pp. 24–46.
29 One commentator claims that the writing of *Materialism and Empirio-Criticism* took

the better part of a year and that in that time Lenin did little else. Ballestrem, *op. cit.*
p. 283.

³⁰ *Ibid.* p. 307.

³¹ Bogdanov, 'Autobiography', p. 287.

³² See Conclusion.

³³ For an account of "Bogdanovists" in the Soviet educational establishment see Sheila
Fitzpatrick, *The Commisariat of Enlightenment*, Cambridge, Cambridge University Press,
1970, *passim.*

³⁴ Bogdanov, 'Autobiography', p. 288.

³⁵ *loc. cit.*

³⁶ For a list of principal works on proletarian culture see *Ibid.* p. 289.

³⁷ Fitzpatrick, *op. cit.* pp. 89–109.

³⁸ *Ibid.* pp. 174–80.

³⁹ *Ibid.* pp. 175, 236–42.

⁴⁰ Haupt, 'Bogdanov', p. 292.

⁴¹ See Michael Csizmas, 'Cybernetics – Marxism – Jurisprudence', *Studies in Soviet
Thought* 2 (June 1971) p. 90.

⁴² Haupt. *op. cit.* p. 292.

⁴³ *loc. cit.*

⁴⁴ Schapiro, *op. cit.* p. 276.

⁴⁵ Haupt, *op. cit.* p. 292.

⁴⁶ Bogdanov, 'Autobiography', p. 288.

⁴⁷ Ballestrem, *op. cit.* p. 292.

⁴⁸ N. I. Bukharin, obituary in *Pravda,* 8 April 1928, p. 3.

⁴⁹ See Stephen F. Cohen, *Bukharin and the Bolshevik Revolution*, New York, Alfred A.
Knopf, 1973, pp. 113, 118–9, 141–4.

⁵⁰ Bogdanov, 'Autobiography', pp. 288–89.

⁵¹ For a partial list of titles see *Ibid.* p. 288.

⁵² Grille, *op. cit.* p. 47.

⁵³ *loc. cit.*; Bogdanov, "Autobiography," p. 288.

⁵⁴ Cohen, *op. cit.* pp. 143–44.

⁵⁵ For a review of these works see Ballestrem, *op. cit.* pp. 302–04.

⁵⁶ *Ibid.* p. 284.

⁵⁷ N. I. Bukharin, *Historical Materialism*, Ann Arbor, Ann Arbor Paperback, 1969,
pp. 104–275 *passim.*

⁵⁸ For a portrait of the polemic see Joravsky, *op. cit.* pp. 26–30.

⁵⁹ *Ibid.* pp. 170–232.

⁶⁰ Ballestrem, *op. cit.* p. 307.

⁶¹ Joravsky, *op. cit.* pp. 93–169.

⁶² This is best seen in the work under consideration in this study, i.e., A. A. Bogdanov,
Filosofija živogo opyta, 3rd ed., St. Petersburg and Moscow, 1923. Unless otherwise
noted, this edition is that which will be cited in short form hereafter.

⁶³ N. Valentinov, *Encounters with Lenin,* London, Oxford University Press, 1968, p. 250.

⁶⁴ Bogdanov, 'Autobiography', p. 289.

⁶⁵ Edward J. Brown, *Russian Literature Since the Revolution,* London, Collier Books,
1969, pp. 137–40.

⁶⁶ Schapiro, *op. cit.* p. 276.

[67] See Eden Paul and Cedar Paul, *Proletcult*, New York, Thomas Seltzer, 1921.

[68] A. A. Bogdanov, *Tektologiia: Vseobshchaia organizatsionnaia nauka*, Tom I (St. Petersburg, 1913); *Tektologiia: Vseobshchaia organizatsionnaia nauka*, Vol. II (Moscow, 1917); *Tektologiia: Vseobshchaia organizatsionnaia nauka*, Vol. III (Berlin, 1922).

[69] See Csizmas, *op. cit.* p. 90.

[70] See Conclusion.

[71] Of the major studies, Grille's and Ballestrem's are the most representative of this. The extreme may be seen in the chief Soviet work on Bogdanov, A. V. Ščeglov, *Bor'ba lenina protiv bogdanovskoj revizii marksizma*, Moscow, 1937.

[72] Grille, *op. cit.* pp. 238–39.

[73] In addition to Grille and Ballestrem see also S. V. Utechin, *Russian Political Thought*, New York, Praeger, 1964, pp. 209–10, and Gustav Wetter, *Dialectial Materialism*, trans. Peter Heath, London, Routledge and Kegan Paul, 1958, p. 92.

[74] While it is true that Bogdanov regarded philosophy and epistemology to be very nearly the same thing and that one gets at his thought as a whole from an epistemological starting-point, it must be said that Lenin's (and, with that, past students') interest in Bogdanov's thought was in epistemological positions in the narrow sense. When we say that Bogdanov's thought is most often reduced to the epistemology Lenin knew, then, we mean that the implications of his point of view on knowledge for what he considered his larger worldview to be are not fully considered.

[75] Although there are many studies on the "empiriocritics", the most informative and readable are John T. Blackmore, *Ernst Mach*, Berkeley, University of California Press, 1972, and Leszek Kołakowski, *The Alienation of Reason*, trans. Norbert Guterman, New York, Doubleday, 1969, pp. 101–28.

[76] Ščeglov, *op. cit.* passim.

[77] Joravsky, *op. cit.* pp. 26–29.

[78] The practice was certainly alive and well as late as 1937. See Ščeglov, *op. cit.* passim.

[79] For a list of "Machists" in all categories see Utechin, *op. cit.* p. 213.

[80] *Ocherki realisticheskaia mirovozzreniia*, ed. A. A. Bogdanov (St. Petersburg, 1904).

[81] Of the greatest interest among them is *Encounters with Lenin* which records the relationship between Lenin, Bogdanov and other Machians before 1909.

[82] Wetter, *op. cit.* pp. 98–100.

[83] Robert S. Cohen, 'Ernst Mach: Physics, Perception and the Philosophy of Science', *Synthese* 18 (April 1968): 132–70.

[84] *Ocherki po filosofii marksizma*, ed. A. A. Bogdanov, St. Petersburg, 1908; *Ocherki po filosofii kollektivizma*, ed. A. A. Bogdanov, St. Petersburg, 1909.

[85] V. I. Lenin, *Materialism and Empirio-criticism*, New York, International Publishers, 1927, pp. 13–31 passim.

[86] For a nearly complete chronological bibliography of Bogdanov's writings, see Dietrich Grille, 'Verläufige Bogdanov-Bibliographie', in Dietrich Grille, *op. cit.* pp. 252–9.

[87] Bogdanov, 'Autobiography', pp. 288–89.

[88] Ballestrem, *op. cit.* pp. 283–306 passim; Grille, *op. cit.* pp. 39–72 passim.

[89] Ballestrem, *op. cit.* p. 293.

[90] A. A. Bogdanov, *Empiriomonizm*, Vol. I. Moscow, 1904; A. A. Bogdanov, *Empiriomonizm*, Vol. II, St. Petersburg, 1906; A. A. Bogdanov, *Empiriomonizm*, Vol. III, St. Petersburg, 1906.

[91] See Bogdanov, *Filosofiia zhivogo opyta*, pp. 328–45.

[92] *Ibid.*, pp. 174–215, 216–66.

[93] Especially good are Utechin, *Russian Political Thought*; Wetter, *Dialectical Materialism*; Ballestrem, 'Lenin and Bogdanov'. Grille, in *Lenins Rivale*, is the most expansive but his analysis is obscure. He has been taken to task for it by others. See Ballestrem, 'Lenin and Bogdanov', p. 311. As far as this writer knows, Grille's work has never been reviewed. It is cited several places for the biographical data it provides on Bogdanov, but no mention is made of its analysis of his thought.

[94] cf. Wetter, *op. cit.* and Ballestrem *op. cit.*

[95] Grille *op. cit.* pp. 171–76.

[96] A. A. Bogdanov, *Vera i nauka (O knige V. Il'ina "Materialism i empiriokrititsizm")*, Moscow, 1910.

[97] See Chapter II.

CHAPTER I

[1] Little is known of Kalinin and Vilonov, let alone their works. Bogdanov tells us only that the first was a weaver and the second a lathe operator. See Bogdanov, *Filosofiia zhivogo opyta*, p. 3. Nikifor Efremovič Vilonov (1883–1910) was a Bolshevik Party member associated with the *Vperedists* during the difficulties of 1908–9. He left the latter group to join Lenin in Paris at the end of 1909, but died soon thereafter, presumably from tuberculosis. The Soviets credit him with taking part in the founding of the Capri school; and he, therefore, must have been a colleague of Bogdanov and perhaps his student. I have not been able to discover any record of his writings. See *Bol'šaja sovetskaja enciklopedija*, 3rd ed., s.v. "Vilonov, Nikifor Efremovič." It may well be that Kalinin was similarly associated with Bogdanov in the years 1908–11, but no record of his life or works exists to my knowledge.

[2] This might be better translated "navigational instrument". However, since Bogdanov wished to portray philosophy as a tool like others in production, we render the phrase in this way.

[3] See Chapter IV, pp. 123–127.

[4] See Chapter V.

[5] These essays are entitled 'What was There before Philosophy?' and 'How did Philosophy Together with Science Proceed from Religion?' Bogdanov, *Filosofiia zhivogo opyta*, pp. 20–39, 39–55.

[6] In an earlier work which gives the same scheme regarding the history of society and thought, Bogdanov actually refers to himself as an historical materialist after the fashion of Marx. See A. A. Bogdanov, *Kratkii Kurs ekonomicheskoi nauki* (Moscow, 1897), p. v.

[7] See Chapter II.

[8] See Chapter IV, pp. 119–123.

[9] See below, pp. 148–159.

[10] See Chapter IV passim.

[11] See Chapter IV, pp. 134–138.

[12] See Chapter III, pp. 96–97.

[13] The term "sociomorphism" appears first in 'The Materialism of the Ancient World'. Bogdanov, *Filosofiia zhivogo optya*, p. 124.

[14] See Chapter IV, pp. 132–134.

[15] See Chapter III.

CHAPTER II

1 See Wetter, *Dialectical Materialism*, pp. 92–98 *passim*; Ballestrem, 'Lenin and Bogdanov', p. 286, Cohen, 'Ernst Mach', p. 163.

2 cf., Blackmore, *Ernst Mach*, pp. 164–203; Kolakowski, *Alienation of Reason*, pp. 101–121.

3 It is tempting because this ection dovetails with the section on science and the proletariat in the work's introduction. See Chapter I, pp. 24–33.

CHAPTER III

1 See Chapter IV *passim*.

2 Wetter, *Dialectical Materialism*, pp. 96–7.

3 A. A. Bogdanov, *Tektologiia: Vseobshchaia organizatsionnaia nauka*, Vol. III (Berlin, 1922), pp. 502–30.

4 Gustav Wetter gives the same quote in his essay on Bogdanov; however, it is mistranslated there. The last phrase is given with the adjective "various" (*raznyj*) translated as "opposite." See Wetter, *op. cit.*, p. 96.

5 Wetter, *op. cit.*; Ščeglov, *Bor'ba lenina*, p. 210.

6 Wetter, *op. cit.*,

7 *Ibid*. p. 97.

8 *Loc. cit.*

9 *Loc. cit.*

10 On account of statements such as this, one supposes, past students of Bogdanov have largely come to designate what we discuss here as "equilibrium theory" rather than as dialectics. While this may be a useful way of contrasting Bogdanov's dialectic with those of, say, Engels or the Soviet diamatists, it does not illuminate what Bogdanov speaks of in this chapter to emphasize the stasis and passivity which "equilibrium" may be taken to imply. Gustav Wetter, incidently, speaks not of equilibrium theory but of Bogdanov's dialectic.

11 Wetter, *op. cit.*, p. 97.

12 See Chapter I, pp. 24–33.

13 See below, pp. 96–97.

14 Marx's eleventh thesis on Feuerbach is quoted in part on these pages.

15 This is said expressly in Bogdanov, *Filosofiia zhivogo opyta*, p. 243.

16 Compare pp. 243–45 with Friedrich Engels, *Herr Eugen Dühring's Revolution in Science*, Moscow, Progress Publishers, 1969, pp. 143–73.

17 The proposal to focus on this is made in Bogdanov, *op. cit.*, p. 243.

18 Joseph Dietzgen (1828–88) was a German-born tanner who arrived at a philosophic perspective similar to that of Marx but independently of his influence. The Soviets generally regard Dietzgen with favor and cite with approval his arguments to support their polemics against positivism, especially of the Machist variety. For a Soviet biography and bibliography see *Bol'saja sovetskaja enciklopedija*, 2nd ed., s.v. "Dicgen, Iosef."

19 A reading of *Materialism and Empirio-Criticism* will suggest that Dietzgen was of similar importance for Lenin. Lenin, however, was quite explicit as to the character of Dietzgen's dialectical materialism. Quite often Lenin measures the Russian Machists against Dietzgen as well as Marx, Engels and Feuerbach as exponents of the correct view of things. See Lenin, *Materialism and Empirio-Criticism*, pp. 13, 115–20, 249–55.

[20] See especially the chapter entitled "Basic Notions and Methods" in Bogdanov, *Tektologiia,* Vol. I., pp. 66–97.

[21] Perhaps, however, the following ought to be said. We fear that the reader may come to the conclusion that, inasmuch as he judged Marx's to be a fully active worldview, getting beyond Marx for Bogdanov could not have been the same sort of thing as getting beyond Mach or the classical materialisms. While this may be true in some part or other, we have to argue, first, that Bogdanov demanded a truly active, *scientific* and *consistent* worldview. Marx's dialectic denied him the possibility of being the possessor of the same, because it was not only inconsistent with the rest of his thought but also at odds with scientific method. Secondly, Bogdanov regarded large contradictions in all philosophies as something like a kiss of death. If Lenin and company were condemned as having no worldview at all for the contradiction of aspiring to be "materialist" in both the Marxist and the eighteenth-century senses, then what of Marxism with its quasi-idealist dialectic? We do not believe, on consideration of what he had to say about organizational versus dialectical views of process, that one can argue that Bogdanov considered what he was doing to be a case of 'Marx and his true successor Bogdanov against the rest'. Compared to what Bogdanov thought *he* knew about the study of process, Marx was more than wrong: he had not got the enterprise very far off the ground. This latter argument will perhaps become more clear in our next chapter, in which positions shared with Marx find their way into a system the intended similarity of which to Marxism has to be regarded as at least highly problematic.

CHAPTER IV

[1] See Chapter III, pp. 94–98.

[2] See, for example, Ballestrem, 'Lenin and Bogdanov' pp. 292–301; and Wetter, *Dialectical Materialism,* pp. 92–98.

[3] See, in particular, A. A. Bogdanov, *Osnovnye elementy istoricheskogo vzgliada na prirodu* [Basic Elements of an Historical View of Nature] (St. Petersburg, 1899); and A. A. Bogdanov, *Poznanie s istoricheskie tochki zreniia* [Knowledge from an Historical Point of View] (St. Petersburg, 1901). Even in these works, "the labor point of view" is not concisely stated. It might be said that "the labor point of view" comes into being in them and is the general result of their creation.

[4] It cannot be denied that his chief legacy was his "negative" effect on the development of Marxism-Leninism.

[5] Compare the following exposition of empiriomonism with those of Wetter, *op. cit.,* pp. 92–98; Ballestrem, *op. cit.,* pp. 293–301; Utechin, *Russian Political Thought,* pp. 209–12.

[6] See below, pp. 119–123.

[7] See below, pp. 123–127.

[8] See Chapter V.

[9] Karl Ballestrem feels particularly comfortable in doing this. See Ballestrem, *op. cit.,* pp. 292–301 passim.

[10] Apparently, Bogdanov was still enough of a partisan of Mach to follow the latter on the issue of the actuality of atoms.

[11] Ballestrem, *op. cit.,* p. 296.

[12] See also Chapter II.

13 Wetter, *op. cit.*, p. 93.
14 Ibid.
15 Ibid.
16 See Chapter I, pp. 24—33.
17 For an account of this see Ščeglov, *Bor'ba lenina*, pp. 77—79.
18 Wetter, *op. cit.*, p. 94.
19 Wetter's comment suggests that, like the materialist, Bogdanov denies objectivity to the contents of the individual mind. However, since "socially organized experience" resides in collective consciousness for him, it was unquestionably the case that Bogdanov proceeded as something other than a materialist in formulating his view of the "physical" and "psychical".
20 See Chapter III.
21 See Chapter I, p. 32.

CHAPTER V

1 See below, p. 159.
2 See Chapter I.
3 See Chapter III.
4 See Chapter III.

CONCLUSION

1 See Introduction, pp. 5—7.
2 See Grille, *Lenins Rivale*, pp. 256—7.
3 A. A. Bogdanov, *Inzhener Menni, fantasticheskii roman*. Moscow, 1913.
4 See Grille *op. cit.* pp. 257—9.
5 A. A. Bogdanov, 'Princip otnositel'nosti i ego filosofskoe istolkovanie [The Principle of Relativity and its Philosophical Interpretation] *Mir* no. 4 (April 1923); A. A. Bogdanov, 'Ob'ektivnoe ponimanie principa otnositel'nosti' (Metodologičeskie tezisy) [The Objective Understanding of the Principle of Relativity (Methodological Theses)], *Vestnik kommunističeskoj akademii* no. 7 (July 1924): 332—47.
6 Csizmas, 'Cybernetics — Marxism — Jurisprudence', p. 90.
7 See Grille *op. cit.* pp. 256—7; also Utechin, *Russian Political Thought*, p. 213.
8 A. A. Bogdanov, *Allgemeine Organisationslehre (Tektologie)*, Vol. I (Berlin, 1922), p. 13; also cited in Csizmas *op. cit.* p. 90.
9 Not only was the third edition of 1923 no different from that of 1913, save for an added footnote on the progress of organizational science and the emendation of 'From Religious to Scientific Monism', the second edition of 1920 remained the same as well. Compare A. A. Bogdanov, *Filosofiia zhivogo opyta*, 2nd. ed. (Petrograd, 1920), and Bogdanov, *Filosofiia zhivogo opyta*, 3rd. ed. The *Tektologiia* appeared in second edition beginning in 1925. See Grille *op. cit.* pp. 258—9.
10 A. A. Bogdanov, *Vera i nauka (O knige V. Il'ina "Materializm i Empiriokrititsizm")* [Belief and Science (On V. Il'ina's Book *Materialism and Empirio-Criticism*)], Moscow, 1910.
11 For a discussion and analysis of Nietzsche which allows Bogdanov's comparison to him as a philosopher for the times see Pamela K. Jensen, 'Nietzsche and Liberation: The

Prelude to a Philosophy of the Future', *Interpretation* 2 (May 1977): 79–106.

[12] Jürgen Habermas, *Knowledge and Human Interests*, trans, Jeremy J. Shapiro, Boston, Beacon Press, 1971.

[13] Alexander Vucinich, *Social Thought in Tsarist Russia. The Quest for a General Science of Society, 1861–1917,* Chicago and London, University of Chicago Press, 1976. Regrettably, I did not have Vucinich's piece on Bogdanov in this book at my disposal until revisions of this manuscript were nearly complete. The informed reader will rightly guess that my remarks on Bogdanov scholarship in the Introduction would have been somewhat different had I been able to take Professor Vucinich's effort into the accounting.

[14] Vucinich *op. cit.* p. viii.

[15] Adam Ulam, *Stalin*, New York, Viking Press, 1973, p. 101.

[16] Georg Lukács, *History and Class Consciousness*, trans. Rodney Livingstone, Cambridge, Mass., The MIT Press, 1971; Karl Korsch, *Marxism and Philosophy*, trans. Fred Halliday, New York, Monthly Review Press, 1971.

[17] See George Lichtheim, *From Marx to Hegel,* New York, Herder and Herder, 1971, especially pp. 1–49.

BIBLIOGRAPHY

GENERAL

Grille, Dietrich. 'Vorläufige Bogdanov-Bibliographie'.
In Grille, Dietrich. *Lenins Rivale*, Cologne, Verlag Wissenschaft und Politik, 1966, pp. 252–9.
In a separate section of his bibliography, Grille gives a nearly complete chronological listing of Bogdanov's works.

WORKS BY BOGDANOV

Bogdanov, A. A. *A Short Course of Economic Science*, Revised and supplemented by S. M. Dvolaitskii. Translated by J. Fineberg. London, Labour Publishing Company, Ltd., 1923.
_____, *Allgemeine Organisationslehre (Tektologie)* [Universal Organizational Science (Tektologiia)], Vol. I. Berlin, 1926.
_____, *Allgemeine Organisationslehre (Tektologie)*, Vol. II. Berlin, 1928.
_____, 'Autobiography'. In Haupt, Georges, and Marie, Jean-Jacques, *Makers of the Russian Revolution*, Translated by C. I. P. Ferdinand and D. M. Bellos. Ithaca, Cornell University Press, 1974, pp. 286–9.
_____, 'Bogdanov, Aleksandr Aleksandrovič, Avtobiografija'. Appears in *Enciklopedičeskij slovar' Granat* [Granat Encyclopedia Dictionary]. Moscow, 1924.
_____, 'The Criticism of Proletarian Art', *The Labour Monthly* no. 5 (1923): 344–56.
_____, *Empiriomonizm: Stat'i po filosofii* [Empiriomonism: Articles on Philosophy], Vol. I. 2nd ed. St. Petersburg, 1906.
_____, *Empiriomonizm: Stat'i po filosofii*. Vol. II. St. Petersburg, 1906.
Bogdanov, A. A. *Empiriomonizm: Stat'i po filosofii*, Vol. III. St. Petersburg, 1906.
_____, *Filosofiia zhivogo opyta* [The Philosophy of Living Experience], St. Petersburg, 1913.
_____, *Filosofiia zhivogo opyta* 2nd ed. Petrograd, 1920.
_____, *Filosofiia zhivogo opyta*, 3rd ed. Petrograd and Moscow, 1923.
The edition cited almost exclusively in this work.
_____, *Inzhener Menni, fantasticheskii roman* [Engineer Menni, A Fantasy Novel], Moscow, 1913.
_____, *Iz psikhologii obshchestva* [From the Psychology of Society], St. Petersburg, 1904.
_____, *Krasnaia zvezda (Jutopia)* [Red Star (Utopia)], St. Petersburg, 1908.
_____, *Kratkii kurs economicheskoi nauki* [Short Course of Economic Science], Moscow, 1897.
_____, *Nauka i rabochii klass* [Science and the Working Class], Moscow, 1922.
_____, *Nauka ob obshchestvennom soznanii* [The Science of Social Consciousness], 3rd ed. Moscow, 1914.

181

——————————, 'Ob'ektivnoe ponimanie principa otnositel'nosti (Metodologičeskie tezisy)' [The Objective Understanding of the Principle of Relativity (Methodological Theses)]. *Vestnik kommunističeskoj akademii* no. 7 (July 1924), 332–47.

——————————, *Osnovnye elementy istoricheskogo vzgliada na prirodu* [Basic Elements of the Historical View of Nature]. St. Petersburg, 1899.

——————————, 'Ot monizma religioznogo k naučnomu (doklad)' [From Religious to Scientific Monism (Lecture)]. In Bogdanov, A. A. *Filosofiia zhivogo opyta*, 3rd ed., Petrograd and Moscow, 1923, pp. 328–345.

Bogdanov, A. A. *Poznanie s istoricheskoi tochki zrenia* [Knowledge from the Historical Point of View], St. Petersburg, 1901.

——————————, 'Princip otnositel'nosti i ego filosofskoe istolkovanie' [The Principle of Relativity and its Philosophical Interpretation], *Mir* no. 4 (April 1923).

——————————, 'Proletarian Poetry', *The Labour Monthly* no. 4 (1923), 275–85, 357–62.

——————————, 'Religion, Art and Marxism', *The Labour Monthly* no. 6 (1924), 489–97.

——————————, *Socializm nauki* [The Socialism of Science], Moscow, 1918.

——————————, *Tektologiia: Vseobshchaia organizatsionnaia nauka* [Tektologiia: Universal Organizational Science], Vol. 1. St. Petersburg, 1913.

——————————, *Tektologiia: Vseobshchaia organizatsionnaia nauka*, Vol. II. Moscow, 1917.

——————————, *Tektologiia: Vseobshchaia organizationnaia nauka*, Vol. III. Berlin, 1922.

——————————, *Tektologiia: Vseobshchaia organizatsionnaia nauka*, Vol. I. 3rd ed. Moscow and Leningrad, 1925.

——————————, *Tektologiia: Vseobshchaia organizatsionnaia nauka*, Vol. II. 3rd ed. Moscow and Leningrad, 1928.

——————————, *Tektologiia: Vseobshchaia organizatsionnaia nauka*, Vol. III. 3rd ed. Leningrad and Moscow, 1929.

——————————, *Vera i nauka (O Knige V. Il'ina "Materializm i empiriokrititsizm")* [Belief and Science (On V. Il'ina's Book *Materialism and Empirio-Criticism*)]. Moscow, 1910.

——————————, 'The Workers' Artistic Inheritance', *The Labour Monthly* no. 6 (1924), 549–56.

SECONDARY MATERIALS: BOOKS

Action, H. B. *The Illusion of the Epoch*, London, Cohen and West, 1955.

Althusser, Louis, *For Marx*, Translated by Ben Brewster, New York, Vintage Books, 1970.

——————————, *Lenin and Philosophy*, Translated by Ben Brewster. New York and London, Monthly Review Press, 1971.

Badaev, Aleksei, *The Bolsheviks in the Tsarist Duma*, New York, International Publishers, 1932.

Ballestrem, Karl G. *Russian Philosophical Terminology*, Dordrecht, D. Reidel Publishing Company, 1964.

Baron, Samuel H. *Plekhanov, The Father of Russian Marxism*, Stanford, Stanford University Press, 1963.

Blackmore, John T. *Ernst Mach*, Berkeley, University of California Press, 1972.

Blakeley. Thomas J. *Soviet Scholasticism*, Dordrecht, D. Reidel Publishing Company, 1961.

_____, *Soviet Theory of Knowledge*, Dordrecht, D. Reidel Publishing Company, 1964.

Bocheński, J. M. *Soviet Russian Dialectical Materialism*, Translated by Nocolas Sollohub, Dordrecht, D. Reidel Publishing Company, 1963.

Brown, Edward J. *Russian Literature Since the Revolution*, New York, Collier Books, 1969.

Bukharin, N. I. *Historical Materialism*, Ann Arbor, Ann Arbor Paperbacks, 1969.

Cassirer, Ernst. *The Problem of Knowledge*, Tranlsated by William H. Woglom and Charles W. Hendel, New Haven, Yale University Press, 1950.

Cohen, Stephen F. *Bukharin and the Bolshevik Revolution*, New York, Alfred A. Knopf, 1973.

Daniels, R. V. *The Conscience of the Revolution: Communist Opposition in Soviet Russia*, Cambridge, Massachusetts, Harvard University Press, 1960.

Deborin, A. M., Bukharin, N. I., Uranovsky, Y. M., Vavilov, S. I., Komarov, V. L., and Tiumeniev, Al. I. *Marxism and Modern Thought*, Translated by Ralph Fox. London, G. Routledge and Sons, Ltd., 1935.

Deborin, A. *Vvedenie v filosofii dialekticheskoso materializma* [An Introduction to the Philosophy of Dialectical Materialism], St. Petersburg, 1916.

De George, Richard T. *Patterns of Soviet Thought: The Origins and Development of Dialectical and Historical Materialism*, Ann Arbor, University of Michigan Press, 1966.

D'Elia, Alfronsina, *Ernst Mach*, Florence, La Nuova Italia Editrice, 1971.
    Like Blackmore, D'Elia includes a section (in appendix) on "Machism" in Russia.

Edie, James M., Scanlan, James P., Zeldin, Mary-Barbara, *Russian Philosophy*, Vol. III. Chicago, Quadrangle, 1965.

Engels, Friedrich, *The Dialectics of Nature*, Translated and edited by J. B. S. Haldane, New York, International Publishers, 1940.

_____, *Herr Eugen Dühring's Revolution in Science,* Moscow, Progress Publishers, 1969.

Fitzpatrick, Sheila, *The Commisariat of Enlightenment*, Cambridge, Cambridge University Press, 1970.

Frank, Philipp, *Modern Science and its Philosophy*, New York, George Braziller, 1955.

Graham, Loren, *Science and Philosophy in the Soviet Union*, New York, Alfred A. Knopf, 1972.

Grille, Dietrich, *Lenins Rivale*, Cologne, Verlag Wissenschaft und Politik, 1966.

Habermas, Jürgen, *Knowledge and Human Interests*, Translated by Jeremy J. Shapiro, Boston, Beacon Press, 1971.

Haimson, Leopold H. *The Russian Marxists and the Origins of Bolshevism*. Cambridge, Massachusetts, Harvard University Press, 1955.

Hecker, J. F. *Russian Sociology*, New York, A. M. Kelley, 1969.

Hughes, H. Stuart, *Consciousness and Society*, New York, Vintage Books, 1961.

Janik, Allen, and Toulmin, Stephen, *Wittgenstein's Vienna*, New York, Simon and Schuster, 1973.

Johnston, William M. *The Austrian Mind, An Intellectual and Social History, 1848–1938*, Berkeley, University of California Press, 1972.

Joravsky, David, *Soviet Marxism and Natural Science*, London, Routlege and Kegan Paul, 1961.

Keep, J. L. *The Rise of Social Democracy in Russia*, London, Oxford University Press, 1963.

Kline, G. G. *Spinoza in Soviet Philosophy*, London, Routledge and Kegan Paul, 1952.

Kołakowski, Leszek, *The Alienation of Reason*, Translated by Norbert Guterman, New York, Doubleday, 1969.

Korsch, Karl, *Marxism and Philosophy*, Translated by Fred Halliday, New York, Monthly Review Press, 1971.

Krupskaia, N. K. *Memories of Lenin*, Translated by E. Verney, 2 vols. New York, International Publishers, 1930.

Lenin, V. I. *Materialism and Empirio-criticism*, New York, International Publishers, 1927.

Levin, Alfred, *The Second Duma*, New Haven, Yale University Press, 1940.

Lichtheim, George, *From Marx to Hegel*, New York, Herder and Herder, 1971.

Lichtheim, George, *Marxism; an Historical and Critical Study*, New York, Praeger, 1961.

Losskii, N. O. *History of Russian Philosophy*, New York, International Universities Press, Inc., 1951.

Lukács, Georg, *History and Class Consciousness*, Translated by Rodney Livingstone, Cambridge, Mass., The MIT Press, 1971.

Mach, Ernst, *The Analysis of Sensations and the Relation of the Physical to the Psychical*, Translated by C. M. Williams, Chicago, Open Court, 1914.

_____, *The Science of Mechanics*, Translated by Thomas J. McCormack, Chicago, Open Court, 1960.

Mandelbaum, Maurice, *History, Man and Reason*, Baltimore, The Johns Hopkins Press, 1971.

Masaryk, T. G. *The Spirit of Russia*, Translated by Eden and Cedar Paul, New York, Macmillan, 1955.

Meyer, Alred G. *Leninism*, New York, Praeger, 1962.

Mises, Richard von, *Positivism*, New York, Dover Publishers, Inc., 1968.

Novack, George, *Empiricism and Its Evolution: A Marxist View*, New York, Merit Books, 1971.

Ocherki filosofii kollektivizma [Essays in the Philosophy of Collectivism], Edited by A. A. Bogdanov, St. Petersburg, 1909.

Ocherki, po filosofii marksizma [Essays in the Philosophy of Marxism], Edited by A. A. Bogdanov, St Petersburg, 1908.

Ocherki realisticheskogo mirovozzreniia [Essays on a Realistic World-View], Edited by A. A. Bogdanov, St. Petersburg, 1904.

Paul, Eden, and Paul, Cedar, *Proletcult*, New York, Thomas Selzer, 1921.

Ratliff, Floyd, *Mach Bands*, San Francisco, Holden-Day, 1965.

Schapiro, Leonard, *The Communist Party of the Soviet Union*, New York, Vintage Books, 1960.

_____, *The Origins of the Communist Autocracy: Political Opposition in the Soviet State, First Period, 1917–1922.* Cambridge, Massachusetts, Harvard University Press, 1955.

Ščeglov, A. V. *Bor'ba lenina protiv bogdanovskoj revizii marksizma* [The Struggle of Lenin against the Bogdanovist Revision of Marxism], Moscow, 1937.

Ulam, Adam B. *The Bolsheviks*, New York, Collier Books, 1965.

Ulam, Adam, *Stalin*, New York, Viking Press, 1973.

Utechin, S. V. *Russian Political Thought: A Concise History*, New York, Praeger, 1964.

Valentinov, N. *E. Mach i marksizm* [E. Mach and Marxism], St. Petersburg, 1908.
——————, *Encounters with Lenin*, London, Oxford University Press, 1968.
Vucinich, Alexander, *Social Thought in Tsarist Russia. The Quest for a General Science of Society, 1861–1917*, Chicago and London, The University of Chicago Press, 1976.
Wetter, Gustav, *Dialectical Materialism*, Translated by Peter Heath, London, Routledge and Kegan Paul, 1958.
——————, *Soviet Ideology Today*, Translated by Peter Heath. New York, Praeger, 1966.
Wolfe, Bertram D. *The Bridge and the Abyss: The Troubled Friendship of Maxim Gorky and V. I. Lenin*, New York, Praeger, 1967.
——————, *Three Who Made a Revolution*, Boston, Beacon Paperbacks, 1960.
Zen'kovskii, V. A. *A History of Russian Philosophy*, London, Routledge and Kegan Paul, 1953.

SECONDARY MATERIALS: ARTICLES

Ballestrem, Karl G. 'Lenin and Bogdanov', *Studies in Soviet Thought* 9 (December 1969), 283–310.
——————, 'Soviet Historiography of Philosophy', *Studies in Soviet Thought* 3 (June 1963), 107–20.
Blakeley, Thomas J. 'Terminology in Soviet Epistemology', *Studies in Soviet Thought* 4 (September 1964), 232–8.
Bol'šaja sovetskaja enciklopedija [Great Soviet Encyclopedia], 1st ed. S. V. 'Bolon'-skaja partijnaja škola' [Bologna Party School].
Bol'šaja sovetskaja enciklopedija, 2nd ed. S.v. 'Ditzgen, Iosef'.
Bol'šaja sovetskaja enciklopedija, 1st ed. S.v. 'Empiriokriticizm'.
Bol'šaja sovetskaja enciklopedija, 1st ed. S.v. 'Empiriomonizm'.
Bol'šaja sovetskaja enciklopedija, 1st ed. S.v. 'Kaprijskaja škola' [Capri School].
Bol'šaja sovetskaja enciklopedija, 1st ed. S.v. 'Malinovskij, Aleksandr Aleksandrovič.'.   '
Bol'šaja sovetskaja enciklopedija, 2nd ed. S.v., 'Malinovskij, Aleksandr Aleksandrovič.'
Bol'šaja sovetskaja enciklopedija, 3rd ed. S.v. 'Vilonov, Nikifor Efremovič.'
Brush, S. G. 'Mach and Atomism', *Synthese* 18 (April 1968), 192–215.
Bukharin, N. I. obituary of Bogdanov in *Pravda*, 8 April, 1928.
Capek, Milic, 'Ernst Mach's Biological Theory of Knowledge', *Synthese* 18 (April 1968), 171–91.
Cohen, Robert S. 'Ernst Mach: Physics, Perception and the Philosophy of Science', *Synthese* 18 (April 1968), 132–70.
Csizmas, Michael, 'Cybernetics – Marxism – Jurisprudence', *Studies in Soviet Thought* 11 (June 1971), 90–108.
Encyclopedia of Philosophy, S.v. 'Mach Ernst', by Peter Alexander.
Feuer, L. S. 'Dialectical Materialism and Soviet Science', *Philosophy of Science* 16 (April 1949), 105–24.
Filosofskaja enciklopedija [Philosophic Encyclopedia]. S.v. 'Malinovskij, Aleksandr Aleksandrovič'.
Haupt, Georges, 'Aleksandr Aleksandrovich Bogdanov (Malinovsky)', In Haupt, Georges and Marie, Jean-Jacques, *Makers of the Russian Revolution*, Translated by C. I. P.

Ferdinand and D. M. Bellos, Ithaca, New York, Cornell University Press, 1974, pp. 289–292.

Jensen, Pamela K. 'Nietzsche and Liberation: The Prelude to a Philosophy of the Future', *Interpretation* 2 (May 1977), 79–106.

Katkov, George, 'Lenin as Philosopher', In *Lenin: The Man, The Theorist, The Leader*, Edited by Leonard Schapiro and Peter Reddaway, New York, Praeger, 1967, pp. 71–86.

Kemball, R. J. 'Nineteenth – and Early Twentieth-Century Russian Thought: A Preliminary Review of the Literature I', *Studies in Soviet Thought* 5 (June 1965), 30–50.

—————, 'Nineteenth – and Early Twentieth Century Russian Thought: A Preliminary Review of the Literature II', *Studies in Soviet Thought* 5 (September 1965), 173–203.

Livshits, S. 'Partijnaja škola v Bolon'e (1910–1911 gg)' [The Party School in Bologna (1910–1911)], *Proletarskaja revoljucija* no. 3 (1926), 109–44.

Paul, G. A. 'Lenin's Theory of Perception', *Analysis* 5 (October 1938), 65–73.

Utechin, S. V. 'Philosophy and Society: Alexander Bogdanov', In *Revisionism*, Edited by Leopold Labedz, New York, Praeger, 1962, pp. 117–125.

INDEX

SOVIETICA

Publications and Monographs of the Institute of East-European Studies
at the University of Fribourg/Switzerland
and the Center for East Europe, Russia and Asia
at Boston College and the Seminar for Political Theory and Philosophy
at the University of Munich

1. BOCHEŃSKI, J. M. and BLAKELEY, TH. J. (eds.): *Bibliographie der sowjetischen Philosophie.* I: *Die 'Voprosy filosofii' 1947–1956.* 1959, VIII + 75 pp.
2. BOCHEŃSKI, J. M. and BLAKELEY, TH. J. (eds.): *Bibliographie der sowjetischen Philosophie.* II: *Bücher 1947–1956; Bücher und Aufsätze 1957–1958; Namenverzeichnis 1947–1958.* 1959, VIII + 109 pp.
3. BOCHEŃSKI, J. M.: *Die dogmatischen Grundlagen der sowjetischen Philosophie (Stand 1958). Zusammenfassung der 'Osnovy Marksistskoj Filosofii' mit Register.* 1959, XII + 84 pp.
4. LOBKOWICZ, NICOLAS (ed.): *Das Widerspruchsprinzip in der neueren sowjetischen Philosophie.* 1960, VI + 89 pp.
5. MÜLLER-MARKUS, SIEGFRIED: *Einstein und die Sowjetphilosophie. Krisis einer Lehre.* I: *Die Grundlagen. Die spezielle Relativitätstheorie.* 1960. (Out of print.)
6. BLAKELEY, TH. J.: *Soviet Scholasticism.* 1961, XIII + 176 pp.
7. BOCHEŃSKI, J. M. and BLAKELEY, TH. J. (eds.): *Studies in Soviet Thought,* I. 1961, IX + 141 pp.
8. LOBKOWICZ, NICOLAS: *Marxismus-Leninismus in der ČSR. Die tschechoslowakische Philosophie seit 1945.* 1962, XVI + 268 pp.
9. BOCHEŃSKI, J. M. and BLAKELFY, TH. J. (eds.): *Bibliographie der sowjetischen Philosophie.* III: *Bücher und Aufsätze 1959–1960.* 1962, X + 73 pp.
10. BOCHEŃSKI, J. M. and BLAKELEY, TH. J. (eds.): *Bibliographie der sowjetischen Philosophie.* IV: *Ergänzungen 1947–1960.* 1963, XII + 158 pp.
11. FLEISCHER, HELMUT: *Kleines Textbuch der kommunistischen Ideologie. Auszüge aus dem Lehrbuch 'Osnovy marksizma-leninizma', mit Register.* 1963, XIII + 116 pp.
12. JORDAN, ZBIGNIEW, A.: *Philosophy and Ideology. The Development of Philosophy and Marxism-Leninism in Poland since the Second World War.* 1963, XII + 600 pp.
13. VRTAČIČ, LUDVIK: *Einführung in den jugoslawischen Marxismus-Leninismus Organisation. Bibliographie.* 1963, X + 208 pp.
14. BOCHEŃSKI, J. M.: *The Dogmatic Principles of Soviet Philosophy (as of 1958). Synopsis of the 'Osnovy Marksistskoj Filosofii' with complete index.* 1963, XII + 78 pp.
15. BIRKUJOV, B. V.: *Two Soviet Studies on Frege.* Translated from the Russian and edited by Ignacio Angelelli. 1964, XXII + 101 pp.

16. BLAKELEY, T. J.: *Soviet Theory of Knowledge.* 1964, VII + 203 pp.
17. BOCHEŃSKI, J. M. and BLAKELEY, TH. J. (eds.): *Bibliographie der sowjetischen Philosophie.* V: *Register 1947–1960.* 1964, VI + 143 pp.
18. BLAKELEY, THOMAS J.: *Soviet Philosophy. A General Introduction to Contemporary Soviet Thought.* 1964, VI + 81 pp.
19. BALLESTREM, KAREL G.: *Russian Philosophical Terminology* (in Russian, English, German, and French). 1964, VIII + 116 pp.
20. FLEISCHER, HELMUT: *Short Handbook of Communist Ideology. Synopsis of the 'Osnovy marksizma-leninizma' with complete index.* 1965, XIII + 97 pp.
21. PLANTY-BONJOUR, G.: *Les catégories du matérialisme dialectique. L'ontologie soviétique contemporaine.* 1965, VI + 206 pp.
22. MÜLLER-MARKUS, SIEGFRIED: *Einstein und die Sowjetphilosophie. Krisis einer Lehre.* II: *Die allgemeine Relativitätstheorie.* 1966, X + 509 pp.
23. LASZLO, ERVIN: *The Communist Ideology in Hungary. Handbook for Basic Research.* 1966, VIII + 351 pp.
24. PLANTY-BONJOUR, G.: *The Categories of Dialectical Materialism. Contemporary Soviet Ontology.* 1967, VI + 182 pp.
25. LASZLO, ERVIN: *Philosophy in the Soviet Union. A Survey of the Mid-Sixties.* 1967, VIII + 208 pp.
26. RAPP, FRIEDRICH: *Gesetz und Determination in der Sowjetphilosophie. Zur Gesetzeskonzeption des dialektischen Materialismus unter besonderer Berücksichtigung der Diskussion über dynamische und statische Gesetzmässigkeit in der zeitgenössischen Sowjetphilosophie.* 1968, XI + 474 pp.
27. BALLESTREM, KARL G.: *Die sowjetische Erkenntnismetaphysik und ihr Verhältnis zu Hegel.* 1968, IX + 189 pp.
28. BOCHEŃSKI, J. M. and BLAKELEY, TH. J. (eds.): *Bibliographie der sowjetischen Philosophie.* VI: *Bücher und Aufsätze 1961–1963.* 1968, XI + 195 pp.
29. BOCHEŃSKI, J. M. and BLAKELEY, TH. J. (eds.): *Bibliographie der sowjetischen Philosophie.* VII: *Bücher und Aufsätze 1964–1966. Register.* 1968, X + 311 pp.
30. PAYNE, T. R.: *S. L. Rubinštejn and the Philosophical Foundations of Soviet Psychology.* 1968, X + 184 pp.
31. KIRSCHENMANN, PETER PAUL: *Information and Reflection. On Some Problems of Cybernetics and How Contemporary Dialectical Materialism Copes with Them.* 1970, XV + 225 pp.
32. O'ROURKE, JAMES J.: *The Problem of Freedom in Marxist Thought.* 1974, XII + 231 pp.
33. SARLEMIJN, ANDRIES: *Hegel's Dialectic.* 1975, XIII + 189 pp.
34. DAHM, HELMUT: *Vladimir Solovyev and Max Scheler: Attempt at a Comparative Interpretation A Contribution to the History of Phenomenology.* 1975, XI + 324 pp.
35. BOESELAGER, WOLFHARD F.: *The Soviet Critique of Neopositivism. The History and Structure of the Critique of Logical Positivism and Related Doctrines by Soviet Philosophers in the Years 1947–1967.* 1965, VII + 157 pp.
36. DEGEORGE, RICHARD T. and SCANLAN, JAMES P. (eds.): *Marxism and Religion in Eastern Europe. Papers Presented at the Banff International Slavic Conference, September 4–7, 1974.* 1976, XVI + 182 pp.
37. BLAKELEY, T. J. (ed.): *Themes in Soviet Marxist Philosophy. Selected Articles from the 'Filosofskaja Enciklopedija'.* 1975, XII + 224 pp.

38. GAVIN, W. J. and BLAKELEY, T. J.: *Russia and America: A Philosophical Comparison. Development and Change of Outlook from the 19th to the 20th Century.* 1976, x + 114 pp.
40. GRIER, P. T.: *Marxist Ethical Theory in the Soviet Union.* 1978, xviii + 271 pp.
41. JENSEN, K. M.: *Beyond Marx and Mach. Aleksandr Bogdanov's* Philosophy of Living Experience. 1978, ix + 189 pp.

In Press:

39. LIEBICH, A.: *Between Ideology and Utopia. The Politics and Philosophy of August Cieszkowski,* 1978.